THE BUSINESS OF HEAVEN

Born in Ireland in 1898, C. S. Lewis was educated at Malvern College for a year and then privately. He gained a triple First at Oxford and was a Fellow and Tutor at Magdalen College 1925–54. In 1954 he became Professor of Mediaeval and Renaissance Literature at Cambridge. He was an outstanding and popular lecturer and had a deep and lasting influence on his pupils.

C. S. Lewis was for many years an atheist, and described his conversion in *Surprised by Joy*: 'In the Trinity Term of 1929 I gave in, and admitted that God was God … perhaps the most dejected and reluctant convert in all England.' It was this experience that helped him to understand not only apathy but active unwillingness to accept religion, and as a Christian writer, gifted with an exceptionally brilliant and logical mind and a lucid, lively style, he was without peer. *The Problem of Pain, The Screwtape Letters, Mere Christianity, The Four Loves* and the posthumous *Prayer: Letters to Malcolm* are only a few of his best-selling works. He also wrote books for children, and some science fiction, besides many works of literary criticism. His works are known to millions of people all over the world in translation. He died on 22 November 1963, at his home in Oxford.

Walter Hooper was secretary to C. S. Lewis and is now the literary advisor to his estate. He lives in Oxford.

C. S. Lewis

THE BUSINESS
OF HEAVEN

DAILY READINGS FROM C. S. LEWIS

Edited by Walter Hooper

Fount
An Imprint of HarperCollins*Publishers*

Fount is an Imprint of
HarperCollins*Religious*
Part of HarperCollins*Publishers*
77–85 Fulham Palace Road, London W6 8JB

First published in Great Britain
in 1984 by Fount Paperbacks
This edition 1999

1 3 5 7 9 10 8 6 4 2

A catalogue record for this book is
available from the British Library

ISBN 0 00 6281486

Printed and bound in Great Britain by
Caledonian International Book Manufacturing Ltd, Glasgow

Contents

Preface

'Humanity does not pass through phases as a train passes through stations: being alive, it has the privilege of always moving yet never leaving anything behind. Whatever we have been, in some sort we are still.' This comes from the opening paragraph of C.S. Lewis's *The Allegory of Love*. I had thought of this observation so often that, no sooner had I been asked to compile a day-to-day anthology of Lewis's theological writings than the two things were in my mind almost at the same moment. The idea of a train suggested a journey. A journey where? While thinking about this I remembered this passage from Lewis's *Reflections on the Psalms* – 'When we carry out our "religious duties" we are like people digging channels in a waterless land, in order that when at last the water comes, it may find them ready . . . There are happy moments, even now, when a trickle creeps along the dry beds; and happy souls to whom this happens often.'

The combination was irresistible and I began imagining what a pleasure it would be to pour the writings of C.S. Lewis into that 'channel' which is called the Christian Year. The Christian Year is like a train which *does* enjoy the 'privilege of always moving yet never leaving anything behind' because it is based on the two great events of history, the Birth and the Resurrection of Our Lord. Strictly speaking, the Christian Year begins with the first Sunday in Advent – which word means the 'coming' of Christ. The Christmas season reaches its culmination on January 6 in the Feast of the Epiphany which is the celebration of Christ's 'manifestation' to the Gentiles in the person of the Magi. The next and greatest

Feast of the Church is that of Easter which lasts forty days and is followed by the feasts of the Ascension, Pentecost, and the Holy Trinity. It is customary to speak of the weeks between Pentecost and Advent as such and such a week 'after Pentecost' or 'after Trinity'. And so it goes on until we return to Advent and begin again. Those of us who take this annual circular journey of the Christian Year find it timeless and yet always refreshingly new.

There may be an odd individual here or there who will say 'New? What's so new about a train journey that returns to its original starting point?' But I doubt if such an objection will be raised by anyone who has lived within the Christian fold. I realize that there are many Christians of churches less liturgical, but not less devout, to whom the ancient form of the Christian Year will seem a little confusing. But if they follow the order in which these readings are arranged I doubt that they will be confused for long. So far as I am able to judge, the Christian Year takes nothing away from what they already believe. More than that, I believe they will find that what they hold best and dearest about the events in the earthly life of Our Lord will be strengthened. Surely it *does* strengthen both our belief and our appreciation of the Resurrection of Jesus to keep it in remembrance for forty days rather than to limit this great event to a single day.

I have never heard any Christian complain 'Christmas again! Easter again!' For most of us know that even the longest human life is not long enough for any attentive Christian to imagine that the Feast of the Resurrection is 'used up'. It was in his book *Letters to Malcolm* that C.S. Lewis said, 'It is well to have specifically holy places, and things and days, for, without these local points or reminders, the belief that all is holy and "big with God" will soon dwindle into a mere sentiment.' This he said in answer to Pantheism which is perhaps the most appealing heresy there is. At least Lewis found it so, as it delayed for some time his conversion to Christianity.

8

And Lewis, who drew so much nourishment from the Christian Year, praises it in the book where we are least likely to look for it – *The Screwtape Letters*. For those who may be meeting these letters for the first time in this anthology I should explain that Screwtape is a senior devil. His 'letters' are addressed to a young devil, Wormwood, whose job it is to secure a young man's soul for Hell. You must remember that when Screwtape speaks of 'Our Father Below' he means Satan. When referring to 'He' or 'The Enemy' Screwtape means God. In the entry of this book for January 17 Screwtape is urging Wormwood to instil in us a horror of 'The Same Old Thing' along with an insatiable desire for Novelty. All this Screwtape admits would be easier if The Enemy had not balanced our 'love of change' by a 'love of permanence'. 'He gives them', complains Screwtape:

the seasons, each season different yet every year the same, so that spring is always felt as a novelty yet always the recurrence of an immemorial theme. He gives them in His Church a spiritual year; they change from a fast to a feast, but it is the same feast as before.

It seemed, then, to me that the theme of the Christian Year would best serve those who like daily readings. And as I began selecting individual passages I came to believe that this theme could, if properly followed, make the most interesting and diversified use of C.S. Lewis's writings. I hoped, too, that it would go a long way towards defeating Screwtape's plans for destroying God's 'spiritual year' and inflaming our horror of 'The Same Old Thing'. 'The Enemy', Screwtape goes on to point out,

loves platitudes. Of a proposed course of action He wants men, so far as I can see, to ask very simple questions; is it righteous? is it prudent? is it possible? Now if we can keep men asking 'Is it in accordance with the general movement of our time? Is it progressive or reactionary? Is this the way that History is going?' they will neglect the relevant questions. And the questions they *do* ask are, of course, unanswerable; for they do not know the future, and what the future will be depends very largely on just those choices which they now invoke the future to help them make. As a result, while their minds are buzzing in this vacuum, we have the better chance to slip in and bend them to the action *we* have decided on.

A man would have to be very blind indeed not to see how many conquests Screwtape has made. I am thinking specially about the widespread apostasy among the clergy. I cannot forget my astonishment when I heard a bishop devote the whole of his Easter sermon to Psychical Research. He was delighted to report that some residue of what is now you and me might – just might – 'survive'. Lewis did not know this bishop, but there is a strikingly accurate portrait of him in the entries for May 22–25. You are fortunate if those entries are not a portrait of someone you know.

As it turned out, this 'Psychical Research Bishop' did me a favour. He made me remember something very important. If you know Church history you must know that whenever heresy has raised its head and pretended to be the way all sensible people think, it has resulted in a stimulation of orthodox Christian doctrine. Have you never noticed that such things as wars, diseases and famines usually have the effect of bringing out the best in many good people who do all they can to find solutions to these awful problems? Ever since the beginning of the Church, God has raised up great Christians to defeat heresy and strengthen the Faith once delivered. This is one of the reasons I have included entries for a number of those whom Lewis so frequently referred to as 'the great saints'.

I could not include entries for all the saints for the very pleasant reason that there are so many. And Lewis did not write about all of them. But there are two reasons why I've included those I have. First, they ought to be there as they stimulated or held fast to the Faith when the world (as now) seemed poised to lapse into Paganism. Second, they are a very necessary reminder that the Church did not begin with you or me, but is a great inheritance which might not be here today in the form Christ intended had it not been for these great ones. The names of the saints' days, and the Feasts and Fasts of the Church – what Lewis called 'holy days' – are printed in a different type to distinguish them from the titles I have given the other entries.

What are Fasts and Feasts? The different bodies of the Church are not agreed as to whether the two major Fasts of the Christian Year – Ash Wednesday, the first day of Lent, and Good Friday, the anniversary of the Crucifixion – should be marked by abstinence from all food or only from meat. Still, almost all believe that some acts of self-denial should be practised during the whole of Lent. When the Apostles witnessed Our Lord cast the evil spirit from the boy as recorded in St Mark 9:17–29 they asked why they could do nothing like this. 'This', replied Jesus, 'can come forth by nothing, but by prayer and fasting.' In the lives of the saints prayer and fasting nearly always go together. Fasting is a penitential practice designed to strengthen the spiritual life by weakening the attractions of sensual pleasures. The forty days of Lent commemorate Our Lord's forty days of temptation in the wilderness. For us the main purpose of Lent is to identify with Our Lord as He goes to the Cross.

Feasts are the anniversaries of the great events in the life of Our Lord and the occasions when we honour the saints. The Resurrection is the major Feast of the Christian Year. And here I suspect it would be a good idea to clear up a possible misunderstanding. When the New Testament writers referred to the Sabbath they meant both the day when God rested from His work of Creation as well as Israel's deliverance from Egypt. This is what the Jewish people still mean by the Sabbath. In New Testament times Sundays replaced Sabbaths. Even for the Apostles Sundays had come to mean a weekly com-

11

memoration of the Resurrection. This explains why fasting is never required on Sundays, not even during Lent, as every Sunday of the year is a commemoration of the Resurrection.

By now I expect you have spotted the one difficulty about arranging an anthology based on the Christian Year. It's plain sailing when one is dealing with what are called 'Immovable Feasts' – such as Christmas Day – because these days are fixed. However, because Easter Day is determined by the Paschal Full Moon it changes with the year, its extreme limits being March 21 and April 25. That causes it to be a 'Movable Feast'. There was no way I could give Easter Day and the fasts and feasts related to it a set place in this book. The solution was to put the readings for what I've called 'The Movable Fasts and Feasts' into a separate section at the end of the book. You should turn to that section for the appropriate readings from Lewis's writings for Ash Wednesday, Maundy Thursday, Good Friday, Holy Saturday, Easter Day, the Ascension, Pentecost, Holy Trinity, and The Body and Blood of Christ. I have provided a fifteen-year calendar in order to make it easy to know exactly when these special days occur.

There has been in recent years a movement to soft-pedal sin and to loud-pedal love, joy and peace. The result of this short cut has, so far as I can see, been disastrous. Those who are really guilty of something can't understand why it is, as they cannot be rid of the guilt which clings to them, that love, joy and peace never seem to amount to much. This effort to make us well without taking our medicine (repentance) seems to me like *looking* for happiness. As if happiness was something you could grasp if only you knew which bush it was hiding behind. You either get disillusioned, or you wake up to the fact that happiness has always been the *result* of something more important than itself.

I believe that those who follow these readings day by day as they were arranged to be read will discover what that 'something' beyond happiness is. You will find that I hammer away pretty hard with passages about morality. But you will find that I hammer away just as hard with passages which are meant to show us – as Lewis said – that 'Joy is the serious business of Heaven'. Lewis forces us to look at the whole of what we are. This is because he was one of the most realistic Christians we are ever likely to meet. He never makes a mountain of a mole hill. But he never pretends that a real mole hill isn't there. Not for a moment will he allow you to pretend that Christianity is less, or different, or other than what it is. Why should he? As he said, when writing of John Bunyan, 'To be born is to be exposed to delights and miseries greater than imagination could have anticipated; that the choice of ways at any cross-road may be more important than we think; and that short cuts may lead to very nasty places.'

But here's the surprise. As Lewis makes very clear in this book, morality – important though it is – was never intended as an end in itself. Morals are the 'ropes and axes' necessary for climbing those great heights from which a greater journey than even the Christian Year begins. That greater journey leads to the 'happy land of the Trinity'. It is there that joys, almost unimaginable in this world, begin. Begin – not *end* – for in that 'happy land' you won't need to have the 'serious business of Heaven' explained to you. You will have forgotten that there ever was anything else.

But C.S. Lewis's journey of the Christian Year comes first.

The Feast of St Mary Magdalen, 1983   Walter Hooper
Oxford

Readings For The Year

Beginning the New Year

I know all about the despair of overcoming chronic temptations. It is not serious, provided self-offended petulance, annoyance at breaking records, impatience etc. don't get the upper hand. *No amount* of falls will really undo us if we keep on picking ourselves up each time. We shall of course be very muddy and tattered children by the time we reach home. But the bathrooms are all ready, the towels put out, and the clean clothes in the airing cupboard. The only fatal thing is to lose one's temper and give it up. It is when we notice the dirt that God is most present in us: it is the very sign of His presence.

The First Job Each Morning

The real problem of the Christian life comes where people do not usually look for it. It comes the very moment you wake up each morning. All your wishes and hopes for the day rush at you like wild animals. And the first job each morning consists simply in shoving them all back; in listening to that other voice, taking that other point of view, letting that other larger, stronger, quieter life come flowing in. And so on, all day. Standing back from all your natural fussings and frettings; coming in out of the wind.

We can only do it for moments at first. But from those moments the new sort of life will be spreading through our system: because now we are letting Him work at the right part of us. It is the difference between paint, which is merely laid on the surface, and a dye or stain which soaks right through. He never talked vague, idealistic gas. When He said, 'Be perfect', He meant it. He meant that we must go in for the full treatment. It is hard; but the sort of compromise we are all hankering after is harder — in fact, it is impossible. It may be hard for an egg to turn into a bird: it would be a jolly sight harder for it to learn to fly while remaining an egg. We are like eggs at present. And you cannot go on indefinitely being just an ordinary, decent egg. We must be hatched or go bad.

Refreshments on the Journey January 3

The settled happiness and security which we all desire, God withholds from us by the very nature of the world: but joy, pleasure, and merriment, He has scattered broadcast. We are never safe, but we have plenty of fun, and some ecstasy. It is not hard to see why. The security we crave would teach us to rest our hearts in this world and oppose an obstacle to our return to God: a few moments of happy love, a landscape, a symphony, a merry meeting with our friends, a bathe or a football match, have no such tendency. Our Father refreshes us on the journey with some pleasant inns, but will not encourage us to mistake them for home.

An Upside Down World January 4

While we are in this 'valley of tears', cursed with labour, hemmed round with necessities, tripped up with frustrations, doomed to perpetual plannings, puzzlings, and anxieties, certain qualities that must belong to the celestial condition have no chance to get through, can project no image of themselves, except in activities which, for us here and now, are frivolous. For surely we must suppose the life of the blessed to be an end in itself, indeed The End: to be utterly spontaneous; to be the complete reconciliation of boundless freedom with order – with the most delicately adjusted, supple, intricate, and beautiful order? How can you find any image of this in the 'serious' activities either of our natural or of our (present) spiritual life? Either in our precarious and heartbroken affections or in the Way which is always, in some degree, a *via crucis*? No. . . . It is only in our 'hours-off', only in our moments of permitted festivity, that we find an analogy. Dance and game *are* frivolous, unimportant down here; for 'down here' is not their natural place. Here they are a moment's rest from the life we were placed here to live. But in this world everything is upside down. That which, if it could be prolonged here, would be a truancy, is likest that which in a better country is the End of ends. Joy is the serious business of Heaven.

The Road   *January 5*

When we are lost in the woods the sight of a signpost is a great matter. He who first sees it cries, 'Look!' The whole party gathers round and stares. But when we have found the road and are passing signposts every few miles, we shall not stop and stare. They will encourage us and we shall be grateful to the authority that set them up. But we shall not stop and stare, or not much; not on this road, though their pillars are of silver and their lettering of gold. 'We would be at Jerusalem.'

The Epiphany of the Lord   *January 6*

We, with our modern democratic and arithmetical pre-suppositions would so have liked and expected all men to start equal in their search for God. One has the picture of great centripetal roads coming from all directions, with well-disposed people, all meaning the same thing, and getting closer and closer together. How shockingly opposite to that is the Christian story! One people picked out of the whole earth; that people purged and proved again and again. Some are lost in the desert before they reach Palestine; some stay in Babylon; some becoming indifferent. The whole thing narrows and narrows, until at last it comes down to a little point, small as the point of a spear – a Jewish girl at her prayers. That is what the whole of human nature has narrowed down to before the Incarnation takes place. Very unlike what we expected, but, of course, not in the least unlike what seems, in general, as shown by Nature, to be God's way of working. . . . The people who are selected are, in a sense, unfairly selected for a supreme honour; but it is also a supreme burden. The People of Israel come to realize that it is their woes which are saving the world.

Waiting to be Called In   *January 7*

At present we are on the outside of the world, the wrong side of the door. We discern the freshness and purity of morning, but they do not make us fresh and pure. We cannot mingle with the splendours we see. But all the leaves of the New Testament are rustling with the rumour that it will not always be so. Some day, God willing, we shall get *in*. When human souls have become as perfect in voluntary obedience as the inanimate creation is in its lifeless obedience, then they will put on its glory, or rather that greater glory of which Nature is only the first sketch. For you must not think that I am putting forward any heathen fancy of being absorbed into Nature. Nature is mortal; we shall outlive her. When all the suns and nebulae have passed away, each one of you will still be alive. Nature is only the image, the symbol; but it is the symbol Scripture invites me to use. We are summoned to pass in through Nature, beyond her, into that splendour which she fitfully reflects.

Into the Presence of God   *January 8*

It is religion itself – prayer and sacrament and repentance and adoration – which is here, in the long run, our sole avenue to the real. Like mathematics, religion can grow from within, or decay. The Jew knows more than the Pagan, the Christian more than the Jew, the modern vaguely religious man less than any of the three. But, like mathematics, it remains simply itself, capable of being applied to any new theory of the material universe and outmoded by none.

When any man comes into the presence of God he will find, whether he wishes it or not, that all those things which seemed to make him so different from the men of other times, or even from his earlier self, have fallen off him. He is back where he always was, where every man always is. . . . No possible complexity which we can give to our picture of the universe can hide us from God: there is no copse, no forest, no jungle thick enough to provide cover. . . . In the twinkling of an eye, in a time too small to be measured, and in any place, all that seems to divide us from God can flee away, vanish, leaving us naked before Him, like the first man, like the only man, as if nothing but He and I existed. And since that contact cannot be avoided for long and since it means either bliss or horror, the business of life is to learn to like it. That is the first and great commandment.

If you asked twenty good men today what they thought the highest of the virtues, nineteen of them would reply, Unselfishness. But if you had asked almost any of the great Christians of old, he would have replied, Love. You see what has happened? A negative term has been substituted for a positive, and this is of more than philological importance. The negative idea of Unselfishness carries with it the suggestion not primarily of securing good things for others, but of going without them ourselves, as if our abstinence and not their happiness was the important point. I do not think this is the Christian virtue of Love. The New Testament has lots to say about self-denial, but not about self-denial as an end in itself. We are told to deny ourselves and to take up our crosses in order that we may follow Christ; and nearly every description of what we shall ultimately find if we do so contains an appeal to desire. If there lurks in most modern minds the notion that to desire our own good and earnestly to hope for the enjoyment of it is a bad thing, I submit that this notion has crept in from Kant and the Stoics and is no part of the Christian faith. Indeed, if we consider the unblushing promises of reward and the staggering nature of the rewards promised in the gospels, it would seem that Our Lord finds our desires, not too strong, but too weak. We are half-hearted creatures, fooling about with drink and sex and ambition when infinite joy is offered us, like an ignorant child who wants to go on making mud pies in a slum because he cannot imagine what is meant by the offer of a holiday at the sea. We are far too easily pleased.

The Difference between Love and Kindness

By the goodness of God we mean nowadays almost exclusively His lovingness; and in this we may be right. And by Love, in this context, most of us mean kindness – the desire to see others than the self happy; not happy in this way or in that, but just happy. What would really satisfy us would be a God who said of anything we happened to like doing, 'What does it matter so long as they are contented?' We want, in fact, not so much a Father in Heaven as a grandfather in heaven – a senile benevolence who, as they say, 'liked to see young people enjoying themselves' and whose plan for the universe was simply that it might be truly said at the end of each day, 'a good time was had by all'. Not many people, I admit, would formulate a theology in precisely those terms: but a conception not very different lurks at the back of many minds. I do not claim to be an exception: I should very much like to live in a universe which was governed on such lines. But since it is abundantly clear that I don't, and since I have reason to believe, nevertheless, that God is Love, I conclude that my conception of love needs correction.

The Intolerable Compliment

There is kindness in Love: but Love and kindness are not coterminous, and when kindness . . . is separated from the other elements of Love, it involves a certain fundamental indifference to its object, and even something like contempt of it. Kindness consents very readily to the removal of its object – we have all met people whose kindness to animals is constantly leading them to kill animals lest they should suffer. Kindness, merely as such, cares not whether its object becomes good or bad, provided only that it escapes suffering. As Scripture points out, it is bastards who are spoiled: the legitimate sons, who are to carry on the family tradition, are punished. It is for people whom we care nothing about that we demand happiness on any terms: with our friends, our lovers, our children, we are exacting and would rather see them suffer much than be happy in contemptible and estranging modes. If God is Love, He is, by definition, something more than mere kindness. And it appears, from all the records, that though He has often rebuked us and condemned us, He has never regarded us with contempt. He has paid us the intolerable compliment of loving us, in the deepest, most tragic, most inexorable sense.

Objects of the Divine Love   *January 12*

When Christianity says that God loves man, it means that God *loves* man: not that He has some 'disinterested', because really indifferent, concern for our welfare, but that, in awful and surprising truth, we are the objects of His love. You asked for a loving God: you have one. The great spirit you so lightly invoked, the 'lord of terrible aspect', is present: not a senile benevolence that drowsily wishes you to be happy in your own way, not the cold philanthropy of a conscientious magistrate, nor the care of a host who feels responsible for the comfort of his guests, but the consuming fire Himself, the Love that made the worlds, persistent as the artist's love for his work and despotic as a man's love for a dog, provident and venerable as a father's love for a child, jealous, inexorable, exacting as love between the sexes. How this should be, I do not know. . . . We were made not primarily that we may love God (though we were made for that too) but that God may love us, that we may become objects in which the Divine love may rest 'well pleased'.

To ask that God's love should be content with us as we are is to ask that God should cease to be God: because He is what He is, His love must, in the nature of things, be impeded and repelled, by certain stains in our present character, and because He already loves us He must labour to make us lovable. We cannot even wish, in our better moments, that He could reconcile Himself to our present impurities.

The Visible Church   *January 13*

If He can be known it will be by self-revelation on His part, not by speculation on ours. We, therefore, look for Him where it is claimed that He has revealed Himself by miracle, by inspired teachers, by enjoined ritual. The traditions conflict, yet the longer and more sympatheti- cally we study them the more we become aware of a common element in many of them: the theme of sacri- fice, of mystical communion through the shed blood, of death and rebirth, of redemption, is too clear to escape notice. We are fully entitled to use moral and intellectual criticism. What we are not, in my opinion, entitled to do is simply to abstract the ethical element and set that up as a religion on its own. Rather in that tradition which is at once more completely ethical and most transcends mere ethics . . . we may still most reasonably believe that we have the consummation of all religion, the fullest message from the wholly other, the living creator, who, if He is at all, must be the God not only of the philosophers, but of mystics and savages, not only of the head and heart, but also of the primitive emotions and the spiritual heights beyond all emotion. We may . . . attach ourselves to the Church, to the only concrete organization which has preserved down to this present time the core of all the messages, pagan and perhaps pre-pagan, that have ever come from beyond the world, and begin to practise the only religion which rests not upon some selection of certain supposedly 'higher' elements in our nature, but on the shattering and rebuilding, the death and rebirth, of that nature in every part: neither Greek nor Jew nor barbarian, but a new creation.

The Divisions of Christendom   *January 14*

If any man is tempted to think – as one might be tempted who read only contemporaries – that 'Christianity' is a word of so many meanings that it means nothing at all, he can learn beyond all doubt, by stepping out of his own century, that this is not so. Measured against the ages 'mere Christianity' turns out to be no insipid inter-denominational transparency, but something positive, self-consistent, and inexhaustible. I know it, indeed, to my cost. In the days when I still hated Christianity, I learned to recognize, like some all too familiar smell, that almost unvarying *something* which met me, now in Puritan Bunyan, now in Anglican Hooker, now in Thomist Dante. . . .

We are all rightly distressed, and ashamed also, at the divisions of Christendom. But those who have always lived within the Christian fold may be too easily dispirited by them. They are bad, but such people do not know what it looks like from without. Seen from there, what is left intact, despite all the divisions, still appears (as it truly is) an immensely formidable unity. I know, for I saw it; and well our enemies know it. That unity any of us can find by going out of his own age. It is not enough, but it is more than you had thought till then. Once you are well soaked in it, if you then venture to speak, you will have an amusing experience. You will be thought a Papist when you are actually reproducing Bunyan, a Pantheist when you are quoting Aquinas, and so forth. For you have now got on to the great level viaduct which crosses the ages and which looks so high from the valleys, so low from the mountains, so narrow compared with the swamps, and so broad compared with the sheeptracks.

The Reunion of Christ's Church   *January 15*

It was never more needed. A united Christendom should be the answer to the new Paganism. But how reconciliation of the churches, as opposed to conversions of individuals from one church to another, is to come about, I confess I cannot see. I am inclined to think that the immediate task is vigorous co-operation on the basis of what even now is common – combined, of course, with full admission of the differences. An *experienced* unity on some things might then prove the prelude to a confessional unity on all things. Nothing would give such strong support to the Papal claims as the spectacle of a Pope actually functioning as head of Christendom.

Christianity v. Christianity-and-Water   *January 16*

The time is always ripe for reunion. Divisions between Christians are a sin and a scandal, and Christians ought at all times to be making contributions towards reunion, if it is only by their prayers. I am only a layman and a recent Christian, and I do not know much about these things, but in all the things which I have written and thought I have always stuck to traditional dogmatic positions. The result is that letters of agreement reach me from what are ordinarily regarded as the most different kinds of Christians; for instance, I get letters from Jesuits, monks, nuns, and also from Quakers and Welsh

Dissenters, and so on. So it seems to me that the 'extremist' elements in every church are nearest one another and the liberal and 'broad-minded' people in each Body could never be united at all. The world of 'broad-mindedness' and watered-down 'religion' is a world where a small number of people (all of the same type) say totally different things and change their minds every few minutes. We shall never get reunion from them.

Screwtape on Hell's Plan for Christians   *January 17*

My dear Wormwood,
    The real trouble about the set your patient is living in is that it is *merely* Christian. They all have individual interests, of course, but the bond remains mere Christianity. What we want, if men become Christians at all, is to keep them in the state of mind I call 'Christianity And'. You know – Christianity and the Crisis, Christianity and the New Psychology, Christianity and the New Order, Christianity and Faith Healing, Christianity and Psychical Research, Christianity and Vegetarianism, Christianity and Spelling Reform. If they must be Christians let them at least be Christians with a difference. Substitute for the faith itself some Fashion with a Christian colouring. Work on their horror of the Same Old Thing.
    The horror of the Same Old Thing is one of the most valuable passions we have produced in the human heart – an endless source of heresies in religion, folly in counsel, infidelity in marriage, and inconstancy in friendship. The humans live in time, and experience reality successively. To experience much of it, therefore, they must experience many different things; in other words, they must experience change. And since they need change, the Enemy (being a hedonist at heart) has made change pleasurable to them, just as He has made eating pleasur-

28

able. But since He does not wish them to make change, any more than eating, an end in itself, He has balanced the love of change in them by a love of permanence. He has contrived to gratify both tastes together in the very world He has made, by that union of change and permanence which we call Rhythm. He gives them the seasons, each season different yet every year the same, so that spring is always felt as a novelty yet always as the recurrence of an immemorial theme. He gives them in His Church a spiritual year; they change from a fast to a feast, but it is the same feast as before. . . . We pick out this natural pleasantness of change and twist it into a demand for absolute novelty.

The Theologian's Danger   *January 18*

There have been men . . . who got so interested in proving the existence of God that they came to care nothing for God Himself . . . as if the good Lord had nothing to do but *exist*! There have been some who were so occupied in spreading Christianity that they never gave a thought to Christ. Man! Ye see it in smaller matters. Did ye never know a lover of books that with all his first editions and signed copies had lost the power to read them? Or an organizer of charities that had lost all love for the poor? It is the subtlest of all the snares.

Advice to the Clergy   *January 19*

There is a danger . . . of the clergy developing a special professional conscience which obscures the very plain moral issue. Men who have passed beyond these boundary lines . . . are apt to protest that they have come by their unorthodox opinions honestly. In defence of those opinions they are prepared to suffer obloquy and to forfeit professional advancement. They thus come to feel like martyrs. But this simply misses the point which so gravely scandalizes the layman. We never doubted that the unorthodox opinions were honestly held: what we complain of is your continuing your ministry after you have come to hold them. We always knew that a man who makes his living as a paid agent of the Conservative Party may honestly change his views and honestly become a Communist. What we deny is that he can honestly continue to be a Conservative agent and to receive money from one party while he supports the policy of another.

True – or False? *January 20*

One of the great difficulties is to keep before the audience's mind the question of Truth. They always think you are recommending Christianity not because it is *true* but because it is *good*. And in the discussion they will at every moment try to escape from the issue 'True – or False' into stuff about the Spanish Inquisition, or France, or Poland – or anything whatever. You have to keep forcing them back, and again back, to the real point. Only thus will you be able to undermine . . . their belief that a certain amount of 'religion' is desirable but one mustn't carry it too far. One must keep on pointing out that Christianity is a statement which, if false, is of no importance, and, if true, of infinite importance. The one thing it cannot be is moderately important.

We are to defend Christianity itself – the faith preached by the Apostles, attested by the Martyrs, embodied in the Creeds, expounded by the Fathers. This must be clearly distinguished from the whole of what any one of us may think about God and Man. Each of us has his individual emphasis: each holds, in addition to the Faith, many opinions which seem to him to be consistent with it and true and important. And so perhaps they are. But as apologists it is not our business to defend *them*. We are defending Christianity; not 'my religion'. When we mention our personal opinions we must always make quite clear the difference between them and the Faith itself. . . .

This distinction, which is demanded by honesty, also gives the apologist a great tactical advantage. The great difficulty is to get modern audiences to realize that you are preaching Christianity solely and simply because you happen to think it *true*; they always suppose you are preaching it because you like it or think it is good for society or something of that sort. . . . This immediately helps them to realize that what is being discussed is a question about objective fact – not gas about ideals and points of view. . . . Do not attempt to water Christianity down. There must be no pretence that you can have it with the Supernatural left out. So far as I can see Christianity is precisely the one religion from which the miraculous cannot be separated. You must frankly argue for supernaturalism from the very outset.

When the Temperature Drops   *January 22*

We who defend Christianity find ourselves constantly opposed not by the irreligion of our hearers but by their real religion. Speak about beauty, truth and goodness, or about a God who is simply the indwelling principle of these three, speak about a great spiritual force pervading all things, a common mind of which we are all parts, a pool of generalized spirituality to which we can all flow, and you will command friendly interest. But the temperature drops as soon as you mention a God who has purposes and performs particular actions, who does one thing and not another, a concrete, choosing, commanding, prohibiting God with a determinate character. People become embarrassed or angry. Such a conception seems to them primitive and crude and even irreverent. The popular 'religion' excludes miracles because it excludes the 'living God' of Christianity and believes instead in a kind of God who obviously would not do miracles, or indeed anything else.

Christian Education in Schools   *January 23*

If we had noticed that the young men of the present day found it harder and harder to get the right answers to sums, we should consider that this had been adequately explained the moment we discovered that schools had for some years ceased to teach arithmetic. After that discovery we should turn a deaf ear to people who offered explanations of a vaguer and larger kind – people who said that the influence of Einstein had sapped the ancestral belief in fixed numerical relations, or that gangster films had undermined the desire to get right answers, or that the evolution of consciousness was now entering on its post-arithmetical phase. Where a clear and simple explanation completely covers the facts no other explanation is in court. If the younger generation have never been told what the Christians say and never heard any arguments in defence of it, then their agnosticism or indifference is fully explained. There is no need to look any further: no need to talk about the general intellectual climate of the age, the influence of mechanistic civilization on the character of urban life. And having discovered that the cause of their ignorance is lack of instruction, we have also discovered the remedy. There is nothing in the nature of the younger generation which incapacitates them for receiving Christianity. If any one is prepared to tell them, they are apparently ready to hear. . . . The young people today are un-Christian because their teachers have been either unwilling or unable to transmit Christianity to them. . . . None can give to another what he does not possess himself.

St François de Sales   January 24

The crude picture of penitence as something like apology or even placation has, for me, the value of making penitence an act. The more high-minded views involve some danger of regarding it simply as a state of feeling. . . . The question is before my mind at present because I've been reading Alexander Whyte. . . . For him, one essential symptom of the regenerate life is a permanent, and permanently horrified, perception of one's natural and (it seems) unalterable corruption. The true Christian's nostril is to be continually attentive to the inner cesspool. . . . Another author, quoted in Haller's *Rise of Puritanism*, says that when he looked into his heart, it was 'as if I had in the heat of summer lookt down into the Filth of a Dungeon, where I discerned Millions of crawling living things in the midst of that Sink and liquid Corruption'.

I won't listen to those who describe that vision as merely pathological. I have seen the 'slimy things that crawled with legs' in my own dungeon. I thought the glimpse taught me sense. But Whyte seems to think it should be not a glimpse but a daily, lifelong scrutiny. Can he be right? It sounds so very unlike the New Testament fruits of the spirit – love, joy, peace. And very unlike the

Pauline programme: 'forgetting those things which are behind and reaching forth unto those things that are before.' And very unlike St François de Sales' green, dewy chapter on *la douceur* towards one's self. Anyway, what's the use of laying down a programme of permanent emotions? They can be permanent only by being factitious. . . . I know that a spiritual emetic at the right moment may be needed. But not a regular diet of emetics! If one survived, one would develop a 'tolerance' of them. This poring over the 'sink' might breed its own perverse pride.

The Conversion of St Paul   January 25

In one sense the road back to God is a road of moral effort, of trying harder and harder. But in another sense it is not trying that is ever going to bring us home. All this trying leads up to the vital moment at which you turn to God and say, 'You must do this. I can't.' Do not, I implore you, start asking yourselves, 'Have I reached that moment?' Do not sit down and start watching your own mind to see if it is coming along. That puts a man quite on the wrong track. When the most important things in our life happen we quite often do not know, at the moment, what is going on. A man does not always say to himself, 'Hullo! I'm growing up.' It is often only when he looks back that he realizes what has happened and recognizes it as what people call 'growing up'. You can see it even in simple matters. A man who starts anxiously watching to see whether he is going to sleep is very likely to remain wide awake. As well, the thing I am talking of now may not happen to every one in a sudden flash – as it did to St Paul or Bunyan: it may be so gradual that no one could ever point to a particular hour or even a particular year. And what matters is the nature of the change in itself, not how we feel while it is happening. It is the change from being confident about our own efforts to the state in which we despair of doing anything for ourselves and leave it to God.

St Timothy and St Titus *January 26*

A most astonishing misconception has long dominated the modern mind on the subject of St Paul. It is to this effect: that Jesus preached a kindly and simple religion (found in the Gospels) and that St Paul afterwards corrupted it into a cruel and complicated religion (found in the Epistles). This is really quite untenable. All the most terrifying texts came from the mouth of Our Lord: all the texts on which we can base such warrant as we have for hoping that all men will be saved come from St Paul. If it could be proved that St Paul altered the teaching of his Master in any way, he altered it in exactly the opposite way to that which is popularly supposed. But there is no real evidence for a pre-Pauline doctrine different from St Paul's. The Epistles are, for the most part, the earliest Christian documents we possess. The Gospels come later. They are not 'the Gospel', the statement of the Christian belief. They were written for those who had already been converted, who had already accepted 'the Gospel'. They leave out many of the 'complications' (that is, the theology) because they are intended for readers who have already been instructed in it. In that sense the Epistles are more primitive and more central than the Gospels – though not, of course, than the great events which the Gospels recount. God's act (the Incarnation, the Crucifixion, and the Resurrection) comes first: the earliest theological analysis of it comes in the Epistles: then, when the generation who had known the Lord was dying out, the Gospels were composed to provide for believers a record of the great Act and of some of the Lord's sayings.

In the earlier history of every rebellion there is a stage at which you do not yet attack the King in person. You say, 'The King is all right. It is his Ministers who are wrong. They misrepresent him and corrupt all his plans – which, I'm sure, are good plans if only the Ministers would let them take effect.' And the first victory consists in beheading a few Ministers: only at a later stage do you go on and behead the King himself. In the same way, the nineteenth-century attack on St Paul was really only a stage in the revolt against Christ. Men were not ready in large numbers to attack Christ Himself. They made the normal first move – that of attacking one of His principal ministers. Everything they disliked in Christianity was therefore attributed to St Paul. It was unfortunate that their case could not impress anyone who had really read the Gospels and the Epistles with attention: but apparently few people had, and so the first victory was won. St Paul was impeached and banished and the world went on to the next step – the attack on the King Himself.

St Thomas Aquinas   *January 28*

We may anticipate a revival of the allegorical sense in biblical criticism. But it will probably be dangerous, and in the Middle Ages I think it was dangerous, to appreciation of the Historical Books as plain heroic narrative.

St Thomas Aquinas throws a little more light on the . . . 'lowness' or 'simplicity' of the Bible. He explains why Scripture expresses divine truths not merely through corporeal images but even through images of vile bodies rather than noble. This is done, he says, to liberate the mind from error, to reduce the danger of any confusion between the symbol and the reality. It is an answer worthy of a profound theologian. At the same time, the passage in which it occurs reveals attitudes most hostile to aesthetic appreciation of the sacred text. It would seem, he says, that Scripture ought not to use metaphors. For what is proper to the lowest kind of learning (*infimae doctrinae*) does not seem suitable to the queen of the sciences. But metaphor is proper to poetry, and poetry is the lowest of all forms of learning. . . . The answer, so far as it concerns us here, is that poetry and Scripture use metaphor for quite different reasons; poetry for delight, and Scripture *propter necessitatem et utilitatem*. Where a nineteenth-century critic might have said that Scripture was itself the highest poetry, St Thomas says rather that the highest and the lowest *doctrinae* have, paradoxically, one point in common, but of course for different reasons.

Restoration of the Bible
on its Own Terms

Unless the religious claims of the Bible are again acknowledged, its literary claims will, I think, be given only 'mouth honour' and that decreasingly. For it is, through and through, a sacred book. Most of its component parts were written, and all of them were brought together, for a purely religious purpose. It contains good literature and bad literature. But even the good literature is so written that we can seldom disregard its sacred character. It is easy enough to read Homer while suspending our disbelief in the Greek pantheon; but then the *Iliad* was not composed chiefly, if at all, to enforce obedience to Zeus and Athene and Poseidon. The Greek tragedians are more religious than Homer, but even there we have only religious speculation or at least the poet's personal religious ideas; not dogma. That is why we can join in. Neither Aeschylus nor even Virgil tacitly prefaces his poetry with the formula 'Thus say the gods'. But

37

in most parts of the Bible everything is implicitly or explicitly introduced with 'Thus saith the Lord'. It is, if you like to put it that way, not merely a sacred book but a book so remorselessly and continuously sacred that it does not invite, it excludes or repels, the merely aesthetic approach. You can read it as literature only by a *tour de force*. You are cutting the wood against the grain, using the tool for a purpose it was not intended to serve. It demands incessantly to be taken on its own terms: it will not continue to give literary delight very long except to those who go to it for something quite different. I predict that it will in the future be read as it always has been read, almost exclusively by Christians.

Other Religions   *January 30*

If you are a Christian you do not have to believe that all the other religions are simply wrong all through. If you are an atheist you do have to believe that the main point in all the religions of the whole world is simply one huge mistake. If you are a Christian, you are free to think that all these religions, even the queerest ones, contain at least some hint of the truth. When I was an atheist I had to try to persuade myself that most of the human race have always been wrong about the question that mattered to them most; when I became a Christian I was able to take a more liberal view. But, of course, being a Christian does mean thinking that where Christianity differs from other religions, Christianity is right and they are wrong. As in arithmetic – there is only one right answer to a sum, and all other answers are wrong: but some of the wrong answers are much nearer being right than others.

There is no half-way house and there is no parallel in other religions. If you had gone to Buddha and asked him 'Are you the son of Bramah?' he would have said, 'My son, you are still in the vale of illusion.' If you had gone to Socrates and asked, 'Are you Zeus?' he would have laughed at you. If you had gone to Mohammed and asked, 'Are you Allah?' he would first have rent his clothes and then cut your head off. If you had asked Confucius, 'Are you Heaven?' I think he would have probably replied, 'Remarks which are not in accordance with nature are in bad taste.' The idea of a great moral teacher saying what Christ said is out of the question. In my opinion, the only person who can say that sort of thing is either God or a complete lunatic suffering from that form of delusion which undermines the whole mind of man. If you think you are a poached egg, when you are looking for a piece of toast to suit you, you may be sane, but if you think you are God, there is no chance for you. We may note in passing that He was never regarded as a mere moral teacher. He did not produce that effect on any of the people who actually met Him. He produced mainly three effects – Hatred – Terror – Adoration. There was no trace of people expressing mild approval.

What are We to Make of Christ?   *February 1*

'What are we to make of Christ?' There is no question of what we can make of Him, it is entirely a question of what He intends to make of us. You must accept or reject the story.

The things He says are very different from what any other teacher has said. Others say, 'This is the truth about the Universe. This is the way you ought to go', but He says, '*I* am the Truth, and the Way, and the Life.' He says, 'No man can reach absolute reality, except through Me. Try to retain your own life and you will be inevitably ruined. Give yourself away and you will be saved.' He says, 'If you are ashamed of Me, if, when you hear this call, you turn the other way, I also will look the other way when I come again as God without disguise. If anything whatever is keeping you from God and from Me, whatever it is, throw it away. If it is your eye, pull it out. If it is your hand, cut it off. If you put yourself first you will be last. Come to Me everyone who is carrying a heavy load, I will set that right. Your sins, all of them, are wiped out, I can do that. I am Re-birth, I am Life. Eat Me, drink Me, I am your Food. And finally, do not be afraid, I have overcome the whole Universe.' That is the issue.

The Presentation of the Lord   *February 2*

When we look into the Selectiveness which the Christians attribute to God we find in it none of that 'favouritism' which we were afraid of. The 'chosen' people are chosen not for their own sake (certainly not for their own honour or pleasure) but for the sake of the unchosen. Abraham is told that 'in his seed' (the chosen nation) 'all nations shall be blest'. That nation has been chosen to bear a heavy burden. Their sufferings are great: but, as Isaiah recognized, their sufferings heal others. On the finally selected Woman falls the utmost depth of maternal anguish. Her Son, the incarnate God, is a 'man of sorrows'; the one Man into whom Deity descended, the one Man who can be lawfully adored, is pre-eminent for suffering.

A Matter of Fairness *February 3*

Is it not frightfully unfair that this new life should be confined to people who have heard of Christ and been able to believe in Him? But the truth is God has not told us what His arrangements about the other people are. We do know that no man can be saved except through Christ; we do not know that only those who know Him can be saved through Him. But in the meantime, if you are worried about the people outside, the most unreasonable thing you can do is to remain outside yourself. Christians are Christ's body, the organism through which He works. Every addition to that body enables Him to do more. If you want to help those outside you must add your own little cell to the body of Christ who alone can help them. Cutting off a man's fingers would be an odd way of getting him to do more work.

Dogma and the Universe *February 4*

It is a common reproach against Christianity that its dogmas are unchanging, while human knowledge is in continual growth. Hence, to unbelievers, we seem to be always engaged in the hopeless task of trying to force the new knowledge into moulds which it has outgrown. I think this feeling alienates the outsider much more than any particular discrepancies between this or that doctrine and this or that scientific theory. We may, as we say, 'get over' dozens of isolated 'difficulties', but that does not alter his sense that the endeavour as a whole is doomed to failure and perverse: indeed, the more ingenious, the more perverse. For it seems to him clear that, if our ancestors had known what we know about the universe, Christianity would never have existed at all: and, however we patch and mend, no system of thought which claims to be immutable can, in the long run, adjust itself to our growing knowledge.

Science and the Dogma of Creation   *February 5*

In one respect, as many Christians have noticed, contemporary science has recently come into line with Christian doctrine, and parted company with the classical forms of materialism. If anything emerges clearly from modern physics, it is that nature is not everlasting. The universe had a beginning, and will have an end. But the great materialistic systems of the past all believed in the eternity, and thence in the self-existence of matter. As Professor Whittaker said in the Riddell Lectures of 1942, 'It was never possible to oppose seriously the dogma of the Creation except by maintaining that the world has existed from all eternity in more or less its present state.' This fundamental ground for materialism has now been withdrawn. We should not lean too heavily on this, for scientific theories change. But at the moment it appears that the burden of proof rests, not on us, but on those who deny that Nature has some cause beyond herself.

In popular thought, however, the origin of the universe has counted (I think) for less than its character – its immense size and its apparent indifference, if not hostility, to human life. And very often this impresses people all the more because it is supposed to be a modern discovery – an excellent example of those things which our ancestors did not know and which, if they had known them, would have prevented the very beginnings of Christianity. Here there is a simple historical falsehood. Ptolemy knew just as well as Eddington that the earth was infinitesimal in comparison with the whole content of space. There is no question here of knowledge having grown until the frame of archaic thought is no longer able

42

to contain it. The real question is why the spatial insignificance of the earth, after being known for centuries, should suddenly in the last century have become an argument against Christianity.

The Argument about Space *February 6*

When the doctor at a post-mortem diagnoses poison, pointing to the state of the dead man's organs, his argument is rational because he has a clear idea of that opposite state in which the organs would have been found if no poison were present. In the same way, if we use the vastness of space and the smallness of earth to disprove the existence of God, we ought to have a clear idea of the sort of universe we should expect if God did exist. But have we? Whatever space may be in itself – and, of course, some moderns think it finite – we certainly perceive it as three-dimensional, and to three-dimensional space we can conceive no boundaries. By the very forms of our perceptions, therefore, we must feel as if we lived somewhere in infinite space. If we discovered no objects in this infinite space except those which are of use to man (our own sun and moon), then this vast emptiness would certainly be used as a strong argument against the existence of God. If we discover other bodies, they must be habitable or uninhabitable: and the odd thing is that both these hypotheses are used as grounds for rejecting Christianity. If the universe is teeming with life, this, we are told, reduces to absurdity the Christian claim – or what is thought to be the Christian claim – that man is unique, and the Christian doctrine that to this one planet God came down and was incarnate for us men and our salvation. If, on the other hand, the earth is really unique, then that proves that life is only an accidental by-product in the universe, and so again disproves our religion. Really, we are hard to please. We

43

treat God as the police treat a man when he is arrested; whatever He does will be used in evidence against Him. I do not think this is due to our wickedness. I suspect there is something in our very mode of thought which makes it inevitable that we should always be baffled by actual existence, *whatever* character actual existence may have.

Size and Value *February 7*

The whole argument from size rests on the assumption that differences of size ought to coincide with differences of value: for unless they do, there is, of course, no reason why the minute earth and the yet smaller human creatures upon it should not be the most important thing in a universe that contains the spiral nebulae. Now, is this assumption rational or emotional? I feel, as well as anyone else, the absurdity of supposing that the galaxy could be of less moment in God's eyes than such an atom as a human being. But I notice that I feel no similar absurdity in supposing that a man of five feet high may be more important than another man who is five feet three and a half – nor that a man may matter more than a tree, or a brain more than a leg. In other words, the feeling of absurdity arises only if the differences of size are very great. But where a relation is perceived by reason it holds good universally. If size and value had any real connection, small differences in size would accompany small differences in value as surely as large differences in size accompany large differences in value. But no sane man could suppose that this is so. I don't think the taller man *slightly* more valuable than the shorter one. I don't allow a slight superiority to trees over men, and then neglect it because it is too small to bother about. I perceive, as long as I am dealing with the small differences of size, that they have no connection with value whatsoever. I therefore conclude that the importance attached to the great differences of size is an affair, not of reason but of emotion – of that peculiar emotion which superiorities in size produce only after a certain point of absolute size has been reached.

We are Inveterate Poets   *February 8*

When a quantity is very great, we cease to regard it as mere quantity. Our imaginations awake. Instead of mere quantity, we now have a quality – the sublime. Unless this were so, the merely arithmetical greatness of the galaxy would be no more impressive than the figures in a telephone directory. It is thus, in a sense, from ourselves that the material universe derives its power to overawe us. To a mind which did not share our emotions, and lacked our imaginative energies, the argument from size would be sheerly meaningless. Men look on the starry heavens with reverence: monkeys do not. The silence of the eternal spaces terrified Pascal, but it was the greatness of Pascal that enabled them to do so. When we are frightened by the greatness of the universe, we are (almost literally) frightened by our own shadows: for these light years and billions of centuries are mere arithmetic until the shadow of man, the poet, the maker of myth, falls upon them. I do not say we are wrong to tremble at his shadow; it is a shadow of an image of God. But if ever the vastness of matter threatens to overcross our spirits, one must remember that it is matter spiritualized which does so. To puny man, the great nebula in Andromeda owes in a sense its greatness.

What Sort of Universe Do We Demand? *February 9*

We are hard to please. If the world in which we found ourselves were not vast and strange enough to give us Pascal's terror, what poor creatures we should be! Being what we are, rational but also animate, amphibians who start from the world of sense and proceed through myth and metaphor to the world of spirit, I do not see how we could have come to know the greatness of God without that hint furnished by the greatness of the material universe. Once again, what sort of universe do we demand? If it were small enough to be cosy, it would not be big enough to be sublime. If it is large enough for us to stretch our spiritual limbs in, it must be large enough to baffle us. Cramped or terrified, we must, in any conceivable world, be one or the other. I prefer terror. I should be suffocated in a universe that I could see to the end of. Have you never, when walking in a wood, turned back deliberately for fear you should come out at the other side and thus make it ever after in your imagination a mere beggarly strip of trees?

Man is Not the Measure of All Things *February 10*

I hope you do not think I am suggesting that God made the spiral nebulae solely or chiefly in order to give me the experience of awe and bewilderment. I have not the faintest idea why He made them; on the whole, I think it would be rather surprising if I had. As far as I understand the matter, Christianity is not wedded to an anthropocentric view of the universe as a whole. The first chapters of Genesis, no doubt, give the story of creation in the form of a folk-tale — a fact recognized as early as the time of St Jerome — and if you take them alone you might get that impression. But it is not confirmed by the Bible as a whole. There are few places in literature where we are more sternly warned against making man the measure of all things than in the Book of Job: 'Canst thou draw out leviathan with an hook? Will he make a covenant with thee? Wilt thou take him for a servant? Shall not one be cast down even at the sight of him?' In St Paul, the powers of the skies seem usually to be hostile to man. It is, of course, the essence of Christianity that God loves man and for his sake became man and died. But that does not prove that man is the sole end of nature. In the parable, it was the one lost sheep that the shepherd went in search of: it was not the only sheep in the flock, and we are not told that it was the most valuable – save in so far as the most desperately in need has, while the need lasts, a peculiar value in the eyes of Love.

God's Love Has no Limits   *February 11*

The doctrine of the Incarnation would conflict with what we know of this vast universe only if we knew also that there were other rational species in it who had, like us, fallen, and who needed redemption in the same mode, and that they had not been vouchsafed it. But we know none of these things. It may be full of life that needs no redemption. It may be full of life that has been redeemed. It may be full of things quite other than life which satisfy the Divine Wisdom in fashions one cannot conceive. We are in no position to draw up maps of God's psychology, and prescribe limits to His interests. We would not do so even for a man whom we knew to be greater than ourselves. The doctrines that God is Love and that He delights in men, are positive doctrines, not limiting doctrines. He is not less than this. What more He may be, we do not know; we know only that He must be more than we can conceive. It is to be expected that His creation should be, in the main, unintelligible to us.

Christians themselves have been much to blame for the misunderstanding on these matters. They have a bad habit of talking as if revelation existed to gratify curiosity by illuminating all creation so that it becomes self-explanatory and all questions are answered. But revelation appears to me to be purely practical, to be addressed to the particular animal, Fallen Man, for the relief of his urgent necessities – not to the spirit of inquiry in man for the gratification of his liberal curiosity. We know that God has visited and redeemed His people, and that tells us just as much about the general character of the creation as a dose given to one sick hen on a big farm tells us about the general character of farming in England. What we must do, which road we must take to the fountain of life, we know, and none who has seriously followed the directions complains that he has been deceived. But whether there are other creatures like ourselves, and how they are dealt with: whether inanimate matter exists only to serve living creatures or for some other reason: whether the immensity of space is a means to some end, or an illusion, or simply the natural mode in which infinite energy might be expected to create – on all these points I think we are left to our own speculations.

No. It is not Christianity which need fear the giant universe. It is those systems which place the whole meaning of existence in biological or social evolution on our own planet. It is the creative evolutionist, the Bergsonian or Shavian, or the Communist, who should tremble when he looks up at the night sky. For he really is committed to a sinking ship. He really is attempting to ignore the discovered nature of things, as though by concentrating on the possibly upward trend in a single planet he could make himself forget the inevitable downward trend in the universe as a whole, the trend to low temperatures and irrevocable disorganization.

How can an unchanging system survive the continual increase of knowledge? Now, in certain cases we know very well how it can. A mature scholar reading a great passage in Plato, and taking in at one glance the metaphysics, the literary beauty, and the place of both in the history of Europe, is in a very different position from a boy learning the Greek alphabet. Yet through that unchanging system of the alphabet all this vast mental and emotional activity is operating. It has not been broken by the new knowledge. It is not outworn. If it changed, all would be chaos. A great Christian statesman, considering the morality of a measure which will affect millions of lives, and which involves economic, geographical and political considerations of the utmost complexity, is in a different position from a boy first learning that one must not cheat or tell lies, or hurt innocent people. But only in so far as that first knowledge of the great moral platitudes survives unimpaired in the statesman will his deliberation be moral at all. If that goes, then there has been no progress, but only mere change. For change is not progress unless the core remains unchanged. A small oak grows into a big oak: if it became a beech, that would not be growth, but mere change. And thirdly, there is a great difference between counting apples and arriving at the mathematical formulae of modern physics. But the multiplication table is used in both and does not grow out of date. . . .

The very possibility of progress demands that there should be an unchanging element. New bottles for new wine, by all means: but not new palates, throats and stomachs, or it would not be, for us, 'wine' at all. I take it we should all agree to find this sort of unchanging element in the simple rules of mathematics. I would add to these the primary principles of morality. And I would also add the fundamental doctrines of Christianity. To put it in rather more technical language, I claim that the positive historical statements made by Christianity have the power, elsewhere found chiefly in formal principles, of receiving, without intrinsic change, the increasing complexity of meaning which increasing knowledge puts into them.

Is God in Outer Space? *February 14*

The Russians, I am told, report that they have not found God in outer space. On the other hand, a good many people in many different times and countries claim to have found God, or been found by God, here on earth.

The conclusion some want us to draw from these data is that God does not exist. As a corollary, those who think they have met Him on earth were suffering from a delusion.

But other conclusions might be drawn:
1. We have not yet gone far enough in space. There had been ships on the Atlantic for a good time before America was discovered.
2. God does exist but is locally confined to this planet.
3. The Russians did find God in space without knowing it, because they lacked the requisite apparatus for detecting Him.
4. God does exist but is not an object either located in a particular part of space nor diffused, as we once thought 'ether' was, throughout space.

The first two conclusions do not interest me. The sort of religion for which they could be a defence would be a religion for savages: the belief in a local deity who can be contained in a particular temple, island or grove. That, in fact, seems to be the sort of religion about which the Russians – or some Russians, and a good many people in the West – are being irreligious. It is not in the least disquieting that no astronauts have discovered a god of that sort. The really disquieting thing would be if they had.

The Author of All Space and Time   *February 15*

Looking for God – or Heaven – by exploring space is like reading or seeing all Shakespeare's plays in the hope that you will find Shakespeare as one of the characters or Stratford as one of the places. Shakespeare is in one sense present at every moment in every play. But he is never present in the same way as Falstaff or Lady Macbeth. Nor is he diffused through the play like a gas. . . . My point is that, if God does exist, He is related to the universe more as an author is related to a play than as one object in the universe is related to another. If God created the universe, He created space-time, which is to the universe as the metre is to a poem or the key is to music. To look for Him as one item within the framework which He Himself invented is nonsensical. If God – such a God as any adult religion believes in – exists, mere movement in space will never bring you any nearer to Him or any farther from Him than you are at this very moment. You can neither reach Him nor avoid Him by travelling to Alpha Centauri or even to other galaxies. A fish is no more, and no less, in the sea after it has swum a thousand miles than it was when it set out. . . . Space-travel really has nothing to do with the matter. To some, God is discoverable everywhere; to others, nowhere. Those who do not find Him on earth are unlikely to find Him in space. (Hang it all, we're in space already; every year we go a huge circular tour in space.) But send a saint up in a spaceship and he'll find God in space as he found God on earth. Much depends on the seeing eye.

If there are species, and rational species, other than man, are any or all of them, like us, fallen? This is the point non-Christians always seem to forget. They seem to think that the Incarnation implies some particular merit or excellence in humanity. But of course it implies just the reverse: a particular demerit and depravity. No creature that deserved Redemption would need to be redeemed. They that are whole need not the physician. Christ died for men precisely because men are *not* worth dying for; to make them worth it. . . .

If we knew that Redemption by an Incarnation and Passion had been denied to creatures in need of it – is it certain that this is the only mode of Redemption that is possible? Here of course we ask for what is not merely unknown but, unless God should reveal it, wholly unknowable. It may be that the further we were permitted to see into His councils, the more clearly we should understand that thus and not otherwise – by the birth at Bethlehem, the cross on Calvary and the empty tomb – a fallen race could be rescued. There may be a necessity for this, insurmountable, rooted in the very nature of God and the very nature of sin. But we don't know. At any rate, I don't know. Spiritual as well as physical conditions might differ widely in different worlds. There might be different sorts and different degrees of fallenness. We must surely believe that the divine charity is as fertile in resource as it is measureless in condescension. To different diseases, or even to different patients sick with the same disease, the great Physician may have applied different remedies; remedies which we should probably not recognize as such even if we ever heard of them.

Can even missionaries be trusted? 'Gun and Gospel' have been horribly combined in the past. The missionary's holy desire to save souls has not always been kept quite distinct from the arrogant desire, the busybody's itch, to (as he calls it) 'civilize' the (as he calls them) 'natives'. Would all our missionaries recognize an unfallen race if they met it? Could they? Would they continue to press upon creatures that did not need to be saved that plan of Salvation which God has appointed to Man? Would they denounce as sins mere differences of behaviour which the spiritual and biological history of these strange creatures fully justified and which God Himself had blessed? Would they try to teach those from whom they had better learn? I do not know.

What I do know is that here and now, as our only possible practical preparation for such a meeting, you and I should resolve to stand firm against all exploitation and all theological imperialism. It will not be fun. We shall be called traitors to our own species. We shall be hated of almost all men; even of some religious men. And we must not give back one single inch. We shall probably fail, but let us go down fighting for the right side. Our loyalty is due not to our species but to God. Those who are, or can become, His sons, are our real brothers even if they have shells or tusks. It is spiritual, not biological, kinship that counts. . . .

If I remember rightly, St Augustine raised a question about the theological position of satyrs, monopods, and other semi-human creatures. He decided it could wait till we knew there were any. So can this.

Chronological Snobbery

'Why – damn it – it's *medieval*', I exclaimed; for I still had all the chronological snobbery of my period and used the names of earlier periods as terms of abuse . . . Barfield made short work of what I have called my 'chronological snobbery', the uncritical acceptance of the intellectual climate common to our own age and the assumption that whatever has gone out of date is on that account discredited. You must find why it went out of date. Was it refuted (and if so by whom, where, and how conclusively) or did it merely die away as fashions do? If the latter, this tells us nothing about its truth or falsehood. From seeing this, one passes to the realization that our own age is also 'a period', and certainly has, like all periods, its own characteristic illusions. They are likeliest to lurk in those widespread assumptions which are so ingrained in the age that no one dares to attack or feels it necessary to defend them . . . We had been, in the technical sense of the term, 'realists'; that is, we accepted as rock-bottom reality the universe revealed by the senses . . . We maintained that abstract thought (if obedient to logical rules) gave indisputable truth.

Approach of the Living God

Men are reluctant to pass over from the notion of an abstract and negative deity to the living God. I do not wonder. . . . The Pantheist's God does nothing, demands nothing. He is there if you wish for Him, like a book on a shelf. He will not pursue you. There is no danger that at any time heaven and earth should flee away at His glance. If He were the truth, then we could really say that all the Christian images of kingship were a historical accident of which our religion ought to be cleansed. It is with a shock that we discover them to be indispensable.

You have had a shock like that before, in connection with smaller matters – when the line pulls at your hand, when something breathes beside you in the darkness. So here; the shock comes at the precise moment when the thrill of *life* is communicated to us along the clue we have been following. It is always shocking to meet life where we thought we were alone. 'Look out!' we cry, 'it's *alive*.' And therefore this is the very point at which so many draw back – I would have done so myself if I could – and proceed no further with Christianity. An 'impersonal God' – well and good. A subjective God of beauty, truth and goodness, inside our own heads – better still. A formless life-force surging through us, a vast power which we can tap – best of all. But God Himself, alive, pulling at the other end of the cord, perhaps approaching at an infinite speed, the hunter, king, husband – that is quite another matter. There comes a moment when the children who have been playing at burglars hush suddenly: was that a *real* footstep in the hall? There comes a moment when people who have been dabbling in religion ('Man's search for God'!) suddenly draw back. Supposing we really found Him? We never meant it to come to *that*! Worse still, supposing He had found us?

The Summons of Lent   *February 20*

It is a matter of common experience that, when one person has got himself into a hole, the trouble of getting him out usually falls on a kind friend. Now what was the sort of 'hole' man had got himself into? He had tried to set up on his own, to behave as if he belonged to himself. In other words, fallen man is not simply an imperfect creature who needs improvement: he is a rebel who must lay down his arms. Laying down your arms, surrendering, saying you are sorry, realizing that you have been on the wrong track and getting ready to start life over again from the ground floor – that is the only way out of a 'hole'. This process of surrender – this movement full speed astern – is what Christians call repentance. Now repentance is no fun at all. It is something much harder than merely eating humble pie. It means unlearning all the self-conceit and self-will that we have been training ourselves into for thousands of years. It means killing part of yourself, undergoing a kind of death. In fact, it needs a good man to repent. And here comes the catch. Only a bad person needs to repent: only a good person can repent perfectly. The worse you are the more you need it and the less you can do it. The only person who could do it perfectly would be a perfect person – and he would not need it.

Help from the Perfect Penitent   *February 21*

This repentance, this willing submission to humiliation and a kind of death, is not something God demands of you before He will take you back and which He could let you off if He chose: it is simply a description of what going back to Him is like. If you ask God to take you back without it, you are really asking Him to let you go back without going back. It cannot happen. Very well, then, we must go through with it. But the same badness which makes us need it, makes us unable to do it. Can we do it if God helps us? Yes, but what do we mean when we talk of God helping us? We mean God putting into us a bit of Himself, so to speak. He lends us a little of His reasoning powers and that is how we think: He puts a little of His love into us and that is how we love one another. When you teach a child writing, you hold its hand while it forms the letters: that is, it forms the letters because you are forming them. We love and reason because God loves and reasons and holds our hand while we do it.

A Complaint from the Ungracious

I have heard some people complain that if Jesus was God as well as man, then His suffering and death lose all value in their eyes, 'because it must have been so easy for him'. Others may (very rightly) rebuke the ingratitude and ungraciousness of this objection; what staggers me is the misunderstanding it betrays. In one sense, of course, those who make it are right. They have even understated their own case. The perfect submission, the perfect suffering, the perfect death were not only easier to Jesus because He was God, but were possible only because He was God. But surely that is a very odd reason for not accepting them? The teacher is able to form the letters for the child because the teacher is grown-up and knows how to write. That, of course, makes it easier for the teacher; and only because it is easier for him can he help the child. If it rejected him because 'it's easy for grown-ups' and waited to learn writing from another child who could not write itself (and so had no 'unfair' advantage), it would not get on very quickly. If I am drowning in a rapid river, a man who still has one foot on the bank may give me a hand which saves my life. Ought I to shout back (between my gasps) 'No, it's not fair! You have an advantage! You're keeping one foot on the bank'? That advantage – call it 'unfair' if you like – is the only reason why he can be of any use to me. To what will you look for help if you will not look to that which is stronger than yourself?

Contrition

The Lenten season is devoted especially to what theologians call contrition. . . . Contrite, as you know, is a word translated from Latin, meaning crushed or pulverized. Now modern people complain that there is too much of that note in our Prayer Book. They do not wish their hearts to be pulverized, and they do not feel that they can sincerely say that they are 'miserable offenders'. I once knew a regular churchgoer who never repeated the words, 'the burden of them [i.e. his sins] is intolerable', because he did not feel that they were intolerable. But he was not understanding the words. I think the Prayer Book is very seldom talking primarily about our feelings; that is (I think) the first mistake we're apt to make about these words 'we are miserable offenders'. I do not think whether we are feeling miserable or not matters. I think it is using the word miserable in the old sense – meaning an object of pity. That a person can be a proper object of pity when he is not feeling miserable, you can easily understand if you imagine yourself looking down from a height on two crowded express trains that are travelling towards one another along the same line at sixty miles an hour. You can see that in forty seconds there will be a head-on collision. I think it would be very natural to say about the passengers of these trains, that they were objects of pity. This would not mean that they felt miserable themselves; but they would certainly be proper objects of pity.

Confession   *February 24*

It is not for me to decide whether you should confess your sins to a priest or not ... but if you do not, you should at least make a list on a piece of paper, and make a serious act of penance about each one of them. There is something about the mere words, you know, provided you avoid two dangers, either of sensational exaggeration – trying to work things up and make melodramatic sins out of small matters – or the opposite danger of slurring things over. It is essential to use the plain, simple, old-fashioned words that you would use about anyone else. I mean words like theft, or fornication, or hatred, instead of 'I did not mean to be dishonest', or 'I was only a boy then', or 'I lost my temper'. I think that this steady facing of what one does know and bringing it before God, without excuses, and seriously asking for Forgiveness and Grace, and resolving as far as in one lies to do better, is the only way.

The Fatal Charm of National Repentance *February 25*

Men fail so often to repent their real sins that the occasional repentance of an imaginary sin might appear almost desirable. But what actually happens . . . to the youthful national penitent is a little more complicated than that. England is not a natural agent, but a civil society. When we speak of England's actions we mean the actions of the British Government. The young man who is called upon to repent of England's foreign policy is really being called upon to repent the acts of his neighbour; for a Foreign Secretary or a Cabinet Minister is certainly a neighbour. And repentance presupposes condemnation. The first and fatal charm of national repentance is, therefore, the encouragement it gives us to turn from the bitter task of repenting our own sins to the congenial one of bewailing – but, first, of denouncing – the conduct of others. If it were clear to the young penitent that this is what he is doing, no doubt he would remember the law of charity. Unfortunately the very terms in which national repentance is recommended to him conceal its true nature. By a dangerous figure of speech, he calls the Government not 'they' but 'we'. And since, as penitents, we are not encouraged to be charitable to our own sins, nor to give ourselves the benefit of any doubt, a Government which is called 'we' is *ipso facto* placed beyond the sphere of charity or even of justice. You can say anything you please about it. You can indulge in the popular vice of detraction without restraint, and yet feel all the time that you are practising contrition.

The Forgiveness of Sins

We say a great many things in church (and out of church too) without thinking of what we are saying. For instance, we say in the Creed 'I believe in the forgiveness of sins'. I had been saying it for several years before I asked myself why it was in the Creed. At first sight it seems hardly worth putting in. 'If one is a Christian,' I thought, 'of course one believes in the forgiveness of sins. It goes without saying.' But the people who compiled the Creed apparently thought that this was a part of our belief which we needed to be reminded of every time we went to church. And I have begun to see that, as far as I am concerned, they were right. To believe in the forgiveness of sins is not nearly so easy as I thought. Real belief in it is the sort of thing that very easily slips away if we don't keep on polishing it up.

We believe that God forgives us our sins; but also that He will not do so unless we forgive other people their sins against us. There is no doubt about the second part of this statement. It is in the Lord's Prayer: it was emphatically stated by Our Lord. If you don't forgive you will not be forgiven. No part of His teaching is clearer: and there are no exceptions to it. He doesn't say that we are to forgive other people's sins provided they are not too frightful, or provided there are extenuating circumstances, or anything of that sort. We are to forgive them all, however spiteful, however mean, however often they are repeated. If we don't, we shall be forgiven none of our own.

Now it seems to me that we often make a mistake both about God's forgiveness of our sins and about the forgiveness we are told to offer to other people's sins. Take it first about God's forgiveness. I find that when I think I am asking God to forgive me I am often in reality (unless I watch myself very carefully) asking Him to do something quite different. I am asking Him not to forgive me but to excuse me. But there is all the difference in the world between forgiving and excusing. Forgiveness says 'Yes, you have done this thing, but I accept your apology, I will never hold it against you and everything between us two will be exactly as it was before.' But excusing says 'I see that you couldn't help it or didn't mean it, you weren't really to blame.' If one was not really to blame then there is nothing to forgive. In that sense forgiveness and excusing are almost opposites. Of course in dozens of cases, either between God and man, or between one man and another, there may be a mixture of the two. Part of what seemed at first to be the sins turns out to be really nobody's fault and is excused; the bit that is left over is forgiven. If you had a perfect excuse you would not need forgiveness: if the whole of your action needs forgiveness then there was no excuse for it. But the trouble is that what we call 'asking God's forgiveness' very often really consists in asking God to accept our excuses. What leads us into this mistake is the fact that there usually is some amount of excuse, some 'extenuating circumstances'. We are so very anxious to point these out to God (and to ourselves) that we are apt to forget the really important thing; that is, the bit left over, the bit which the excuses don't cover, the bit which is inexcusable but not, thank God, unforgivable. And if we forget this we shall go away imagining that we have repented and been forgiven when all that has really happened is that we have satisfied ourselves with our own excuses.

There are two remedies for this danger. One is to remember that God knows all the real excuses very much better than we do. If there are real 'extenuating circumstances' there is no fear that He will overlook them. Often He must know many excuses that we have never thought of, and therefore humble souls will, after death, have the delightful surprise of discovering that on certain occasions they sinned much less than they had thought. All the real excusing He will do. What we have got to take to Him is the inexcusable bit, the sin. We are only wasting time by talking about all the parts which can (we think) be excused. When you go to a doctor you show him the bit of you that is wrong – say, a broken arm. It would be a mere waste of time to keep on explaining that your legs and eyes and throat are all right. You may be mistaken in thinking so; and anyway, if they are really all right, the doctor will know that.

The second remedy is really and truly to believe in the forgiveness of sins. A great deal of our anxiety to make excuses comes from not really believing in it: from thinking that God will not take us to Himself again unless He is satisfied that some sort of case can be made out in our favour. But that would not be forgiveness at all. Real forgiveness means looking steadily at the sin, the sin that is left over without any excuse, after all allowances have been made, and seeing it in all its horror, dirt, meanness and malice, and nevertheless being wholly reconciled to the man who has done it. That, and only that, is forgiveness; and that we can always have from God if we ask for it.

When it comes to a question of our forgiving other people, it is partly the same and partly different. It is the same because, here also, forgiving does not mean excusing. Many people seem to think it does. They think that if you ask them to forgive someone who has cheated or bullied them you are trying to make out that there was really no cheating or no bullying. But if that were so, there would be nothing to forgive. They keep on replying, 'But I tell you the man broke a most solemn promise.' Exactly: that is precisely what you have to forgive. (This doesn't mean you must necessarily believe his next promise. It does mean that you must make every effort to kill every trace of resentment in your own heart – every wish to humiliate or hurt him or to pay him out.) The difference between this situation and the one in which you are asking God's forgiveness is this. In our own case we accept excuses too easily, in other people's we do not accept them easily enough. As regards my own sins it is a safe bet (though not a certainty) that the excuses are not really so good as I think: as regards other men's sins against me it is a safe bet (though not a certainty) that the excuses are better than I think. One must therefore begin by attending carefully to everything which may show that the other man was not so much to blame as we thought. But even if he is absolutely fully to blame we still have to forgive him; and even if ninety-nine per cent of his apparent guilt can be explained away by really good excuses, the problem of forgiveness begins with the one per cent of guilt which is left over. To excuse what can really produce good excuses is not Christian charity; it is only fairness. To be a Christian means to forgive the inexcusable, because God has forgiven the inexcusable in you.

This is hard. It is perhaps not so hard to forgive a single great injury. But to forgive the incessant provocations of daily life – to keep on forgiving the bossy mother-in-law, the bullying husband, the nagging wife, the selfish daughter, the deceitful son – how can we do it? Only, I think, by remembering where we stand, by meaning our words when we say in our prayers each night 'Forgive us our trespasses as we forgive those that trespass against us.' We are offered forgiveness on no other terms. To refuse it is to refuse God's mercy for ourselves. There is no hint of exceptions and God means what He says.

The Three Parts of Morality   *March 2*

There is a story about a schoolboy who was asked what he thought God was like. He replied that, as far as he could make out, God was 'The sort of person who is always snooping round to see if anyone is enjoying himself and then trying to stop it.' And I am afraid that is the sort of idea that the word Morality raises in a good many people's minds: something that interferes, something that stops you having a good time. In reality, moral rules are directions for running the human machine. Every moral rule is there to prevent a breakdown, or a strain, or a friction, in the running of that machine. That is why these rules at first seem to be constantly interfering with our natural inclinations. When you are being taught how to use any machine, the instructor keeps on saying, 'No, don't do it like that', because, of course, there are all sorts of things that look all right and seem to you the natural way of treating the machine, but do not really work. . . .

There are two ways in which the human machine goes wrong. One is when human individuals drift apart from one another, or else collide with one another and do one another damage, by cheating or bullying. The other is when things go wrong inside the individual – when the different parts of him (his different faculties and desires and so on) either drift apart or interfere with one another.

When people say in the newspapers that we are striving for Christian moral standards, they usually mean that we are striving for kindness and fair play between nations, and classes, and individuals. . . . When a man says about something he wants to do, 'It can't be wrong because it doesn't do anyone else any harm', he is thinking . . . it does not matter what his ship is like inside provided that he does not run into the next ship. And it is quite natural, when we start thinking about morality, to begin with social relations. For one thing, the results of bad morality in that sphere are so obvious and press on us every day: war and poverty and graft and lies and shoddy work. . . . Almost all people at all times have agreed (in theory) that human beings ought to be honest and kind and helpful to one another. But though it is natural to begin with all that, if our thinking about morality stops there, we might just as well not have thought at all. Unless we go on to the second thing – the tidying up inside each human being – we are only deceiving ourselves.

Immortality Makes a Great Difference *March 4*

Religion involves a series of statements about facts, which must be either true or false. If they are true, one set of conclusions will follow about the right sailing of the human fleet: if they are false, quite a different set. For example, let us go back to the man who says that a thing cannot be wrong unless it hurts some other human being. He quite understands that he must not damage the other ships in the convoy, but he honestly thinks that what he does to his own ship is simply his own business. But does it not make a great difference whether his ship is his own property or not? Does it not make a great difference whether I am, so to speak, the landlord of my own mind and body, or only a tenant, responsible to the real landlord? If somebody else made me, for his own purposes, then I shall have a lot of duties which I should not have if I simply belonged to myself. . . .

Christianity asserts that every individual human being is going to live for ever, and this must be either true or false. Now there are a good many things which would not be worth bothering about if I were going to live only seventy years, but which I had better bother about very seriously if I am going to live for ever. Perhaps my bad temper or my jealousy are gradually getting worse – so gradually that the increase in seventy years will not be very noticeable. But it might be absolute hell in a million years: in fact, if Christianity is true, Hell is the precisely correct technical term for what it would be.

Social Morality   *March 5*

The first thing to get clear about Christian morality between man and man is that in this department Christ did not come to preach any brand new morality. The Golden Rule of the New Testament (Do as you would be done by) is a summing up of what everyone, at bottom, had always known to be right. Really great moral teachers never do introduce new moralities: it is quacks and cranks who do that. As Dr Johnson said, 'People need to be reminded more often than they need to be instructed.' The real job of every moral teacher is to keep on bringing us back, time after time, to the old simple principles which we are all so anxious not to see; like bringing a horse back and back to the fence it has refused to jump or bringing a child back and back to the bit in its lesson that it wants to shirk.

The second thing to get clear is that Christianity has not, and does not profess to have, a detailed political programme for applying 'Do as you would be done by' to a particular society at a particular moment. It could not have. It is meant for all men at all times and the particular programme which suited one place or time would not suit another. And, anyhow, that is not how Christianity works. When it tells you to feed the hungry it does not give you lessons in cookery. When it tells you to read the Scriptures it does not give you lessons in Hebrew and Greek, or even in English grammar. It was never intended to replace or supersede the ordinary human arts and sciences: it is rather a director which will set them all to the right jobs, and a source of energy which will give them all new life, if only they will put themselves at its disposal.

The Duty of the Laymen   *March 6*

People say, 'The Church ought to give us a lead.' That is true if they mean it in the right way, but false if they mean it in the wrong way. By the Church they ought to mean the whole body of practising Christians. And when they say that the Church should give us a lead, they ought to mean that some Christians – those who happen to have the right talents – should be economists and statesmen, and that all economists and statesmen should be Christians, and that their whole efforts in politics and economics should be directed to putting 'Do as you would be done by' into action. If that happened, and if we others were really ready to take it, then we should find the Christian solution for our own social problems pretty quickly. But, of course, when they ask for a lead from the Church most people mean they want the clergy to put out a political programme. That is silly. The clergy are those particular people within the whole Church who have been specially trained and set aside to look after what concerns us as creatures who are going to live for ever: and we are asking them to do a quite different job for which they have not been trained. The job is really on us, on the laymen. The application of Christian principles, say, to trade unionism or education, must come from Christian trade unionists and Christian schoolmasters: just as Christian literature comes from Christian novelists and dramatists – not from the bench of bishops getting together and trying to write plays and novels in their spare time.

A Fully Christian Society   *March 7*

The New Testament, without going into details, gives us a pretty clear hint of what a fully Christian society would be like. Perhaps it gives us more than we can take. It tells us that there are to be no passengers or parasites: if a man does no work, he ought not to eat. Everyone is to work with his own hands, and what is more, everyone's work is to produce something good: there will be no manufacture of silly luxuries and then of sillier advertisements to persuade us to buy them. And there is to be no 'swank' or 'side', no putting on airs. To that extent a Christian society would be what we now call Leftist. On the other hand, it is always insisting on obedience – obedience (and outward marks of respect) from all of us to properly appointed magistrates, from children to parents, and (I am afraid this is going to be very unpopular) from wives to husbands. Thirdly, it is to be a cheerful society: full of singing and rejoicing, and regarding worry or anxiety as wrong. Courtesy is one of the Christian virtues; and the New Testament hates what it calls 'busybodies'.

If there were such a society in existence and you or I visited it, I think we should come away with a curious impression. We should feel that its economic life was very socialistic and, in that sense, 'advanced', but that its family life and its code of manners were rather old-fashioned – perhaps even ceremonious and aristocratic. Each of us would like some bits of it, but I am afraid very few of us would like the whole thing. That is just what one would expect if Christianity is the total plan for the human machine. We have all departed from that total plan in different ways, and each of us wants to make out that his own modification of the original plan is the plan itself. You will find this again and again about anything that is really Christian: everyone is attracted by bits of it and wants to pick out those bits and leave the rest. That is why we do not get much further: and that is why people who are fighting for quite opposite things can both say they are fighting for Christianity.

The Modern Economic System   *March 8*

There is one bit of advice given to us by the ancient heathen Greeks, and by the Jews in the Old Testament, and by the great Christian teachers of the Middle Ages, which the modern economic system has completely disobeyed. All these people told us not to lend money at interest: and lending money at interest – what we call investment – is the basis of our whole system. Now it may not absolutely follow that we are wrong. Some people say that when Moses and Aristotle and the Christians agreed in forbidding interest (or 'usury' as they called it), they could not foresee the joint stock company, and were only thinking of the private moneylender, and that, therefore, we need not bother about what they said. That is a question I cannot decide on. I am not an economist and I simply do not know whether the investment system is responsible for the state we are in or not. That is where we want the Christian economist. But I should not have been honest if I had not told you that three great civilizations had agreed (or so it seems at first sight) in condemning the very thing on which we have based our whole life.

Giving to the Poor

In the passage where the New Testament says that everyone must work, it gives as a reason 'in order that he may have something to give to those in need'. Charity – giving to the poor – is an essential part of Christian morality: in the frightening parable of the sheep and the goats it seems to be the point on which everything turns. Some people nowadays say that charity ought to be unnecessary and that instead of giving to the poor we ought to be producing a society in which there were no poor to give to. They may be quite right in saying that we ought to produce that kind of society. But if anyone thinks that, as a consequence, you can stop giving in the meantime, then he has parted company with all Christian morality. I do not believe one can settle how much we ought to give. I am afraid the only safe rule is to give more than we can spare. In other words, if our expenditure on comforts, luxuries, amusements, etc., is up to the standard common among those with the same income as our own, we are probably giving away too little. If our charities do not at all pinch or hamper us, I should say they are too small.

Morality and Psychoanalysis

You want to distinguish very clearly between two things: between the actual medical theories and technique of the psychoanalysts, and the general philosophical view of the world which Freud and some others have gone on to add to this. The second thing – the philosophy of Freud – is in direct contradiction to Christianity: and also in direct contradiction to the other great psychologist, Jung. And furthermore, when Freud is talking about how to cure neurotics he is speaking as a specialist on his own subject, but when he goes on to talk general philosophy he is speaking as an amateur. It is therefore quite sensible to attend to him with respect in the one case and not in the other – and that is what I do. I am all the readier to do it because I have found that when he is talking off his own subject and on a subject I do know something about (namely, languages) he is very ignorant. But psychoanalysis itself, apart from all the philosophical additions that Freud and others have made to it, is not in the least contradictory to Christianity. Its technique overlaps with Christian morality at some points and it would not be a bad thing if every parson knew something about it: but it does not run the same course all the way, for the two techniques are doing rather different things.

When a man makes a moral choice two things are involved. One is the act of choosing. The other is the various feelings, impulses and so on which his psychological outfit presents him with, and which are the raw material of his choice. Now this raw material may be of two kinds. Either it may be what we would call normal: it may consist of the sort of feelings that are common to all men. Or else it may consist of quite unnatural feelings due to things that have gone wrong in his subconscious. . . . Now what psychoanalysis undertakes to do is to remove the abnormal feelings, that is, to give the man better raw material for his acts of choice: morality is concerned with the acts of choice themselves.

Freedom of the Will   *March 11*

Imagine three men who go to war. One has the ordinary natural fear of danger that any man has and he subdues it by moral effort and becomes a brave man. Let us suppose that the other two have, as a result of things in their subconsciousness, exaggerated, irrational fears, which no amount of moral effort can do anything about. Now suppose that a psychoanalyst comes along and cures these two: that is, he puts them both back in the position of the first man. Well it is just then that the psychoanalytical problem is over and the moral problem begins. Because, now that they are cured, these two men might take quite different lines. The first might say, 'Thank goodness I've got rid of all those doo-dahs. Now at last I can do what I always wanted to do – my duty to the cause of freedom.' But the other might say, 'Well, I'm very glad that I now feel moderately cool under fire, but, of course, that doesn't alter the fact that I'm still jolly well determined to look after Number One and let the other chap do the dangerous job whenever I can. Indeed one of the good things about feeling less frightened is that I can now look after myself much more efficiently and can be much cleverer at hiding the fact from the others.' Now this difference is a purely moral one and psychoanalysis cannot do anything about it. However much you improve the man's raw material, you have still got something else: the real, free choice of the man, on the material presented to him, either to put his own advantage first or to put it last. And this free choice is the only thing that morality is concerned with.

Screwtape on Will and Fantasy   *March 12*

Do what you will, there is going to be some benevolence, as well as some malice, in your patient's soul. The great thing is to direct the malice to his immediate neighbours whom he meets every day and to thrust his benevolence out to the remote circumference, to people he does not know. The malice thus becomes wholly real and the benevolence largely imaginary. There is no good at all in inflaming his hatred of Germans if, at the same time, a pernicious habit of charity is growing up between him and his mother, his employer, and the man he meets in the train. Think of your man as a series of concentric circles, his will being the innermost, his intellect coming next, and finally his fantasy. You can hardly hope, at once, to exclude from all the circles everything that smells of the Enemy: but you must keep on shoving all the virtues outward till they are finally located in the circle of fantasy, and all the desirable qualities inward into the will. It is only in so far as they reach the will and are there embodied in habits that the virtues are really fatal to us.

Prudence   *March 13*

Prudence means practical common sense, taking the trouble to think out what you are doing and what is likely to come of it. Nowadays most people hardly think of Prudence as one of the 'virtues'. In fact, because Christ said we could only get into His world by being like children, many Christians have the idea that, provided you are 'good', it does not matter being a fool. But that is a misunderstanding. In the first place, most children show plenty of 'prudence' about doing the things they are really interested in, and think them out quite sensibly. In the second place, as St Paul points out, Christ never meant that we were to remain children in *intelligence*: on the contrary, He told us to be not only 'as harmless as doves', but also 'as wise as serpents'. He wants a child's heart, but a grown-up's head. He wants us to be simple, single-minded, affectionate, and teachable, as good children are; but He also wants every bit of intelligence we have to be alert at its job, and in first-class fighting trim.

Temperance

Temperance is, unfortunately, one of those words that has changed its meaning. It now usually means teetotalism. But in the days when the second Cardinal virtue was christened 'Temperance', it meant nothing of the sort. Temperance referred not specially to drink, but to all pleasures; and it meant not abstaining, but going the right length and no further. It is a mistake to think that Christians ought all to be teetotallers; Mohammedanism, not Christianity, is the teetotal religion. Of course it may be the duty of a particular Christian, or of any Christian, at a particular time, to abstain from strong drink, either because he is the sort of man who cannot drink at all without drinking too much, or because he wants to give the money to the poor, or because he is with people who are inclined to drunkenness and must not encourage them by drinking himself. But the whole point is that he is abstaining, for a good reason, from something which he does not condemn and which he likes to see other people enjoying. One of the marks of a certain type of bad man is that he cannot give up a thing himself without wanting everyone else to give it up. That is not the Christian way. An individual Christian may see fit to give up all sorts of things for special reasons – marriage, or meat, or beer, or the cinema; but the moment he starts saying the things are bad in themselves, or looking down his nose at other people who do use them, he has taken the wrong turning.

One great piece of mischief has been done by the modern restriction of the word Temperance to the question of drink. It helps people to forget that you can be just as intemperate about lots of other things. A man who makes his golf or his motor bicycle the centre of his life, or a woman who devotes all her thoughts to clothes or bridge or her dog, is being just as 'intemperate' as someone who gets drunk every evening. Of course, it does not show on the outside so easily: bridge-mania or golf-mania do not make you fall down in the middle of the road. But God is not deceived by externals.

Justice means much more than the sort of thing that goes on in law courts. It is the old name for everything we should now call 'fairness'; it includes honesty, give and take, truthfulness, keeping promises, and all that side of life. And Fortitude includes both kinds of courage – the kind that faces danger as well as the kind that 'sticks it' under pain. 'Guts' is perhaps the nearest modern English. You will notice, of course, that you cannot practise any of the other virtues very long without bringing this one into play. . . .

We might think that the 'virtues' were necessary only for this present life – that in the other world we could stop being just because there is nothing to quarrel about and stop being brave because there is no danger. Now it is quite true that there will probably be no occasion for just or courageous acts in the next world, but there will be every occasion for being the sort of people that we can become only as a result of doing such acts here. The point is not that God will refuse you admission to His eternal world if you have not got certain qualities of character: the point is that if people have not got at least the beginnings of those qualities inside them, then no possible external conditions could make a 'Heaven' for them – that is, could make them happy with the deep, strong, unshakable kind of happiness God intends for us.

Faith *March 16*

Faith seems to be used by Christians in two senses or on two levels. . . . In the first sense it means simply Belief – accepting or regarding as true the doctrines of Christianity. That is fairly simple. But what does puzzle people – at least it used to puzzle me – is the fact that Christians regard faith in this sense as a virtue. I used to ask how on earth it can be a virtue – what is there moral or immoral about believing or not believing a set of statements? ... What I did not see then – and a good many people do not see still – was this. I was assuming that if the human mind once accepts a thing as true it will automatically go on regarding it as true, until some real reason for reconsidering it turns up. In fact, I was assuming that the human mind is completely ruled by reason. But that is not so. For example, my reason is perfectly convinced by good evidence that anaesthetics do not smother me and that properly trained surgeons do not start operating until I am unconscious. But that does not alter the fact that when they have me down on the table and clap their horrible mask over my face, a mere childish panic begins inside me. I start thinking I am going to choke, and I am afraid they will start cutting me up before I am properly under. In other words, I lose my faith in anaesthetics. It is not reason that is taking away my faith: on the contrary, my faith is based on reason. It is my imagination and emotions. The battle is between faith and reason on one side and emotion and imagination on the other.

Training the Habit of Faith *March 17*

Faith, in the sense in which I am here using the word, is the art of holding on to things your reason has once accepted, in spite of your changing moods. For moods will change, whatever view your reason takes. I know that by experience. Now that I am a Christian I do have moods in which the whole thing looks very improbable: but when I was an atheist I had moods in which Christianity looked terribly probable. This rebellion of your moods against your real self is going to come anyway. That is why Faith is such a necessary virtue: unless you teach your moods 'where they get off', you can never be either a sound Christian or even a sound atheist, but just a creature dithering to and fro, with its beliefs really dependent on the weather and the state of its digestion. Consequently one must train the habit of Faith.

The first step is to recognize the fact that your moods change. The next step is to make sure that, if you have once accepted Christianity, then some of its main doctrines shall be deliberately held before your mind for some time every day. That is why daily prayers and religious readings and churchgoing are necessary parts of the Christian life. We have to be continually reminded of what we believe. Neither this belief nor any other will automatically remain alive in the mind. It must be fed. And as a matter of fact, if you examined a hundred people who had lost their faith in Christianity, I wonder how many of them would turn out to have been reasoned out of it by honest argument? Do not most people simply drift away?

Christ – the Only Complete Realist   *March 18*

No man knows how bad he is till he has tried very hard to be good. A silly idea is current that good people do not know what temptation means. This is an obvious lie. Only those who try to resist temptation know how strong it is. After all, you find out the strength of the German army by fighting it, not by giving in. You find out the strength of a wind by trying to walk against it, not by lying down. A man who gives in to temptation after five minutes simply does not know what it would have been like an hour later. That is why bad people, in one sense, know very little about badness. They have lived a sheltered life by always giving in. We never find out the strength of the evil impulse inside us until we try to fight it: and Christ, because He was the only man who never yielded to temptation, is also the only man who knows to the full what temptation means – the only complete realist.

St Joseph, Husband of the Blessed Virgin Mary

You will hear people say, 'The early Christians believed that Christ was the son of a virgin, but we know that this is a scientific impossibility.' Such people seem to have an idea that belief in miracles arose at a period when men were so ignorant of the course of nature that they did not perceive a miracle to be contrary to it. A moment's thought shows this to be nonsense: and the story of the Virgin Birth is a particularly striking example. When St Joseph discovered that his fiancée was going to have a baby, he not unnaturally decided to repudiate her. Why? Because he knew just as well as any modern gynaecologist that in the ordinary course of nature women do not have babies unless they have lain with men. No doubt the modern gynaecologist knows several things about birth and begetting which St Joseph did not know. But those things do not concern the main point – that a virgin birth is contrary to the course of nature. And St Joseph obviously knew *that*. In any sense in which it is true to say now, 'The thing is scientifically impossible', he would have said the same: the thing always was, and was always known to be, impossible *unless* the regular processes of nature were, in this particular case, being overruled or supplemented by something from beyond nature. When St Joseph finally accepted the view that his fiancée's pregnancy was due not to unchastity but to a miracle, he accepted the miracle as something contrary to the known order of nature. All records of miracles teach the same thing. . . . If they were not known to be contrary to the laws of nature how could they suggest the presence of the supernatural? How could they be surprising unless they were seen to be exceptions to the rules? . . . Nothing can seem extraordinary until you have discovered what is ordinary.

Hope *March 20*

We must not be troubled by unbelievers when they say that this promise of reward makes the Christian life a mercenary affair. There are different kinds of reward. There is the reward which has no natural connection with the things you do to earn it, and is quite foreign to the desires that ought to accompany those things. Money is not the natural reward of love; that is why we call a man mercenary if he marries a woman for the sake of her money. But marriage is the proper reward for a real lover, and he is not mercenary for desiring it. A general who fights well in order to get a peerage is mercenary; a general who fights for victory is not, victory being the proper reward of battle as marriage is the proper reward of love. The proper rewards are not simply tacked on to the activity for which they are given, but are the activity itself in consummation. There is also a third case, which is more complicated. An enjoyment of Greek poetry is certainly a proper, and not a mercenary, reward for learning Greek; but only those who have reached the stage of enjoying Greek poetry can tell from their own experience that this is so. The schoolboy beginning Greek grammar cannot look forward to his adult enjoyment of Sophocles as a lover looks forward to marriage or a general to victory. . . . But it is just in so far as he approaches the reward that he becomes able to desire it for its own sake; indeed, the power of so desiring it is itself a preliminary reward.

The Christian, in relation to Heaven, is in much the same position as this schoolboy. Those who have attained everlasting life in the vision of God doubtless know very well that it is no mere bribe, but the very consummation of their earthly discipleship; but we who have not yet attained it cannot know this in the same way, and cannot even begin to know it at all except by continuing to obey and finding the first reward of our obedience in our increasing power to desire the ultimate reward. Just in proportion as the desire grows, our fear lest it should be a mercenary desire will die away and finally be recognized as an absurdity. But probably this will not, for most of us, happen in a day; poetry replaces grammar, Gospel replaces Law, longing transforms obedience, as gradually as the tide lifts a grounded ship.

Loving and Liking   *March 21*

Try to understand exactly what loving your neighbour as yourself means. I have to love him as I love myself. Well, how exactly do I love myself? Now that I come to think of it, I have not exactly got a feeling of fondness or affection for myself, and I do not even always enjoy my own society. So apparently 'Love your neighbour' does not mean 'feel fond of him' or 'find him attractive'. I ought to have seen that before, because, of course, you cannot feel fond of a person by trying. Do I think well of myself, think myself a nice chap? Well, I am afraid I sometimes do . . . but that is not why I love myself. So loving my enemies does not apparently mean thinking them nice either. That is an enormous relief. For a good many people imagine that forgiving your enemies means making out that they are really not such bad fellows after all, when it is quite plain that they are. Go a step further. In my most clearsighted moments not only do I not think myself a nice man, but I know that I am a very nasty one. I can look at some of the things I have done with horror and loathing. So apparently I am allowed to loathe and hate some of the things my enemies do. Now that I come to think of it, I remember Christian teachers telling me long ago that I must hate a bad man's actions, but not hate the bad man: or, as they would say, hate the sin but not the sinner.

Charity March 22

Though natural likings should normally be encouraged, it would be quite wrong to think that the way to become charitable is to sit trying to manufacture affectionate feelings. Some people are 'cold' by temperament; that may be a misfortune for them, but it is no more a sin than having a bad digestion is a sin; and it does not cut them out from the chance, or excuse them from the duty, of learning charity. The rule for all of us is perfectly simple. Do not waste time bothering whether you 'love' your neighbour; act as if you did. As soon as we do this we find one of the great secrets. When you are behaving as if you loved someone, you will presently come to love him. If you injure someone you dislike, you will find yourself disliking him more. If you do him a good turn, you will find yourself disliking him less. There is, indeed, one exception. If you do him a good turn, not to please God and obey the law of charity, but to show him what a fine forgiving chap you are, and to put him in your debt, and then sit down to wait for his 'gratitude', you will probably be disappointed. (People are not fools: they have a very quick eye for anything like showing off, or patronage.) But whenever we do good to another self, just because it is a self, made (like us) by God, and desiring its own happiness as we desire ours, we shall have learned to love it a little more or, at least, to dislike it less. . . .

Some writers use the word charity to describe not only Christian love between human beings, but also God's love for man and man's love for God. About the second of these two, people are often worried. They are told they ought to love God. They cannot find any such feeling in themselves. What are they to do? The answer is the same as before. Act as if you did. Do not sit trying to manufacture feelings. Ask yourself, 'If I were sure that I loved God, what would I do?' When you have found the answer, go and do it.

Faith or Good Works? *March 23*

Christians have often disputed as to whether what leads the Christian home is good actions, or Faith in Christ. I have no right really to speak on such a difficult question, but it does seem to me like asking which blade in a pair of scissors is most necessary. A serious moral effort is the only thing that will bring you to the point where you throw up the sponge. Faith in Christ is the only thing to save you from despair at that point: and out of that Faith in Him good actions must inevitably come. There are two parodies of the truth which different sets of Christians have, in the past, been accused by other Christians of believing: perhaps they may make the truth clearer. One set were accused of saying, 'Good actions are all that matters. The best good action is charity. The best kind of charity is giving money. The best thing to give money to is the Church. So hand us over £10,000 and we will see you through.' The answer to that nonsense, of course, would be that good actions done for that motive, done with the idea that Heaven can be bought, would not be good actions at all, but only commercial speculations. The other set were accused of saying, 'Faith is all that matters. Consequently, if you have faith, it doesn't matter what you do. Sin away, my lad, and have a good time and Christ will see that it makes no difference in the end.' The answer to that nonsense is that, if what you call your 'faith' in Christ does not involve taking the slightest notice of what He says, then it is not Faith at all

– not faith or truth in Him, but only intellectual acceptance of some theory about Him.

Faith and Good Works are Inseparable   *March 24*

The Bible really seems to clinch the matter when it puts the two things together into one amazing sentence. The first half is, 'Work out your own salvation with fear and trembling' – which looks as if everything depended on us and our good actions: but the second half goes on, 'For it is God who worketh in you' – which looks as if God did everything and we nothing. I am afraid that is the sort of thing we come up against in Christianity. I am puzzled, but I am not surprised. You see, we are now trying to understand, and to separate into watertight compartments, what exactly God does and what man does when God and man are working together. And, of course, we begin by thinking it is like two men working together, so that you could say, 'He did this bit and I did that.' But this way of thinking breaks down. God is not like that. He is inside you as well as outside: even if we could understand who did what, I do not think human language could properly express it. In the attempt to express it different churches say different things. But you will find that even those who insist most strongly on the importance of good actions tell you you need Faith; and even those who insist most strongly on Faith tell you to do good actions. At any rate that is as far as I go.

The resemblance between the *Magnificat* and traditional Hebrew poetry . . . is not mere literary curiosity. There is, of course, a difference. There are no cursings here, no hatred, no self-righteousness. Instead, there is mere statement. He has scattered the proud, cast down the mighty, sent the rich empty away. I spoke . . . of the ironic contrast between the fierce psalmists and the choirboy's treble. The contrast is here brought up to a higher level. Once more we have the treble voice, a girl's voice, announcing without sin that the sinful prayers of her ancestors do not remain entirely unheard; and doing this, not indeed with fierce exultation, yet – who can mistake the tone? – in a calm and terrible gladness. . . .

Christians are unhappily divided about the kind of honour in which the Mother of the Lord should be held, but there is one truth about which no doubt seems admissible. If we believe in the Virgin Birth and if we believe in Our Lord's human nature, psychological as well as physical (for it is heretical to think Him a human body which had the Second Person of the Trinity *instead of* a human soul) we must also believe in a human heredity for that human nature. There is only one source for it (though in that source all the true Israel is summed up). If there is an iron element in Jesus may we not without irreverence guess whence, humanly speaking, it came? Did neighbours say, in His boyhood, 'He's His Mother's Son'? This might set in a new and less painful light the severity of some things He said to, or about His Mother. We may suppose that she understood them very well.

'I have come to give myself up', he said.

'It is well', said Mother Kirk. 'You have come a long way round to reach this place, whither I would have carried you in a few moments. But it is very well.'

'What must I do?' said John.

'You must take off your rags,' said she, 'as your friend has done already, and then you must dive into this water.'

'Alas,' said he, 'I have never learned to dive.'

'There is nothing to learn', said she. 'The art of diving is not to do anything new but simply to cease doing something. You have only to let yourself go.'

Chastity   *March 27*

Chastity is the most unpopular of the Christian virtues. There is no getting away from it: the old Christian rule is, 'Either marriage, with complete faithfulness to your partner, or else total abstinence.' Now this is so difficult and so contrary to our instincts, that obviously either Christianity is wrong or our sexual instinct, as it now is, has gone wrong. One or the other. Of course, being a Christian, I think it is the instinct which has gone wrong.

But I have other reasons for thinking so. The biological purpose of sex is children, just as the biological purpose of eating is to repair the body. Now if we eat whenever we feel inclined and just as much as we want, it is quite true that most of us will eat too much: but not terrifically too much. One man may eat enough for two, but he does not eat enough for ten. The appetite goes a little beyond its biological purpose, but not enormously. But if a healthy young man indulged his sexual appetite whenever he felt inclined, and if each act produced a baby, then in ten years he might easily populate a small village.

This appetite is in ludicrous and preposterous excess of its function.

Or take it another way. You can get a large audience together for a striptease act – that is, to watch a girl undress on the stage. Now suppose you came to a country where you could fill a theatre by simply bringing a covered plate on to the stage and then slowly lifting the cover so as to let everyone see, just before the lights went out, that it contained a mutton chop or a bit of bacon, would you not think that in that country something had gone wrong with the appetite for food? And would not anyone who had grown up in a different world think there was something equally queer about the state of the sex instinct among us?

Sexual Morality   *March 28*

They tell you sex has become a mess because it was hushed up. But for the last twenty years it has not been hushed up. It has been chattered about all day long. Yet it is still in a mess. If hushing up had been the cause of the trouble, ventilation would have set it right. But it has not. I think it is the other way round. I think the human race originally hushed it up because it had become such a mess. Modern people are always saying, 'Sex is nothing to be ashamed of.' They may mean two things. They may mean 'There is nothing to be ashamed of in the fact that the human race reproduces itself in a certain way, nor in the fact that it gives pleasure.' If they mean that, they are right. Christianity says the same. It is not the thing, nor the pleasure, that is the trouble. The old Christian teachers said that if man had never fallen, sexual pleasure, instead of being less than it is now, would actually have been greater. I know some muddle-headed Christians have talked as if Christianity thought that sex, or the body, or pleasure, were bad in themselves. But they were wrong. Christianity is almost the only one of the great religions which thoroughly approves of the body – which believes that matter is good, that God Himself once took on a human body, that some kind of body is going to be given to us even in Heaven and is going to be an essential part of our happiness, our beauty, and our energy. Christianity has glorified marriage more than any other religion: and nearly all the greatest love poetry in the world has been produced by Christians. If anyone says that sex, in itself, is bad, Christianity contradicts him at once. But, of course, when people say, 'Sex is nothing to be ashamed of', they may mean 'the state into which the sexual instinct has now got is nothing to be ashamed of'. . . .

I think it is everything to be ashamed of. There is nothing to be ashamed of in enjoying your food: there would be everything to be ashamed of if half the world made food the main interest of their lives. . . . There are people who want to keep our sex instinct inflamed in order to make money out of us. Because, of course, a man with an obsession is a man who has very little sales resistance.

Screwtape Explains Hell's View of Pleasures

Never forget that when we are dealing with any pleasure in its healthy and normal and satisfying form, we are, in a sense, on the Enemy's ground. I know we have won many a soul through pleasure. All the same, it is His invention, not ours. He made the pleasures: all our research so far has not enabled us to produce one. All we can do is to encourage the humans to take the pleasures which our Enemy has produced, at times, or in ways, or in degrees, which He has forbidden. Hence we always try to work away from the natural condition of any pleasure to that in which it is least natural, least redolent of its Maker, and least pleasurable. An ever-increasing craving for an ever-diminishing pleasure is the formula. It is more certain; and it's better *style*. To get the man's soul and give him *nothing* in return – that is what really gladdens our Father's heart.

The Great Lie about Sex   *March 30*

Our warped natures, the devils who tempt us, and all the contemporary propaganda for lust, combine to make us feel that the desires we are resisting are so 'natural', so 'healthy', and so reasonable, that it is almost perverse and abnormal to resist them. Poster after poster, film after film, novel after novel, associate the idea of sexual indulgence with the ideas of health, normality, youth, frankness, and good humour. Now this association is a lie. Like all powerful lies, it is based on a truth – the truth . . . that sex in itself (apart from the excesses and obsessions that have grown round it) is 'normal' and 'healthy', and all the rest of it. The lie consists in the suggestion that any sexual act to which you are tempted at the moment is also healthy and normal. Now this, on any conceivable view, and quite apart from Christianity, must be nonsense. Surrender to all our desires obviously leads to impotence, disease, jealousies, lies, concealment, and everything that is the reverse of health, good humour, and frankness. For any happiness, even in this world, quite a lot of restraint is going to be necessary; so the claim made by every desire, when it is strong, to be healthy and reasonable, counts for nothing. Every sane and civilized man must have some set of principles by which he chooses to reject some of his desires and to permit others. One man does this on Christian principles, another on hygienic principles, another on sociological principles. The real conflict is not between

Christianity and 'nature', but between Christian principles and other principles in the control of 'nature'. For 'nature' (in the sense of natural desire) will have to be controlled anyway, unless you are going to ruin your whole life.

The Animal Self and the Diabolical Self   *March 31*

People often misunderstand what psychology teaches about 'repressions'. It teaches us that 'repressed' sex is dangerous. But 'repressed' is here a technical term: it does not mean 'suppressed' in the sense of 'denied' or 'resisted'. A repressed desire or thought is one which has been thrust into the subconscious (usually at a very early age) and can now come before the mind only in a disguised and unrecognizable form. Repressed sexuality does not appear to the patient to be sexuality at all. When an adolescent or an adult is engaged in resisting a conscious desire, he is not dealing with a repression nor is he in the least danger of creating a repression. On the contrary, those who are seriously attempting chastity are more conscious, and soon know a great deal more about their own sexuality than anyone else. They come to know their desires as Wellington knew Napoleon, or as Sherlock Holmes knew Moriarty; as a ratcatcher knows rats or a plumber knows about leaky pipes. Virtue – even attempted virtue – brings light: indulgence brings fog.

Finally, though I have had to speak at some length about sex, I want to make it as clear as I possibly can that the centre of Christian morality is not here. If anyone thinks that Christians regard unchastity as the supreme vice, he is quite wrong. The sins of the flesh are bad, but they are the least bad of all sins. All the worst pleasures are purely spiritual: the pleasure of putting other people in the wrong, of bossing and patronizing and spoiling sport, and backbiting; the pleasures of power, of hatred.

For there are two things inside me, competing with the human self which I must try to become. They are the Animal self, and the Diabolical self. The Diabolical self is the worse of the two. That is why a cold, self-righteous prig who goes regularly to church may be far nearer to hell than a prostitute. But, of course, it is better to be neither.

Pride   *April 1*

According to Christian teachers, the essential vice, the utmost evil, is Pride. Unchastity, anger, greed, drunkenness, and all that, are mere fleabites in comparison: it was through Pride that the devil became the devil: Pride leads to every other vice: it is the complete anti-God state of mind. . . . If you want to find out how proud you are the easiest way is to ask yourself, 'How much do I dislike it when other people snub me, or refuse to take any notice of me, or shove their oar in, or patronize me, or show off?' The point is that each person's pride is in competition with everyone else's pride. It is because I wanted to be the big noise at the party that I am so annoyed at someone else being the big noise. Two of a trade never agree. Now what you want to get clear is that Pride is *essentially* competitive – is competitive by its very nature – while the other vices are competitive only, so to speak, by accident. Pride gets no pleasure out of having something, only out of having more of it than the next man. We say that people are proud of being rich, or clever, or good-looking, but they are not. They are proud of being richer, or cleverer, or better-looking than others. If everyone else became equally rich, or clever, or good-looking there would be nothing to be proud about. It is the comparison that makes you proud: the pleasure of being above the rest. Once the element of competition has gone, pride has gone. That is why I say that Pride is essentially competitive in a way the other vices are not.

The Chief Cause of Misery

It is Pride which has been the chief cause of misery in every nation and every family since the world began. Other vices may sometimes bring people together: you may find good fellowship and jokes and friendliness among drunken people or unchaste people. But Pride always means enmity – it *is* enmity. And not only enmity between man and man, but enmity to God.

In God you come up against something which is in every respect immeasurably superior to yourself. Unless you know God as that – and, therefore, know yourself as nothing in comparison – you do not know God. A proud man is always looking down on things and people: and, of course, as long as you are looking down, you cannot see something that is above you.

That raises a terrible question. How is it that people who are quite obviously eaten up with Pride can say they believe in God and appear to themselves very religious? I am afraid it means they are worshipping an imaginary God. They theoretically admit themselves to be nothing in the presence of this phantom God, but are really all the time imagining how He approves of them and thinks them far better than ordinary people: that is, they pay a pennyworth of imaginary humility to Him and get out of it a pound's worth of Pride towards their fellow men. I suppose it was of those people Christ was thinking when He said that some would preach about Him and cast out devils in His name, only to be told at the end of the world that He had never known them. And any of us may at any moment be in this deathtrap. Luckily, we have a test. Whenever we find that our religious life is making us feel that we are good – above all, that we are better than someone else – I think we may be sure that we are being acted on, not by God, but by the devil. The real test of being in the presence of God is that you either forget about yourself altogether or see yourself as a small, dirty object. It is better to forget about yourself altogether.

Direct from Hell

It is a terrible thing that the worst of all the vices can
smuggle itself into the very centre of our religious life.
But you can see why. The other, and less bad, vices come
from the devil working on us through our animal nature.
But this does not come through our animal nature at all.
It comes direct from Hell. It is purely spiritual: consequently, it is far more subtle and deadly. For the same
reason, Pride can often be used to beat down the simpler
vices. Teachers, in fact, often appeal to a boy's Pride, or,
as they call it, his self-respect, to make him behave de-
cently: many a man has overcome cowardice, or lust, or
ill-temper by learning to think that they are beneath his
dignity – that is, by Pride. The devil laughs. He is
perfectly content to see you becoming chaste and brave
and self-controlled provided, all the time, he is setting up
in you the Dictatorship of Pride – just as he would be
quite content to see your chilblains cured if he was
allowed, in return, to give you cancer. For Pride is spiritual cancer: it eats up the very possibility of love, or
contentment, or even common sense.

The Difference between Pride and Vanity

Pleasure in being praised is not Pride. The child who is
patted on the back for doing a lesson well, the woman
whose beauty is praised by her lover, the saved soul to
whom Christ says 'Well done', are pleased and ought to
be. For here the pleasure lies not in what you are but in
the fact that you have pleased someone you wanted (and
rightly wanted) to please. The trouble begins when you
pass from thinking, 'I have pleased him; all is well', to
thinking, 'What a fine person I must be to have done it.'
The more you delight in yourself and the less you delight
in the praise, the worse you are becoming. When you

delight wholly in yourself and do not care about the praise at all, you have reached the bottom. That is why vanity, though it is the sort of Pride which shows most on the surface, is really the least bad and most pardonable sort. The vain person wants praise, applause, admiration, too much and is always angling for it. It is a fault, but a childlike and even (in an odd way) a humble fault. It shows that you are not yet completely contented with your own admiration. You value other people enough to want them to look at you. You are, in fact, still human. The real black, diabolical Pride comes when you look down on others so much that you do not care what they think of you.

Our Share in the Passion of Christ   *April 5*

Some people feel guilty about their anxieties and regard them as a defect of faith. I don't agree at all. They are afflictions, not sins. Like all afflictions, they are, if we can so take them, our share in the Passion of Christ. For the beginning of the Passion – the first move, so to speak – is in Gethsemane. In Gethsemane a very strange and significant thing seems to have happened.

It is clear from many of His sayings that Our Lord had long foreseen His death. He knew what conduct such as His, in a world such as we have made of this, must inevitably lead to. But it is clear that this knowledge must somehow have been withdrawn from Him before He prayed in Gethsemane. He could not, with whatever reservation about the Father's will, have prayed that the cup might pass and simultaneously known that it would not. That is both a logical and a psychological impossibility. You see what this involves? Lest any trial incident to humanity should be lacking, the torments of hope – of suspense, anxiety – were at the last moment loosed upon Him – the supposed possibility that, after

all, He might, He just conceivably might, be spared the
supreme horror. There was precedent. Isaac had been
spared: he too at the last moment, he also against all
apparent probability. It was not quite impossible . . . and
doubtless He had seen other men crucified . . . a sight
very unlike most of our religious pictures and images.

But for this last (and erroneous) hope against hope, and
the consequent tumult of the soul, the sweat of blood,
perhaps He would not have been very Man. To live in a
fully predictable world is not to be a man.

At the end, I know, we are told that an angel appeared
'comforting' Him. . . . 'Strengthening' is more the word.
May not the strengthening have consisted in the renewed
certainty – cold comfort this – that the thing must be
endured and therefore could be?

Christ Suffering for His World   *April 6*

Does not every movement in the Passion write large
some common element in the sufferings of our race?
First, the prayer of anguish; not granted. Then He turns
to His friends. They are asleep – as ours, or we, are so
often, or busy, or away, or preoccupied. Then He faces
the Church; the very Church that He brought into existence. It condemns Him. This also is characteristic. In
every Church, in every institution, there is something
which sooner or later works against the very purpose for
which it came into existence. But there seems to be
another chance. There is the State; in this case, the
Roman state. Its pretensions are far lower than those of
the Jewish church, but for that very reason it may be free
from local fanaticisms. It claims to be just on a rough,
worldly level. Yes, but only so far as is consistent with
political expediency and *raison d'état*. One becomes a
counter in a complicated game. But even now all is not
lost. There is still an appeal to the People – the poor and

simple whom He had blessed, whom He had healed and fed and taught, to whom He Himself belongs. But they have become overnight (it is nothing unusual) a murderous rabble shouting for His blood. There is, then, nothing left but God. And to God, God's last words are 'Why hast thou forsaken me?'

You see how characteristic, how representative, it all is. The human situation writ large. These are among the things it means to be a man. Every rope breaks when you seize it. Every door is slammed shut as you reach it. To be like the fox at the end of the run; the earths all staked.

The 'Hiddenness' of God   *April 7*

As for the last dereliction of all, how can we either understand or endure it? Is it that God Himself cannot be Man unless God seems to vanish at His greatest need? And if so, why? I sometimes wonder if we have ever begun to understand what is involved in the very concept of creation. If God will create, He will make something to be, and yet to be not Himself. To be created is, in some sense, to be ejected or separated. Can it be that the more perfect the creature is, the further this separation must at some point be pushed? It is saints, not common people, who experience the 'dark night'. It is men and angels, not beasts, who rebel. Inanimate matter sleeps in the bosom of the Father. The 'hiddenness' of God perhaps presses most painfully on those who are in another way nearest to Him, and therefore God Himself, made man, will of all men be by God most forsaken? One of the seventeenth-century divines says, 'By pretending to be visible God could only deceive the world.' Perhaps He does pretend just a little to simple souls who need a full measure of 'sensible consolation'. Not deceiving them, but tempering the wind to the shorn lamb. Of course I'm not saying like Niebuhr that evil is inherent in finitude. That would identify the creation with the fall and make God the author of evil. But perhaps there is an anguish, an alienation, a crucifixion involved in the creative act. Yet He who alone can judge judges the far-off consummation to be worth it.

Miracles *April 8*

I have known only one person in my life who claimed to have seen a ghost. It was a woman; and the interesting thing is that she disbelieved in the immortality of the soul before seeing the ghost and still disbelieves after having seen it. She thinks it was a hallucination. In other words, seeing is not believing. This is the first thing to get clear in talking about miracles. Whatever experiences we may have, we shall not regard them as miraculous if we already hold a philosophy which excludes the supernatural. Any event which is claimed as a miracle is, in the last resort, an experience received from the senses; and the senses are not infallible. We can always say we have been the victims of an illusion; if we disbelieve in the supernatural this is what we always shall say. Hence, whether miracles have really ceased or not, they would certainly appear to cease in Western Europe as materialism became the popular creed. For let us make no mistake. If the end of the world appeared in all the literal trappings of the Apocalypse, if the modern materialist saw with his own eyes the heavens rolled up and the great white throne appearing, if he had the sensation of being himself hurled into the Lake of Fire, he would continue forever, in that lake itself, to regard his experience as an illusion and to find the explanation of it in psychoanalysis, or cerebral pathology. Experience by itself proves nothing. If a man doubts whether he is dreaming or waking, no experiment can solve his doubt, since every experiment may itself be part of the dream.

Experience proves this, or that, or nothing, according to the preconceptions we bring to it.

The Snag about Materialism   *April 9*

If the solar system was brought about by an accidental collision, then the appearance of organic life on this planet was also an accident, and the whole evolution of Man was an accident too. If so, then all our present thoughts are mere accidents – the accidental by-product of the movement of atoms. And this holds for the thoughts of the materialists and astronomers as well as for anyone else's. But if *their* thoughts – i.e. of materialism and astronomy – are merely accidental by-products, why should we believe them to be true? I see no reason for believing that one accident should be able to give me a correct account of all the other accidents. It's like expecting that the accidental shape taken by the splash when you upset a milkjug should give you a correct account of how the jug was made and why it was upset.

The Natural and the Supernatural   *April 10*

The experience of a miracle in fact requires two conditions. First we must believe in a normal stability of Nature, which means we must recognize that the data offered by our senses recur in regular patterns. Secondly, we must believe in some reality beyond Nature. When both beliefs are held, and not till then, we can approach with an open mind the various reports which claim that this super- or extra-natural reality has sometimes invaded and disturbed the sensuous content of space and time which makes our 'natural' world. The belief in such a supernatural reality itself can neither be proved nor disproved by experience. The arguments for its existence are metaphysical, and to me conclusive. They turn on the fact that even to think and act in the natural world we have to assume something beyond it and even assume that we partly belong to that something. In order to think we must claim for our own reasoning a validity which is not credible if our own thought is merely a function of our brain, and our brains a by-product of irrational physical processes. In order to act, above the level of mere impulse, we must claim a similar validity for our judgements of good and evil. In both cases we get the same disquieting result. The concept of Nature itself is one we have reached only tacitly by claiming a sort of *supernatural* status for ourselves.

The Miracles of Our Lord   *April 11*

This is what St Athanasius says in his little book *On the Incarnation*: 'Our Lord took a body like to ours and lived as a man in order that those who had refused to recognize Him in His superintendence and captaincy of the whole universe might come to recognize from the works He did here below in the body that what dwelled in this body was the Word of God.' This accords exactly with Christ's account of His miracles: 'The Son can do nothing of Himself, but what He seeth the Father do.' The doctrine, as I understand it, is something like this:

There is an activity of God displayed throughout creation, a wholesale activity let us say which men refuse to recognize. The miracles done by God incarnate, living as a man in Palestine, perform the very same things as this wholesale activity, but at a different speed and on a smaller scale. One of their chief purposes is that men, having seen a thing done by personal power on the small scale, may recognize, when they see the same thing done on the larger scale, that the power behind it is also personal – is indeed the very same person who lived among us two thousand years ago. The miracles in fact are a retelling in small letters of the very same story which is written across the whole world in letters too large for some of us to see. Of that larger script part is already visible, part is still unsolved. In other words, some of the miracles do locally what God has already done universally: others do locally what He has not yet done, but will do. In that sense, and from our human point of view, some are reminders and others prophecies.

The Miracle at Cana   *April 12*

Firstly to Miracles of *Fertility*. The earliest of these was the conversion of water into wine at the wedding feast in Cana. This miracle proclaims that the God of all wine is present. The vine is one of the blessings sent by Jahweh: He is the reality behind the false god Bacchus. Every year, as part of the Natural order, God makes wine. He does so by creating a vegetable organism that can turn water, soil, and sunlight into a juice which will, under proper conditions, become wine. Thus, in a certain sense, He constantly turns water into wine, for wine, like all drinks, is but water modified. Once, and in one year only, God, now incarnate, short-circuits the process: makes wine in a moment: uses earthenware jars instead of vegetable fibres to hold the water. But uses them to do what He is always doing. The Miracle consists in the short cut; but the event to which it leads is the usual one. If the thing happened, then we know that what has come into Nature is no anti-Natural spirit, no God who loves tragedy and tears and fasting *for their own sake* (however He may permit or demand them for special purposes) but the God of Israel who has through all these centuries given us wine to gladden the heart of man.

99

Other miracles that fall in this class are the two instances of miraculous feeding. They involve the multiplication of a little bread and a little fish into much bread and much fish. Once in the desert Satan had tempted Him to make bread of stones: He refused the suggestion. 'The Son does nothing except what He sees the Father do'; perhaps one may without boldness surmise that the direct change from stone to bread appeared to the Son to be not quite in the hereditary style. Little bread into much bread is quite a different matter. Every year God makes a little corn into much corn: the seed is sown and there is an increase. And men say, according to their several fashions, 'It is the laws of Nature', or 'It is Ceres, it is Adonis, it is the Corn-King.' But the laws of Nature are only a pattern: nothing will come of them unless they can, so to speak, take over the universe as a going concern. And as for Adonis, no man can tell us where he died or when he rose again. Here, at the feeding of the five thousand, is He whom we have ignorantly worshipped: the *real* Corn-King who will die once and rise once at Jerusalem during the term of office of Pontius Pilate.

That same day He also multiplied fish. Look down into every bay and almost every river. This swarming, undulating fecundity shows He is still at work 'thronging the seas with spawn innumerable'. The ancients had a god called Genius; the god of animal and human fertility, the patron of gynaecology, embryology, and the marriage bed – the 'genial' bed as they called it after its god Genius. But Genius is only another mask for the God of Israel, for it was He who at the beginning commanded all species 'to be fruitful and multiply and replenish the earth'. And now, that day, at the feeding of the thousands, incarnate God does the same: does close and small, under His human hands, a workman's hands, what He has always been doing in the seas, the lakes and the little brooks.

The Miracles of Healing   *April 14*

Without deciding in detail which of the healings must
(apart from acceptance of the Christian faith) be regarded
as miraculous, we can however indicate the kind of miracle involved. Its character can easily be obscured by the
somewhat magical view which many people still take of
ordinary and medical healing. There is a sense in which
no doctor ever heals. The doctors themselves would be
the first to admit this. The magic is not in the medicine
but in the patient's body – in the *vis medicatrix naturae*,
the recuperative or self-corrective energy of Nature.
What the treatment does is to stimulate Natural functions or to remove what hinders them. We speak for
convenience of the doctor, or the dressing, healing a cut.
But in another sense every cut heals itself: no cut can be
healed in a corpse. That same mysterious force which we
call gravitational when it steers the planets and
biochemical when it heals a live body, is the efficient
cause of all recoveries. And that energy proceeds from
God in the first instance. All who are cured are cured by
Him, not merely in the sense that His providence provides them with medical assistance and wholesome en-
vironments, but also in the sense that their very tissues
are repaired by the far-descending energy which, flowing
from Him, energizes the whole system of Nature. But
once He did it visibly to the sick in Palestine, a Man
meeting with men. What in its general operations we
refer to laws of Nature or once referred to Apollo or
Aesculapius thus reveals itself. The Power that always
was behind all healings puts on a face and hands. Hence,
of course, the apparent chanciness of the miracles. It is
idle to complain that He heals those whom He happens
to meet, not those whom He doesn't. To be a man means
to be in one place and not in another. The world which
would not know Him as present everywhere was saved
by His becoming *local*.

The Miracle of Destruction April 15

Christ's single miracle of Destruction, the withering of the figtree, has proved troublesome to some people, but I think its significance is plain enough. The miracle is an acted parable, a symbol of God's sentence on all that is 'fruitless' and specially, no doubt, on the official Judaism of that age. That is its moral significance. As a miracle, it again does in focus, repeats small and close, what God does constantly and throughout Nature. . . . God, twisting Satan's weapon out of his hand, had become, since the Fall, the God even of human death. But much more, and perhaps ever since the creation, He has been the God of the death of organisms. In both cases, though in somewhat different ways, He is the God of death because He is the God of Life: the God of human death because through it increase of life now comes – the God of merely organic death because death is part of the very mode by which organic life spreads itself out in Time and yet remains new. A forest a thousand years deep is still collectively alive because some trees are dying and others are growing up. His human face, turned with negation in its eyes upon that one figtree, did once what His unincarnate action does to all trees. No tree died that year in Palestine, or any year anywhere, except because God did – or rather ceased to do – something to it.

What the Apostles Meant by the Resurrection April 16

When modern writers talk of the Resurrection they usually mean one particular moment – the discovery of the Empty Tomb and the appearance of Jesus a few yards away from it. The story of that moment is what Christian apologists now chiefly try to support and sceptics chiefly try to impugn. But this almost exclusive concentration on the first five minutes or so of the Resurrection would have astonished the earliest Christian teachers. In claiming to have seen the Resurrection they were not necessarily claiming to have seen *that*. Some of them had, some of them had not. It had no more importance than any of the other appearances of the risen Jesus – apart from the poetic and dramatic importance which the beginnings of things must always have. What they were claiming was that they had all, at one time or another, met Jesus during the six or seven weeks that followed His death. Sometimes they seem to have been alone when they did so, but on one occasion twelve of them saw Him together, and on another occasion about five hundred of them. St Paul says that the majority of the five hundred were still alive when he wrote the *First Letter to the Corinthians*, i.e. in about A.D. 55.

The 'Resurrection' to which they bore witness was, in fact, not the action of rising from the dead but the state of having risen; a state, as they held, attested by intermittent meetings during a limited period. . . . This termination of the period is important, for, as we shall see, there is no possibility of isolating the doctrine of the Resurrection from that of the Ascension.

Christ's Triumph Over Death   *April 17*

The next point to notice is that the Resurrection was not regarded simply or chiefly as evidence for the immortality of the soul. It is, of course, often so regarded today: I have heard a man maintain that 'the importance of the Resurrection is that it proves *survival*'. Such a view cannot at any point be reconciled with the language of the New Testament. On such a view Christ would simply have done what all men do when they die: the only novelty would have been that in His case we were allowed to see it happening. But there is not in Scripture

the faintest suggestion that the Resurrection was new
evidence for something that had *in fact* been always
happening. The New Testament writers speak as if
Christ's achievement in rising from the dead was the first
event of its kind in the whole history of the universe. He
is the 'first fruits', the 'pioneer of life'. He has forced open
a door that has been locked since the death of the first
man. He has met, fought, and beaten the King of Death.
Everything is different because He has done so. This is
the beginning of the New Creation: a new chapter in
cosmic history has opened.

The Resurrection and 'Survival'   *April 18*

I do not mean, of course, that the writers of the New
Testament disbelieved in 'survival'. On the contrary they
believed in it so readily that Jesus on more than one
occasion had to assure them that He was not a ghost.
From the earliest times the Jews, like many other nations, had believed that man possessed a 'soul' or
Nephesh separable from the body, which went at death
into the shadowy world called *Sheol*: a land of forgetful-
ness and imbecility where none called upon Jehovah any
more, a land half unreal and melancholy like the Hades
of the Greeks or the Niflheim of the Norsemen. From it
shades could return and appear to the living, as Samuel's
shade had done at the command of the Witch of Endor. In
much more recent times there had arisen a more cheerful
belief that the righteous passed at death to 'heaven'. Both
doctrines are doctrines of 'the immortality of the soul' as
a Greek or a modern Englishman understands it: and
both are quite irrelevant to the story of the Resurrection.
The writers look upon this event as an absolute novelty.
Quite clearly they do not think they have been haunted
by a ghost from Sheol, nor even that they have had a
vision of a 'soul' in 'heaven'. It must be clearly under-

stood that if the Psychical Researchers succeeded in proving 'survival' and showed that the Resurrection was an instance of it, they would not be supporting the Christian faith but refuting it. If that were all that had happened the original 'Gospel' would have been untrue.

Spiritualism and Psychical Research   *April 19*

It seems to me that both beliefs, unless reinforced by something else, will be to modern man very shadowy and inoperative. If indeed we knew that God were righteous, that He had purposes for us, that He was the leader in a cosmic battle and that some real issue hung on our conduct in the field, then it would be something to the purpose. Or if, again, the utterances which purport to come from the other world ever had the accent which really *suggests* another world, ever spoke (as even the inferior actual religions do) with that voice before which our mortal nature trembles with awe or joy, then that also would be to the purpose. But the god of minimal Theism remains powerless to excite either fear or love. . . . As for the utterances of the mediums . . . I do not wish to be offensive. But will even the most convinced spiritualist claim that one sentence from that source has ever taken its place among the golden sayings of mankind, has ever approached (much less equalled) in power to elevate, strengthen or correct even the second rank of such sayings? Will anyone deny that the vast majority of spirit messages sink pitiably below the best that has been thought and said even in this world?

There are, I allow, certain respects in which the risen Christ resembles the 'ghost' of popular tradition. Like a ghost He 'appears' and 'disappears': locked doors are no obstacle to Him. On the other hand He Himself vigorously asserts that He is corporeal (Luke 24:39–40) and eats boiled fish. It is at this point that the modern reader becomes uncomfortable. He becomes more uncomfortable still at the words, 'Don't touch me; I have not yet gone up to the Father' (John 20:17). For voices and apparitions we are, in some measure, prepared. But what is this that must not be touched? What is all this about going 'up' to the Father? Is He not already 'with the Father' in the only sense that matters? What can 'going up' be except a metaphor for *that*? And if so, why has He 'not yet' gone? These discomforts arise because the story the apostles actually had to tell begins at this point to conflict with the story we expect and are determined beforehand to read into their narrative.

We expect them to tell of a risen life which is purely 'spiritual' in the negative sense of that word: that is, we use the word 'spiritual' to mean not what it is but what it is not. We mean a life without space, without history, without environment, with no sensuous elements in it. We also, in our heart of hearts, tend to slur over the risen *manhood* of Jesus, to conceive Him, after death, simply returning into Deity, so that the Resurrection would be no more than the reversal or undoing of the Incarnation. That being so, all references to the risen *body* make us uneasy: they raise awkward questions.

As long as we hold the negatively spiritual view, we have not really been believing in that body at all. We have thought (whether we acknowledged it or not) that the body was not objective: that it was an appearance sent by God to assure the disciples of truths otherwise incommunicable. But what truths? If the truth is that after death there comes a negatively spiritual life, an eternity of mystical experience, what more misleading way of communicating it could possibly be found than the appearance of a human form which eats boiled fish? Again, on such a view, the body would really be a hallucination. And any theory of hallucination breaks down on the fact (and if it is invention it is the oddest invention that ever entered the mind of man) that on three separate occasions this hallucination was not immediately recognized as Jesus (Luke 24:13–31; John 20:15, 21:4). Even granting that God sent a holy hallucination to teach truths already widely believed without it, and far more easily taught by other methods, and certain to be completely obscured by this, might we not at least hope that He would get the face of the hallucination *right*? Is He who made all faces such a bungler that He cannot even work up a recognizable likeness of the Man who was Himself?

The Imperishable Body of the Risen Lord   *April 22*

The records represent Christ as passing after death (as no man had passed before) neither into a purely, that is, negatively, 'spiritual' mode of existence nor into a 'natural' life such as we know, but into a life which has its own, new Nature. It represents Him as withdrawing six weeks later, into some different mode of existence. It says – He says – that He goes 'to prepare a place for us'.

This presumably means that He is about to create that whole new Nature which will provide the environment or conditions for His glorified humanity and, in Him, for ours. The picture is not what we expected – though whether it is less or more probable and philosophical on that account is another question. It is not the picture of an escape from any and every kind of Nature into some unconditioned and utterly transcendent life. It is the picture of a new human nature, and a new Nature in general, being brought into existence. We must, indeed, believe the risen body to be extremely different from the mortal body: but the existence, in that new state, of anything that could in any sense be described as 'body' at all, involves some sort of spatial relations and in the long run a whole new universe. That is the picture – not of unmaking but of remaking. The old field of space, time, matter, and the senses is to be weeded, dug, and sown for a new crop. We may be tired of that old field: God is not.

St George, Patron of England   April 23

A serious attack on the fairy tale as children's literature comes from those who do not wish children to be frightened. . . . Those who say that children must not be frightened may mean two things. They may mean (1) that we must not do anything likely to give the child those haunting, disabling, pathological fears against which ordinary courage is helpless: in fact, *phobias*. . . . Or they may mean (2) that we must try to keep out of his mind the knowledge that he is born into a world of death, violence, wounds, adventure, heroism and cowardice, good and evil. If they mean the first I agree with them: but not if they mean the second. The second would indeed be to give children a false impression and feed them on escapism in the bad sense. There is something ludicrous in the idea of so educating a generation which is born to the Ogpu and the atomic bomb. Since it is so likely that they will meet cruel enemies, let them at least have heard of brave knights and heroic courage. . . . By confining your child to blameless stories of child life in which nothing at all alarming ever happens, you would fail to banish the terrors, and would succeed in banishing all that can ennoble them or make them endurable. For in the fairy tales, side by side with the terrible figures, we find the immemorial comforters and protectors, the radiant ones; and the terrible figures are not merely terrible, but sublime. It would be nice if no little boy in bed, hearing, or thinking he hears, a sound, were ever at all frightened. But if he is going to be frightened, I think it better that he should think of giants and dragons than merely of burglars. And I think St George, or any bright champion in armour, is a better comfort than the idea of the police.

And So We Shall Rise   *April 24*

The miracles that have already happened are, of course, as Scripture so often says, the first fruits of that cosmic summer which is presently coming on. Christ has risen, and so we shall rise. St Peter for a few seconds walked on the water; and the day will come when there will be a remade universe, infinitely obedient to the will of glorified and obedient men, when we can do all things, when we shall be those gods that we are described as being in Scripture. To be sure, it feels wintry enough still: but often in the very early spring it feels like that. Two thousand years are only a day or two by this scale. A man really ought to say, 'The Resurrection happened two thousand years ago' in the same spirit in which he says, 'I saw a crocus yesterday.' Because we know what is coming behind the crocus. The spring comes slowly down this way; but the great thing is that the corner has been turned. There is, of course, this difference, that in the natural spring the crocus cannot choose whether it will respond or not. We can. We have the power either of withstanding the spring, and sinking back into the cosmic winter, or of going on into those 'high mid-summer pomps' in which our Leader, the Son of Man, already dwells, and to which He is calling us. It remains with us to follow or not, to die in this winter, or to go on into that spring and that summer.

St Mark, Evangelist   April 25

'Say what you like,' we shall be told, 'the apocalyptic beliefs of the first Christians have been proved to be false. It is clear from the New Testament that they all expected the Second Coming in their own lifetime. And, worse still, they had a reason, and one you will find very embarrassing. Their Master had told them so. He shared, and indeed created, their delusion. He said in so many words, "This generation shall not pass till all these things be done." And He was wrong. He clearly knew no more about the end of the world than anyone else.'

It is certainly the most embarrassing verse in the Bible. Yet how teasing, also, that within fourteen words of it should come the statement 'But of that day and that hour knoweth no man, no, not the angels which are in heaven, neither the Son, but the Father.' The one exhibition of error and the one confession of ignorance grow side by side. That they stood thus in the mouth of Jesus Himself, and were not merely placed thus by the reporter, we surely need not doubt. Unless the reporter were perfectly honest he would never have recorded the confession of ignorance at all; he could have had no motive for doing so except a desire to tell the whole truth. And unless later copyists were equally honest they would never have preserved the (apparently) mistaken prediction about 'this generation' after the passage of time had shown the (apparent) mistake. This passage (Mark 13:30–32) and the cry 'Why hast thou forsaken me?' (Mark 15:34) together make up the strongest proof that the New Testament is historically reliable. The evangelists have the first great characteristic of honest witnesses: they mention facts which are, at first sight, damaging to their main contention.

The Full Healing of an Old Disease   *April 26*

Let us confess that probably every Christian now alive finds a difficulty in reconciling the two things he has been told about 'heaven' – that it is, on the one hand, a life in Christ, a vision of God, a ceaseless adoration, and that it is, on the other hand, a bodily life. When we seem nearest to the vision of God in this life, the body seems almost an irrelevance. And if we try to conceive our eternal life as one in a body (any kind of body) we tend to find that some vague dream of Platonic paradises and gardens of the Hesperides has substituted itself for that mystical approach which we feel (and I think rightly) to be more important. But if that discrepancy were final then it would follow – which is absurd – that God was originally mistaken when He introduced our spirits into the Natural order at all. We must conclude that the discrepancy itself is precisely one of the disorders which the New Creation comes to heal. The fact that the body, and locality and locomotion and time, now feel irrelevant to the highest reaches of the spiritual life is . . . a *symptom*. Spirit and Nature have quarrelled in us; that is our disease.

The letter and spirit of Scripture, and of all Christianity, forbid us to suppose that life in the New Creation will be a sexual life; and this reduces our imagination to the withering alternative either of bodies which are hardly recognizable as human bodies at all or else of a perpetual fast. As regards the fast, I think our present outlook might be like that of a small boy who, on being told that the sexual act was the highest bodily pleasure, should immediately ask whether you ate chocolates at the same time. On receiving the answer 'No', he might regard absence of chocolates as the chief characteristic of sexuality. In vain would you tell him that the reason why lovers in their carnal raptures don't bother about chocolates is that they have something better to think of. The boy knows chocolate: he does not know the positive thing that excludes it. We are in the same position. We know the sexual life; we do not know, except in glimpses, the other thing which, in Heaven, will leave no room for it. Hence where fulness awaits us we anticipate fasting. In denying that sexual life, as we now understand it, makes any part of the final beatitude, it is not of course necessary to suppose that the distinction of sexes will disappear. What is no longer needed for biological purposes may be expected to survive for splendour. Sexuality is the instrument both of virginity and of conjugal virtue; neither men nor women will be asked to throw away weapons they have used victoriously. It is the beaten and the fugitives who throw away their swords. The conquerors sheathe theirs and retain them. 'Trans-sexual' would be a better word than 'sexless' for the heavenly life.

Will We be *Bored* by Heaven?

Our notion of Heaven involves perpetual negations: no food, no drink, no sex, no movement, no mirth, no events, no time, no art. Against all these, to be sure, we set one positive: the vision and enjoyment of God. And since this is an infinite good, we hold (rightly) that it outweighs them all. That is, the reality of the Beatific Vision would or will outweigh, would infinitely outweigh, the reality of the negations. But can our present notion of it outweigh our present notion of them? That is quite a different question. And for most of us at most times the answer is No. How it may be for great saints and mystics I cannot tell. But for others the conception of that Vision is a difficult, precarious, and fugitive extrapolation from a very few and ambiguous moments in our earthly experience, while our idea of the negated natural goods is vivid and persistent, loaded with the memories of a lifetime, built into our nerves and muscles and therefore into our imaginations.

Thus the negatives have, so to speak, an unfair advantage in every competition with the positive. What is worse, their presence – and most when we most resolutely try to suppress or ignore them – vitiates even such a faint and ghostlike notion of the positive as we might have had. The exclusion of the lower goods begins to seem the essential characteristic of the higher good. We feel, if we do not say, that the vision of God will come not to fulfil but to destroy our nature; this bleak fantasy often underlies our very use of such words as 'holy' or 'pure' or 'spiritual'.

We must not allow this to happen if we can possibly prevent it. We must believe – and therefore in some degree imagine – that every negation will be only the reverse side of a fulfilling. And we must mean by that the fulfilling, precisely, of our humanity; not our transformation into angels nor our absorption into Deity. For though we shall be 'as the angels' and made 'like unto' our Master, I think this means 'like with the likeness

113

proper to men': as different instruments that play the same air but each in its own fashion. How far the life of the risen man will be sensory, we do not know. But I surmise that it will differ from the sensory life we know here, not as emptiness differs from water or water from wine but as a flower differs from a bulb or a cathedral from an architect's drawing.

A Fable about a Very Likely Misconception *April 29*

Let us picture a woman thrown into a dungeon. There she bears and rears a son. He grows up seeing nothing but the dungeon walls, the straw on the floor, and a little patch of the sky seen through the grating, which is too high up to show anything except sky. This unfortunate woman was an artist, and when they imprisoned her she managed to bring with her a drawing pad and a box of pencils. As she never loses the hope of deliverance she is constantly teaching her son about that outer world which he has never seen. She does it very largely by drawing him pictures. With her pencil she attempts to show him what fields, rivers, mountains, cities and waves on a beach are like. He is a dutiful boy and he does his best to believe her when she tells him that that outer world is far more interesting and glorious than anything in the dungeon. At times he succeeds. On the whole he gets on tolerably well until, one day, he says something that gives his mother pause. For a minute or two they are at cross-purposes. Finally it dawns on her that he has, all these years, lived under a misconception. 'But', she gasps, 'you didn't think that the real world was full of lines drawn in lead pencil?' 'What?' says the boy. 'No pencil marks there?' And instantly his whole notion of the outer world becomes a blank. For the lines, by which alone he was imagining it, have now been denied of it. He has no idea of that which will exclude and dispense with the lines, that of which the lines were merely a transposition – the waving treetops, the light dancing on the weir, the coloured three-dimensional realities which are not enclosed in lines but define their own shapes at every moment with a delicacy and multiplicity which no drawing could ever achieve. The child will get the idea that the real world is somehow less visible than his mother's pictures. In reality it lacks lines because it is incomparably more visible.

So with us. 'We know now what we shall be'; but we may be sure we shall be more, not less, than we were on earth. Our natural experiences (sensory, emotional, imaginative) are only like the drawing, like pencilled lines on flat paper. If they vanish in the risen life, they will vanish only as pencil lines vanish from the real landscape; not as a candle flame that is put out but as a candle flame which becomes invisible because someone has pulled up the blind, thrown open the shutters, and let in the blaze of the risen sun.

A Gallop with the King   *April 30*

The thought at the back of all this negative spirituality is really one forbidden to Christians. They, of all men, must not conceive spiritual joy and worth as things that need to be rescued or tenderly protected from time and place and matter and the senses. Their God is the God of corn and oil and wine. He is the glad Creator. He has become Himself incarnate. The Sacraments have been instituted. Certain spiritual gifts are offered us only on condition that we perform certain bodily acts. After that we cannot really be in doubt of His intention. To shrink back from all that can be called Nature into negative spirituality is as if we ran away from horses instead of learning to ride. There is in our present pilgrim condition plenty of room (more room than most of us like) for abstinence and renunciation and mortifying our natural desires. But behind all asceticism the thought should be, 'Who will trust us with the true wealth if we cannot be trusted even with the wealth that perishes?' Who will trust me with a spiritual body if I cannot control even an earthly body? These small and perishable bodies we now have were given to us as ponies are given to schoolboys. We must learn to manage: not that we may some day be free of horses altogether but that some day we may ride bareback, confident and rejoicing, those greater mounts, those winged, shining and world-shaking horses which perhaps even now expect us with impatience, pawing and snorting in the King's stables. Not that the gallop would be of any value unless it were a gallop with the King; but how else – since He has retained His own charger – should we accompany Him?

St Joseph the Worker   *May 1*

'Good Works' in the plural is an expression much more familiar to modern Christendom than 'good work'. Good works are chiefly alms-giving or 'helping' in the parish. They are quite separate from one's 'work'. And good works need not be good work, as anyone can see by inspecting some of the objects made to be sold at bazaars for charitable purposes. This is not according to our example. When Our Lord provided a poor wedding party with an extra glass of wine all round, He was doing good works. But also good work; it was a wine really worth drinking. Nor is the neglect of goodness in our 'work', our job, according to precept. The Apostle says every one must not only work but work to produce what is 'good'.

The idea of Good Work is not quite extinct among us, though it is not, I fear, especially characteristic of religious people. I have found it among cabinet-makers, cobblers, and sailors. It is no use at all trying to impress sailors with a new liner because she is the biggest or costliest ship afloat. They look for what they call her 'lines': they predict how she will behave in a heavy sea. Artists also talk of Good Work; but decreasingly. They begin to prefer words like 'significant', 'important', 'contemporary', or 'daring'. These are not, to my mind, good symptoms.

St Athanasius   May 2

His epitaph is *Athanasius contra mundum*, 'Athanasius against the world'. We are proud that our country has more than once stood against the world. Athanasius did the same. He stood for the Trinitarian doctrine, 'whole and undefiled', when it looked as if all the civilized world was slipping back from Christianity into the religion of Arius – into one of those 'sensible' synthetic religions which are so strongly recommended today and which, then as now, included among their devotees many highly cultivated clergymen. It is his glory that he did not move with the times; it is his reward that he now remains when those times, as all times do, have moved away.

When I first opened his *De Incarnatione* I soon discovered . . . that I was reading a masterpiece. . . . We cannot, I admit, appropriate all its confidence today. We cannot point to the high virtue of Christian living and the gay, almost mocking, courage of Christian martyrdom, as a proof of our doctrines with quite that assurance which Athanasius takes as a matter of course. But whoever may be to blame for that, it is not Athanasius.

We are taught that the Incarnation itself proceeded 'not by the conversion of the godhead into flesh, but by taking of [the] manhood into God'; in it human life becomes the vehicle of Divine life. If the Scriptures proceed not by conversion of God's word into a literature but by taking up of a literature to be the vehicle of God's word, this is not anomalous. . . .

If the Old Testament is a literature thus 'taken up', made the vehicle of what is more than human, we can of course set no limit to the weight or multiplicity of meanings which may have been laid upon it. . . . We are committed to it in principle by Our Lord Himself. On that famous journey to Emmaus He found fault with the two disciples for not believing what the prophets had said. They ought to have known from their Bibles that the Anointed One, when He came, would enter His glory through suffering. He then explained, from 'Moses' (i.e. the Pentateuch) down, all the places in the Old Testament 'concerning Himself'. . . . We do not know – or anyway I do not know – what all these passages were. We can be pretty sure about one of them. The Ethiopian eunuch who met Philip (Acts 8:27–38) was reading Isaiah 53. He did not know whether in that passage the prophet was talking about himself or about someone else. Philip, in answering his question, 'preached unto him Jesus'. The answer, in fact, was 'Isaiah is speaking of Jesus'. We need have no doubt that Philip's authority for this interpretation was Our Lord.

The Resurrection of Our Bodies *May 4*

The raising of Lazarus differs from the Resurrection of Christ Himself because Lazarus, so far as we know, was not raised to a new and more glorious mode of existence but merely restored to the sort of life he had had before. The fitness of the miracle lies in the fact that He who will raise all men at the general resurrection here does it small and close, and in an inferior – a merely anticipatory – fashion. For the mere restoration of Lazarus is as inferior in splendour to the *glorious* resurrection of the New Humanity as stone jars are to the green and growing vine, or five little barley loaves to all the waving bronze and gold of a fat valley ripe for harvest. The resuscitation of Lazarus, so far as we can see, is simple reversal: a series of changes working in the direction opposite to that we have always experienced. At death, matter which has been organic begins to flow away into the inorganic, to be finally scattered and used (some of it) by other organisms. The resurrection of Lazarus involves the reverse process. The general resurrection involves the reverse process universalized – a rush of matter towards organization at the call of spirits which require it. It is presumably a foolish fancy (not justified by the words of Scripture) that each spirit should recover those particular units of matter which he ruled before. For one thing, they would not be enough to go round: we all live in secondhand suits and there are doubtless atoms in my chin which have served many another man, many a dog, many an eel, many a dinosaur. Nor does the unity of our bodies, even in this present life, consist in retaining the same particles. My form remains one, though the matter in it changes continually. I am, in that respect, like a curve in a waterfall.

The Resurrection of the Senses   *May 5*

The old picture of the soul re-assuming the corpse – perhaps blown to bits or long since usefully dissipated through Nature – is absurd. Nor is it what St Paul's words imply. And I admit that if you ask me what I substitute for this, I have only speculations to offer.

The principle behind these speculations is this. We are not, in this doctrine, concerned with matter as such at all; with waves and atoms and all that. What the soul cries out for is the resurrection of the senses. Even in this life matter would be nothing to us if it were not the source of sensations. . . .

But don't run away with the idea that when I speak of the resurrection of the body I mean merely that the blessed dead will have excellent memories of their sensuous experience on earth. I mean it the other way round: that memory as we now know it is a dim foretaste, a mirage even, of a power which the soul, or rather Christ in the soul (He went to 'prepare a place for us'), will exercise hereafter. It need no longer be intermittent. Above all, it need no longer be private to the soul in which it occurs. . . .

At present we tend to think of the soul as somehow 'inside' the body. But the glorified body of the resurrection as I conceive it – the sensuous life raised from its death – will be inside the soul. As God is not in space but space is in God. . . .

I don't say the resurrection of this body will happen at once. It may well be that this part of us sleeps in death, and the intellectual soul is sent to Lenten lands where she fasts in naked spirituality – a ghostlike and imperfectly human condition. I don't imply that an angel is a ghost. But naked spirituality is in accordance with his nature; not, I think, with ours. (A two-legged horse is maimed, but not a two-legged man.) Yet from that fact my hope is that we shall return and re-assume the wealth we have laid down.

Then the new earth and sky, the same yet not the same as these, will rise in us as we have risen in Christ. And once again, after who knows what aeons of the silence and the dark, the birds will sing and the waters flow, and lights and shadows move across the hills, and the faces of our friends laugh upon us with amazed recognition.

Guesses, of course, only guesses. If they are not true, something better will be. For 'we know that we shall be made like Him, for we shall see Him as He is'.

The Lenten Lands: Purgatory

Our souls *demand* Purgatory, don't they? Would it not break the heart if God said to us, 'It is true, my son, that your breath smells and your rags drip with mud and slime, but we are charitable here and no one will upbraid you with these things, nor draw away from you. Enter into the joy'? Should we not reply, 'With submission, Sir, and if there is no objection, I'd *rather* be cleaned first.' 'It may hurt, you know.' – 'Even so, Sir.'

I assume that the process of purification will normally involve suffering. Partly from tradition; partly because most real good that has been done me in this life has involved it. But I don't think suffering is the purpose of the purgation. I can well believe that people neither much worse nor much better than I will suffer less than I or more. 'No nonsense about merit.' The treatment given will be the one required, whether it hurts little or much.

My favourite image on this matter comes from the dentist's chair. I hope that when the tooth of life is drawn and I am 'coming round', a voice will say, 'Rinse your mouth out with this.' *This* will be Purgatory.

The Second Coming

There are many reasons why the modern Christian and even the modern theologian may hesitate to give to the doctrine of Christ's Second Coming that emphasis which was usually laid on it by our ancestors. Yet it seems to me impossible to retain in any recognizable form our belief in the Divinity of Christ and the truth of the Christian revelation while abandoning, or even persistently neglecting, the promised, and threatened, Return. 'He shall come again to judge the quick and the dead', says the Apostles' Creed. 'This same Jesus', said the angels in Acts, 'shall so come in like manner as ye have seen Him go into heaven.' 'Hereafter', said Our Lord Himself (by those words inviting crucifixion), 'shall ye see the Son of Man . . . coming in the clouds of Heaven.' If this is not an integral part of the faith once given to the saints, I do not know what it is. . . .

Many are shy of this doctrine because they are reacting against a school of thought which is associated with the great name of Dr Albert Schweitzer. According to that school, Christ's teaching about His own return and the end of the world – what theologians call His 'apocalyptic' – was the very essence of His message. . . . Hence, from fear of that extreme, arises a tendency to soft-pedal what Schweitzer's school has over-emphasized.

For my own part I hate and distrust reactions not only in religion but in everything. Luther surely spoke very good sense when he compared humanity to a drunkard who, after falling off his horse on the right, falls off it next time on the left. I am convinced that those who find in Christ's apocalyptic the whole of His message are mistaken. But a thing does not vanish – it is not even discredited – because someone has spoken of it with exaggeration. It remains exactly where it was. The only difference is that if it has recently been exaggerated, we must now take special care not to overlook it; for that is the side on which the drunk man is now most likely to fall off.

The Modern Conception of Progress   *May 8*

No one looking at world history without some precon-ception in favour of progress could find in it a steady up gradient. There is often progress within a given field over a limited period. A school of pottery or painting, a moral effort in a particular direction, a practical art like sanita-tion or shipbuilding, may continuously improve over a number of years. If this process could spread to all departments of life and continue indefinitely, there would be 'Progress' of the sort our fathers believed in. But it never seems to do so. Either it is interrupted (by barbarian irruption or the even less resistible infiltration of modern industrialism) or else, more mysteriously, it decays. The idea which here shuts out the Second Coming from our minds, the idea of the world slowly ripening to perfection, is a myth, not a generalization from experience. And it is a myth which distracts us from our real duties and our real interest. It is our attempt to guess the plot of a drama in which we are the characters. But how can the characters in a play guess the plot? We are not the playwright, we are not the producer, we are not even the audience. We are on the stage. To play well the scenes in which we are 'on' concerns us much more than to guess about the scenes that follow it.

When the World Drama Ends   *May 9*

In *King Lear* (III: vii) there is a man who is such a minor character that Shakespeare has not given him even a name: he is merely 'First Servant'. All the characters around him – Regan, Cornwall, and Edmund – have fine, longterm plans. They think they know how the story is going to end, and they are quite wrong. The servant has no such delusions. He has no notion how the play is going to go. But he understands the present scene. He sees an abomination (the blinding of old Gloucester) taking place. He will not stand it. His sword is out and pointed at his master's breast in a moment: then Regan stabs him dead from behind. That is his whole part: eight lines all told. But if it were real life and not a play, that is the part it would be best to have acted.

The doctrine of the Second Coming teaches us that we do not and cannot know when the world drama will end. The curtain may be rung down at any moment: say, before you have finished reading this paragraph. This seems to some people intolerably frustrating. So many things would be interrupted. Perhaps you were going to get married next month, perhaps you were going to get a rise next week: you may be on the verge of a great scientific discovery; you may be maturing great social and political reforms. Surely no good and wise God would be so very unreasonable as to cut all this short? Not *now*, of all moments!

The Play that God Wrote   *May 10*

We think thus because we keep on assuming that we know the play. We do not know the play. We do not even know whether we are in Act I or Act V. We do not know who are the major and who the minor characters. The Author knows. The audience, if there is an audience (if angels and archangels and all the company of heaven fill the pit and the stalls), may have an inkling. But we, never seeing the play from outside, never meeting any characters except the tiny minority who are 'on' in the same scenes as ourselves, wholly ignorant of the future and very imperfectly informed about the past, cannot tell at what moment the end ought to come. That it will come when it ought, we may be sure; but we waste our time in guessing when that will be. That it has a meaning we may be sure, but we cannot see it. When it is over, we may be told. We are led to expect that the Author will have something to say to each of us on the part that each of us has played. The playing it well is what matters infinitely.

The doctrine of the Second Coming, then, is not to be rejected because it conflicts with our favourite modern mythology. It is, for that very reason, to be the more valued and made more frequently the subject of meditation. It is the medicine our condition especially needs.

Many people find it difficult to believe in this great event without trying to guess its date, or even without accepting as a certainty the date that any quack or hysteric offers them. To write a history of all these exploded predictions would need a book, and a sad, sordid, tragicomical book it would be. One such prediction was circulating when St Paul wrote his second letter to the Thessalonians. Someone had told them that 'the Day' was 'at hand'. This was apparently having the result which such predictions usually have: people were idling and playing the busybody. One of the most famous predictions was that of poor William Miller in 1843. Miller (whom I take to have been an honest fanatic) dated the Second Coming to the year, the day, and the very minute. A timely comet fostered the delusion. Thousands waited for the Lord at midnight on March 21, and went home to a late breakfast on the 22nd followed by the jeers of a drunkard.

Clearly, no one wishes to say anything that will reawaken such mass hysteria. We must never speak to simple, excitable people about 'the Day' without emphasizing again and again the utter impossibility of prediction. We must try to show them that that impossibility is an essential part of the doctrine. If you do not believe Our Lord's words, why do you believe in His return at all? And if you do believe them must you not put away from you, utterly and forever, any hope of dating that return? His teaching on the subject quite clearly consisted of three propositions: (1) That He will certainly return; (2) That we cannot possibly find out when; (3) And that therefore we must always be ready for Him.

Precisely because we cannot predict the moment, we must be ready at all moments. Our Lord repeated this practical conclusion again and again; as if the promise of the Return had been made for the sake of this conclusion alone. Watch, watch, is the burden of His advice. I shall come like a thief. You will not, I most solemnly assure you, you will not see me approaching. If the householder had known at what time the burglar would arrive, he would have been ready for him. If the servant had known when his absent employer would come home, he would not have been found drunk in the kitchen. But they didn't. Nor will you. Therefore you must be ready at all times. The point is surely simple enough. The schoolboy does not know which part of his Virgil lesson he will be made to translate: that is why he must be prepared to translate *any* passage. The sentry does not know at what time an enemy will attack, or an officer inspect, his post: that is why he must keep awake *all* the time. The Return is wholly unpredictable. There will be wars and rumours of wars and all kinds of catastrophes, as there always are. Things will be, in that sense, normal, the hour before the heavens roll up like a scroll. You cannot guess it. If you could, one chief purpose for which it was foretold would be frustrated. And God's purposes are not so easily frustrated as that. One's ears should be closed against any future William Miller in advance. The folly of listening to him at all is almost equal to the folly of believing him. He *couldn't* know what he pretends, or thinks, he knows.

The doctrine of the Second Coming has failed, so far as we are concerned, if it does not make us realize that at every moment of every year in our lives Donne's question 'What if this present were the world's last night?' is equally relevant.

Sometimes this question has been pressed upon our minds with the purpose of exciting fear. I do not think that is its right use. I am, indeed, far from agreeing with those who think all religious fear barbarous and degrading, and demand that it should be banished from the spiritual life. Perfect love, we know, casteth out fear. But so do several other things – ignorance, alcohol, passion, presumption, and stupidity. It is very desirable that we should all advance to that perfection of love in which we shall fear no longer; but it is very undesirable, until we have reached that stage, that we should allow any inferior agent to cast out fear. The objection to any attempt at perpetual trepidation about the Second Coming is, in my view, quite a different one: namely, that it will certainly not succeed. Fear is an emotion: and it is quite impossible – even physically impossible – to maintain any emotion for very long. A perpetual excitement of hope about the Second Coming is impossible for the same reason. Crisis-feeling of any sort is essentially transitory. Feelings come and go, and when they come a good use can be made of them: they cannot be our regular spiritual diet.

In the earliest days of Christianity an 'apostle' was first and foremost a man who claimed to be an eye-witness of the Resurrection. Only a few days after the Crucifixion when two candidates were nominated for the vacancy created by the treachery of Judas, their qualification was that they had known Jesus personally both before and after His death, and could offer first-hand evidence of the Resurrection in addressing the outer world (Acts 1:22). A few days later St Peter, preaching the first Christian sermon, makes the same claim – 'God raised Jesus, of which we all [we Christians] are witnesses' (Acts 2:32). In the first *Letter to the Corinthians* St Paul bases his claim to apostleship on the same ground – 'Am I not an apostle? Have I not seen the Lord Jesus?'

As this qualification suggests, to preach Christianity meant primarily to preach the Resurrection. . . . The Resurrection, and its consequences, were the 'Gospel' or good news which the Christians brought: what we call the 'gospels', the narratives of Our Lord's life and death, were composed later for the benefit of those who had already accepted the *Gospel*. They were in no sense the basis of Christianity: they were written for those already converted. . . . Nothing could be more unhistorical than to pick out selected sayings of Christ from the gospels and to regard those as the datum and the rest of the New Testament as a construction upon it. The first fact in the history of Christendom is a number of people who say they have seen the Resurrection. If they had died without making anyone else believe this 'Gospel' no gospels would ever have been written.

What if this Present were the World's Last night? *May 15*

What is important is not that we should always fear (or hope) about the End but that we should always remember, always take it into account. An analogy may help here. A man of seventy need not be always feeling (much less talking) about his approaching death: but a wise man of seventy should always take it into account. He would be foolish to embark on schemes which presuppose twenty more years of life: he would be criminally foolish not to make – indeed, not to have made long since – his will. Now, what death is to each man, the Second Coming is to the whole human race. We all believe, I suppose, that a man should 'sit loose' to his own individual life, should remember how short, precarious, temporary, and provisional a thing it is; should never give all his heart to anything which will end when his life ends. What modern Christians find it harder to remember is that the whole life of humanity in this world is also precarious, temporary, provisional.

The Death of Lazarus   *May 16*

The world, knowing how all our real investments are beyond the grave, might expect us to be less concerned than other people who go in for what is called Higher Thought and tell us that 'death doesn't matter'; but we 'are not high-minded', and we follow One who stood and wept at the grave of Lazarus – not, surely, because He was grieved that Mary and Martha wept, and sorrowed for their lack of faith (though some thus interpret) but because death, the punishment of sin, is even more horrible in His eyes than in ours. The nature which He had created as God, the nature which He had assumed as Man, lay there before Him in its ignominy; a foul smell, food for worms. Though He was to revive it a moment later, He wept at the shame. . . . Of all men, we hope most of death; yet nothing will reconcile us to – well, its *unnaturalness*. We know that we were not made for it; we know how it crept into our destiny as an intruder; and we know Who has defeated it. Because Our Lord is risen we know that on one level it is an enemy already disarmed; but because we know that the natural level also is God's creation we cannot cease to fight against the death

129

which mars it, as against all other blemishes upon it, against pain and poverty, barbarism and ignorance. Because we love something else more than this world we love even this world better than those who know no other.

Death   *May 17*

As suicide is the typical expression of the stoic spirit, and battle of the warrior spirit, martyrdom always remains the supreme enacting and perfection of Christianity. This great action has been initiated for us, done on our behalf, exemplified for our imitation, and inconceivably communicated to all believers, by Christ on Calvary. There the degree of accepted Death reaches the utmost bounds of the imaginable and perhaps goes beyond them; not only all natural supports, but the presence of the very Father to whom the sacrifice is made deserts the victim, and surrender to God does not falter though God 'forsakes' it. . . .

Christianity teaches us that the terrible task has already in some sense been accomplished for us – that a master's hand is holding ours as we attempt to trace the difficult letters and that our script need only be a 'copy', not an original. Again, where other systems expose our total nature to death (as in Buddhist renunciation) Christianity demands only that we set right a *misdirection* of our nature, and has no quarrel, like Plato, with the body as such, nor with the psychical elements in our make-up. And sacrifice in its supreme realization is not exacted of all. Confessors as well as martyrs are saved, and some old people whose state of grace we can hardly doubt seem to have got through their seventy years surprisingly easily. The sacrifice of Christ is repeated, or re-echoed, among His followers in very varying degrees, from the cruellest martyrdom down to a self-submission of intention whose outward signs have nothing to distinguish them from the ordinary fruits of temperance and 'sweet reasonableness'. The causes of this distribution I do not know; but from our present point of view it ought to be clear that the real problem is not why some humble, pious, believing people suffer, but why some do *not*. Our Lord Himself, it will be remembered, explained the salvation of those who are fortunate in this world only by referring to the unsearchable omnipotence of God.

God's Verdict   *May 18*

Some moderns talk as though duties to posterity were the only duties we had. I can imagine no man who will look with more horror on the End than a conscientious revolutionary who has, in a sense sincerely, been justifying cruelties and injustices inflicted on millions of his contemporaries by the benefits which he hopes to confer on future generations: generations who, as one terrible moment now reveals to him, were never going to exist. Then he will see the massacres, the faked trials, the deportations, to be all ineffaceably real, an essential part, his part, in the drama that has just ended: while the future Utopia had never been anything but a fantasy.

Frantic administration of panaceas to the world is certainly discouraged by the reflection that 'this present' might be 'the world's last night'; sober work for the future, within the limits of ordinary morality and prudence, is not. For what comes is Judgement: happy are those whom it finds labouring in their vocations, whether they were merely going out to feed the pigs or laying good plans to deliver humanity a hundred years hence from some great evil. The curtain has indeed now fallen. Those pigs will never in fact be fed, the great campaign against White Slavery or Governmental Tyranny will never in fact proceed to victory. No matter: you were at your post when the Inspection came.

Our ancestors had a habit of using the word 'Judgement' in this context as if it meant simply 'punishment': hence the popular expression, 'It's a judgement on him'. I believe we can sometimes render the thing more vivid to ourselves by taking judgement in a stricter sense: not as the sentence or award, but as the Verdict. Some day (and 'What if this present were the world's last night?') an absolutely correct verdict — if you like, a perfect critique — will be passed on what each of us is.

The Final Judgement   *May 19*

It will be infallible judgement. If it is favourable we shall have no fear, if unfavourable, no hope, that it is wrong. We shall not only believe, we shall know, know beyond doubt in every fibre of our appalled or delighted being, that as the Judge has said, so we are: neither more nor less nor other. We shall perhaps even realize that in some dim fashion we could have known it all along. We shall know and all creation will know too: our ancestors, our parents, our wives or husbands, our children. The unanswerable and (by then) self-evident truth about each will be known to all.

I do not find that pictures of physical catastrophe — that sign in the clouds, those heavens rolled up like a scroll — help one so much as the naked idea of Judgement. We cannot always be excited. We can, perhaps, train ourselves to ask more and more often how the thing which we are saying or doing (or failing to do) at each moment will look when the irresistible light streams in upon it; that light which is so different from the light of this world — and yet, even now, we know just enough of it to take it into account. Women sometimes have the problem of trying to judge by artificial light how a dress will look by daylight. That is very like the problem of all of us: to dress our souls not for the electric lights of the present world but for the daylight of the next. The good dress is the one that will face that light. For that light will last longer.

The Divorce of Heaven and Hell   *May 20*

Blake wrote the Marriage of Heaven and Hell. If I have written of their Divorce, this is not because I think myself a fit antagonist for so great a genius, nor even because I feel at all sure that I know what he meant. But in some sense or other the attempt to make that marriage is perennial. The attempt is based on the belief that reality never presents us with an absolutely unavoidable 'either-or'; that, granted skill and patience and (above all) time enough, some way of embracing both alternatives can always be found; that mere development or adjustment or refinement will somehow turn evil into good without our being called on for a final and total rejection of anything we should like to retain. This belief I take to be a disastrous error. You cannot take all luggage with you on all journeys; on one journey even your right hand and your right eye may be among the things you have to leave behind. We are not living in a world where all roads are radii of a circle and where all, if followed long enough, will therefore draw gradually nearer and finally meet at the centre: rather in a world where every road, after a few miles, forks into two, and each of those two again, and at each fork you must make a decision. Even on the biological level life is not like a river but like a tree. It does not move towards unity but away from it and the creatures grow further apart as they increase in perfection. Good, as it ripens, becomes continually more different not only from evil but from other good.

Evil Cannot 'Develop' into Good *May 21*

I do not think that all who choose wrong roads perish; but their rescue consists in being put back on the right road. A wrong sum can be put right: but only by going back till you find the error and working it afresh from that point, never by simply *going on*. Evil can be undone, but it cannot 'develop' into good. Time does not heal it. The spell must be unwound, bit by bit, 'with backward mutters of dissevering power' – or else not. It is still 'either-or'. If we insist on keeping Hell (or even earth) we shall not see Heaven: if we accept Heaven we shall not be able to retain even the smallest and most intimate souvenirs of Hell. I believe, to be sure, that any man who reaches Heaven will find that what he abandoned (even in plucking out his right eye) has not been lost: that the kernel of what he was really seeking even in his most depraved wishes will be there, beyond expectation, waiting for him in 'the High Countries'. In that sense it will be true for those who have completed the journey (and for no others) to say that good is everything and Heaven everywhere. But we, at this end of the road, must not try to anticipate that retrospective vision. If we do, we are likely to embrace the false and disastrous converse and fancy that everything is good and everywhere is Heaven.

But what, you ask, of earth? Earth, I think, will not be found by anyone to be in the end a very distinct place. I think earth, if chosen instead of Heaven, will turn out to have been, all along, only a region in Hell: and earth, if put second to Heaven, to have been from the beginning a part of Heaven itself.

A Bishop from Hell Meets a Friend from Heaven

I saw another of the Bright People in conversation with a ghost. It was that fat ghost with the cultured voice . . . and it seemed to be wearing gaiters.

'My dear boy, I'm delighted to see you', it was saying to the Spirit, who was naked and almost blindingly white. 'I was talking to your poor father the other day and wondering where you were.'

'You didn't bring him?' said the other.

'Well, no. He lives a long way from the bus, and, to be quite frank, he's been getting a little eccentric lately. . . . Ah, Dick, I shall never forget some of our talks. I expect you've changed your views a bit since then. You became rather narrow-minded towards the end of your life: but no doubt you've broadened out again.'

'How do you mean?'

'Well, it's obvious by now, isn't it, that you weren't quite right. Why, my dear boy, you were coming to believe in a literal Heaven and Hell!'

'But wasn't I right?'

'Oh, in a spiritual sense, to be sure. I still believe in them in that way. I am still, my dear boy, looking for the Kingdom. But nothing superstitious or mythological . . .'

'Excuse me. Where do you imagine you've been?'

'Ah, I see. You mean that the grey town with its continual hope of morning (we must all live by hope, must we not?), with its field for indefinite progress, is, in a sense, Heaven, if only we have eyes to see it? That is a beautiful idea.'

'I didn't mean that at all. Is it possible you don't know where you've been?'

'Now that you mention it, I don't think we ever do give it a name. What do you call it?'

'We call it Hell.'

'There is no need to be profane, my dear boy. I may not be very orthodox, in your sense of that word, but I do feel that these matters ought to be discussed simply, and seriously, and reverently.'

'Discuss Hell *reverently*? . . . You have been in Hell: though if you don't go back you may call it Purgatory.'

The Bishop Questions His Friend   *May 23*

'Go on, my dear boy. . . . No doubt you'll tell me why I was sent there.'

'But don't you know? You went there because you are an apostate.' . . .

'Dick, this is unworthy of you. What are you suggesting?'

'Friend, I am not suggesting at all. You see, I *know* now. Let us be frank. Our opinions were not honestly come by. We simply found ourselves in contact with a certain current of ideas and plunged into it because it seemed modern and successful. . . . When, in our whole lives, did we honestly face, in solitude, the one question on which all turned: whether after all the Supernatural might not in fact occur? When did we put up one moment's real resistance to the loss of our faith?'

'If this is meant to be a sketch of the genesis of liberal theology in general, I reply that it is a mere libel. Do you suggest that men like . . .'

'I have nothing to do with any generality. Nor with any man but you and me. . . . You know that you and I were playing with loaded dice. We didn't *want* the other to be true. We were afraid of crude salvationism, afraid of a breach with the spirit of the age, afraid of ridicule, afraid (above all) of real spiritual fears and hopes.'

'I'm far from denying that young men may make mistakes. They may well be influenced by current fashions of thought. But it's not a question of how the opinions are formed. The point is that they were my honest opinions, sincerely expressed.'

'Of course. Having allowed oneself to drift, unresisting, unpraying, accepting every half-conscious solicitation from our desires, we reached a point where we no longer believed the Faith. Just in the same way, a jealous man, drifting and unresisting, reaches a point at which he believes lies about his best friend: a drunkard reaches a point at which (for a moment) he actually believes that another glass will do him no harm. The beliefs are sincere in the sense that they do occur as psychological events in the man's mind. If that's what you mean by sincerity they are sincere, and so were ours. But errors which are sincere in that sense are not innocent.'

The Bishop is Urged to Come to Heaven   *May 24*

'Well, that is a plan. I am perfectly ready to consider it. Of course I should require some assurances. . . . I should want a guarantee that you are taking me to a place where I shall find a wider sphere of usefulness – and scope for the talents that God has given me – and an atmosphere of free inquiry – in short, all that one means by civilization and – er – the spiritual life.'

'No', said the other. 'I can promise you none of these things. No sphere of usefulness: you are not needed there at all. No scope for your talents: only forgiveness for having perverted them. No atmosphere of inquiry, for I will bring you to the land not of questions but of answers, and you shall see the face of God.'

'Ah, but we must all interpret those beautiful words in our own way! For me there is no such thing as a final answer. The free wind of inquiry must *always* continue to blow through the mind, must it not? "Prove all things" . . . to travel hopefully is better than to arrive.'

'If that were true, and known to be true, how could anyone travel hopefully? There would be nothing to hope for.'. . .

'The suggestion that I should return at my age to the mere factual inquisitiveness of boyhood strikes me as

137

preposterous. In any case, that question-and-answer conception of thought only applies to matters of fact. Religious and speculative questions are surely on a different level.'. . .

'Do you not even believe that He exists?'

'Exists? What does Existence mean? You *will* keep on implying some sort of static, ready-made reality which is, so to speak, "there", and to which our minds have simply to conform. These great mysteries cannot be approached in that way. If there were such a thing (there is no need to interrupt, my dear boy), quite frankly, I should not be interested in it. It would be of no *religious* significance. God, for me, is something purely spiritual. The spirit of sweetness and light and tolerance – and, er, Dick, service. We mustn't forget that, you know.'

The Bishop Makes up His Mind   May 25

'Happiness, my dear Dick,' said the Ghost placidly, 'happiness, as you will come to see when you are older, lies in the path of duty. Which reminds me. . . . Bless my soul, I'd nearly forgotten. Of course I can't come with you. I have to be back next Friday to read a paper. We have a little Theological Society down there. Oh, yes! there is plenty of intellectual life. Not of a very high quality, perhaps. One notices a certain lack of grip – a certain confusion of mind. That is where I can be of some use to them. There are even regrettable jealousies. . . . I don't know why, but tempers seem less controlled than they used to be. Still, one mustn't expect too much of human nature. I feel I can do a great work among them. But you've never asked me what my paper is about! I'm taking the text about growing up to the measure of the stature of Christ and working out an idea which I feel sure you'll be interested in. I'm going to point out how people always forget that Jesus [here the Ghost bowed] was a comparatively young man when he died. He would have outgrown some of his earlier views, you know, if he'd lived. As he might have done, with a little more tact and patience. I am going to ask my audience to consider what his mature views would have been. A profoundly interesting question. What a different Christianity we might have had if only the Founder had reached his full stature! I shall end up by pointing out how this deepens the significance of the Crucifixion. One feels for the first time what a disaster it was: what a tragic waste . . . so much promise cut short. Oh, must you be going? Well, so must I. Goodbye, my dear boy. It has been a great pleasure. Most stimulating and provocative. . . .'

The Ghost nodded its head and beamed on the Spirit with a bright clerical smile – or with the best approach to it which such unsubstantial lips could manage – and then turned away humming softly to itself 'City of God, how broad and far'.

Lewis's Guide on Good and Evil   *May 26*

'Son,' he said, 'ye cannot in your present state understand eternity. . . . But ye can get some likeness of it if ye say that both good and evil, when they are full grown, become retrospective. . . . That is what mortals misunderstand. They say of some temporal suffering, "No future bliss can make up for it", not knowing that Heaven, once attained, will work backwards and turn even that agony into a glory. And of some sinful pleasure they say, "Let me but have *this* and I'll take the consequences": little dreaming how damnation will spread back and back into their past and contaminate the pleasure of the sin. Both processes begin even before death. The good man's past begins to change so that his forgiven sins and remembered sorrows take on the quality of Heaven: the bad man's past already conforms to his badness and is filled only with dreariness. And that is why, at the end of all thing . . . the Blessed will say, "We have never lived anywhere except in Heaven", and the Lost, "We were always in Hell". And both will speak truly.'

Grumbling

'The whole difficulty of understanding Hell is that the thing to be understood is so nearly Nothing. But ye'll have had experiences. . . . It begins with a grumbling mood, and yourself still distinct from it: perhaps criticizing it. And yourself, in a dark hour, may will that mood, embrace it. Ye can repent and come out of it again. But there may come a day when you can do that no longer. Then there will be no *you* left to criticize the mood, nor even to enjoy it, but just the grumble itself going on forever like a machine.'

The Tyranny of 'Sensitivity'

Did we pretend to be 'hurt' in our sensitive and tender feelings (fine natures like ours are so vulnerable) when envy, ungratified vanity, or thwarted self-will was our real problem? Such tactics often succeed. The other parties give in. They give in not because they don't know what is really wrong with us, but because they have long known it only too well, and that sleeping dog can be roused, that skeleton brought out of its cupboard, only at the cost of imperilling their whole relationship with us. It needs surgery which they know we will never face. And so we win; by cheating. But the unfairness is very deeply felt. Indeed what is commonly called 'sensitiveness' is the most powerful engine of domestic tyranny, sometimes a lifelong tyranny. How we should deal with it in others I am not sure; but we should be merciless to its first appearances in ourselves.

Can You be Happy when Some Reject God?   *May 29*

'What some people say on earth is that the final loss of one soul gives the lie to all the joy of those who are saved.'

'Ye see it does not.'

'I feel in a way that it ought to.'

'That sounds very merciful: but see what lurks behind it.'

'What?'

'The demand of the loveless and the self-imprisoned that they should be allowed to blackmail the universe: that till they consent to be happy (on their own terms) no one else shall taste joy: that theirs should be the final power; that Hell should be able to *veto* Heaven.'

'I don't know what I want, Sir.'

'Son, son, it must be one way or the other. Either the day must come when joy prevails and all the makers of misery are no longer able to infect it: or else for ever and ever the makers of misery can destroy in others the happiness they reject for themselves. I know it has a grand sound to say ye'll accept no salvation which leaves even one creature in the dark outside. But watch that sophistry or ye'll make a Dog in a Manger the tyrant of the universe.'

'But dare one say – it is horrible to say – that Pity must ever die?'

'Ye must distinguish. The action of Pity will live for ever: but the passion of Pity will not. The passion of pity, the pity we merely suffer, the ache that draws men to concede what should not be condeded and to flatter when they should speak truth, the pity that has cheated many a woman out of her virginity and many a statesman out of his honesty – that will die. It was used as a weapon by bad men against good ones: their weapon will be broken.'

'And what is the other kind – the action?'

'It's a weapon on the other side. It leaps quicker than light from the highest place to the lowest to bring healing and joy, whatever the cost to itself. It changes darkness into light and evil into good. But it will not, at the cunning tears of Hell, impose on good the tyranny of evil. Every disease that submits to a cure shall be cured: but we will not call blue yellow to please those who insist on still having jaundice, nor make a midden of the world's garden for the sake of some who cannot abide the smell of roses.'

Two Kinds of People in the End   *May 31*

There are only two kinds of people in the end: those who say to God, 'Thy will be done', and those to whom God says, in the end, '*Thy* will be done.' All that are in Hell, choose it. Without that self-choice there could be no Hell. No soul that seriously and constantly desires joy will ever miss it. Those who seek find. To those who knock it is opened.

The Choice   *June 1*

As he lay there, still unable and perhaps unwilling to rise,
it came into his mind that in certain old philosophers and
poets he had read that the mere sight of the devils was
one of the greatest among the torments of Hell. It had
seemed to him till now merely a quaint fancy. And yet
(as he now saw) even the children know better: no child
would have any difficulty in understanding that there
might be a face the mere beholding of which was final
calamity. The children, the poets, and the philosophers
were right. As there is one Face above all worlds merely
to see which is irrevocable joy, so at the bottom of all
worlds that face is waiting whose sight alone is the misery from which none who beholds it can recover. And
though there seemed to be, and indeed were, a thousand
roads by which a man could walk through the world,
there was not a single one which did not lead sooner or
later either to the Beatific or the Miserific Vision.

The Weight of Glory   *June 2*

In the end that Face which is the delight or the terror of
the universe must be turned upon each of us either with
one expression or with the other, either conferring glory
inexpressible or inflicting shame that can never be cured
or disguised. I read in a periodical the other day that the
fundamental thing is how we think of God. By God
Himself, it is not! How God thinks of us is not only more
important, but infinitely more important. Indeed, how
we think of Him is of no importance except in so far as it
is related to how He thinks of us. It is written that we
shall 'stand before' Him, shall appear, shall be inspected.
The promise of glory is the promise, almost incredible
and only possible by the work of Christ, that some of us,
that any of us who really chooses, shall actually survive

that examination, shall find approval, shall please God. To please God . . . to be a real ingredient in the divine happiness . . . to be loved by God, not merely pitied, but delighted in as an artist delights in his work or a father in a son – it seems impossible, a weight or burden of glory which our thoughts can hardly sustain. But so it is.

Heaven

We were made for God. Only by being in some respect like Him, only by being a manifestation of His beauty, lovingkindness, wisdom or goodness, has any earthly Beloved excited our love. It is not that we have loved them too much, but that we did not quite understand what we were loving. It is not that we shall be asked to turn from them, so dearly familiar, to a Stranger. When we see the face of God we shall know that we have always known it. He has been a party to, has made, sustained and moved moment by moment within, all our earthly experiences of innocent love. All that was true love in them was, even on earth, far more His than ours, and ours only because His. In Heaven there will be no anguish and no duty of turning away from our earthly Beloveds. First, because we shall have turned already; from the portraits to the Original, from the rivulets to the Fountain, from the creatures He made lovable to Love Himself. But secondly, because we shall find them all in Him. By loving Him more than them we shall love them more than we now do.

There is no doctrine which I would more willingly remove from Christianity than this, if it lay in my power. But it has the full support of Scripture and, specially, of Our Lord's own words; it has always been held by Christendom; and it has the support of reason. If a game is played, it must be possible to lose it. If the happiness of a creature lies in self-surrender, no one can make that surrender but himself (though many can help him to make it) and he may refuse. I would pay any price to be able to say truthfully 'All will be saved'. But my reason retorts, 'Without their will, or with it?' If I say 'Without their will', I at once perceive a contradiction; how can the supreme voluntary act of self-surrender be involuntary? If I say 'With their will', my reason replies 'How if they *will not* give in?'

The Dominical utterances about Hell, like all Dominical sayings, are addressed to the conscience and the will, not to our intellectual curiosity. When they have roused us into action by convincing us of a terrible possibility, they have done, probably, all they were intended to do; and if all the world were convinced Christians it would be unnecessary to say a word more on the subject. As things are, however, this doctrine is one of the chief grounds on which Christianity is attacked as barbarous, and the goodness of God impugned. We are told that it is a detestable doctrine – and indeed, I too detest it from the bottom of my heart – and are reminded of the tragedies in human life which have come from believing it. Of the other tragedies which come from not believing it we are told less.

Let us try to be honest with ourselves. Picture to yourself a man who has risen to wealth or power by a continued course of treachery and cruelty, by exploiting for purely selfish ends the noble motions of his victims, laughing the while at their simplicity; who, having thus attained success, uses it for the gratification of lust and hatred and finally parts with the last rag of honour among thieves by betraying his own accomplices and jeering at their last moments of bewildered disillusionment. Suppose, further, that he does all this, not (as we like to imagine) tormented by remorse or even misgiving, but eating like a schoolboy and sleeping like a healthy infant – a jolly, ruddy-cheeked man, without a care in the world, unshakably confident to the very end that he alone has found the answer to the riddle of life, that God and man are fools whom he has got the better of, that his way of life is utterly successful, satisfactory, unassailable. We must be careful at this point. The least indulgence of the passion for revenge is very deadly sin. Christian charity counsels us to make every effort for the conversion of such a man: to prefer his conversion, at the peril of our own lives, perhaps of our own souls, to his punishment; to prefer it infinitely. But that is not the question. Supposing he *will* not be converted, what destiny in the eternal world can you regard as proper for him? Can you really desire that such a man, *remaining what he is* (and he must be able to do that if he has free will), should be confirmed forever in his present happiness – should continue, for all eternity, to be perfectly convinced that the laugh is on his side?

The demand that God should forgive such a man while he remains what he is, is based on a confusion between condoning and forgiving. To condone an evil is simply to ignore it, to treat it as if it were good. But forgiveness needs to be accepted as well as offered if it is to be complete: and a man who admits no guilt can accept no forgiveness. . . .

I willingly believe that the damned are, in one sense, successful, rebels to the end; that the doors of Hell are locked on the *inside*. I do not mean that the ghosts may not *wish* to come out of Hell, in the vague fashion wherein an envious man 'wishes' to be happy: but they certainly do not will even the first preliminary stages of that self-abandonment through which alone the soul can reach any good. They enjoy forever the horrible freedom they have demanded, and are therefore self-enslaved: just as the blessed, forever submitting to obedience, become through all eternity more and more free.

In the long run the answer to all those who object to the doctrine of Hell, is itself a question: 'What are you asking God to do?' To wipe out their past sins and, at all costs, to give them a fresh start, smoothing every difficulty and offering every miraculous help? But He has done so, on Calvary. To forgive them? They will not be forgiven. To leave them alone? Alas, I am afraid that is what He does.

There are no *Ordinary* People   *June 7*

It is a serious thing to live in a society of possible gods and goddesses, to remember that the dullest and most uninteresting person you can talk to may one day be a creature which, if you saw it now, you would be strongly tempted to worship, or else a horror and a corruption such as you now meet, if at all, only in a nightmare. All day long we are, in some degree, helping each other to one or other of these destinations. It is in the light of these overwhelming possibilities, it is with the awe and the circumspection proper to them, that we should conduct all our dealings with one another, all friendships, all loves, all play, all politics. There are no *ordinary* people. You have never talked to a mere mortal. Nations, cultures, arts, civilizations – these are mortal, and their life is to ours as the life of a gnat. But it is immortals whom we joke with, work with, marry, snub, and exploit – immortal horrors or everlasting splendours. This does not mean that we are to be perpetually solemn. We must play. But our merriment must be of that kind (and it is, in fact, the merriest kind) which exists between people who have, from the outset, taken each other seriously – no flippancy, no superiority, no presumption. And our charity must be a real and costly love, with deep feeling for the sins in spite of which we love the sinner – no mere tolerance, or indulgence which parodies love as flippancy parodies merriment. Next to the Blessed Sacrament itself, your neighbour is the holiest object presented to your senses. If he is your Christian neighbour, he is holy in almost the same way, for in him also Christ *vere latitat* – the glorifier and the glorified, Glory Himself – is truly hidden.

Gift-Love and Need-Love   *June 8*

'God is love', says St John. When I first tried to write this book [*The Four Loves*] I thought that his maxim would provide me with a very plain highroad through the whole subject. I thought I should be able to say that human loves deserved to be called loves at all just in so far as they resembled that Love which is God. The first distinction I made was therefore between what I called Gift-love and Need-love. The typical example of Gift-love would be that love which moves a man to work and plan and save for the future well-being of his family which he will die without sharing or seeing; of the second, that which sends a lonely or frightened child to its mother's arms.

There was no doubt which was more like Love Himself. Divine Love is Gift-love. The Father gives all He is and has to the Son. The Son gives Himself back to the Father, and gives Himself to the world, and for the world to the Father, and thus gives the world (in Himself) back to the Father too.

And what, on the other hand, can be less like anything we believe of God's life than Need-love? He lacks nothing, but our Need-love, as Plato saw, is 'the son of Poverty'. It is the accurate reflection in consciousness of our actual nature. We are born helpless. As soon as we are fully conscious we discover loneliness. We need others physically, emotionally, intellectually; we need them if we are to know anything, even ourselves.

God – the Only Real Giver   *June 9*

Every Christian would agree that a man's spiritual health is exactly proportional to his love for God. But man's love for God, from the very nature of the case, must always be very largely, and must often be entirely, a Need-love. This is obvious when we implore forgiveness for our sins or support in our tribulations. But in the long run it is perhaps even more apparent in our growing – for it ought to be growing – awareness that our whole being by its very nature is one vast need; incomplete, preparatory, empty yet cluttered, crying out for Him who can untie things that are now knotted together and tie up things that are still dangling loose. I do not say that man can never bring to God anything at all but sheer Need-love. Exalted souls may tell us of a reach beyond that. But they would also, I think, be the first to tell us that those heights would cease to be true Graces, would become Neo-Platonic or finally diabolical illusions, the moment a man dared to think that he could live on them and henceforth drop out the element of need. 'The highest', says the *Imitation*, 'does not stand without the lowest.' It would be a bold and silly creature that came before its Creator with the boast 'I'm no beggar. I love you disinterestedly.' Those who come nearest to a Gift-love for God will next moment, even at the very same moment, be beating their breasts with the publican and laying their indigence before the only real Giver. And God will have it so. He addresses our Need-love: 'Come unto me all ye that travail and are heavy-laden', or, in the Old Testament, 'Open your mouth wide and I will fill it.'

Nearness to God   *June 10*

We must distinguish two things which might both possibly be called 'nearness to God'. One is likeness to God. God has impressed some sort of likeness to Himself, I suppose, in all that He has made. Space and time, in their own fashion, mirror His greatness; all life, His fecundity; animal life, His activity. Man has a more important likeness than these by being rational. Angels, we believe, have likenesses which Man lacks: immortality and intuitive knowledge. In that way all men, whether good or bad, all angels including those that fell, are more like God than the animals are. Their natures are in this sense 'nearer' to the Divine Nature. But, secondly, there is what we may call nearness of approach. If this is what we mean, the states in which a man is 'nearest' to God are those in which he is most surely and swiftly approaching his final union with God, vision of God and enjoyment of God. And as soon as we distinguish nearness-by-likeness and nearness-of-approach, we see that they do not necessarily coincide. They may or may not.

Perhaps an analogy may help. Let us suppose that we are doing a mountain walk to the village which is our home. At midday we come to the top of a cliff where we are, in space, very near it because it is just below us. We could drop a stone into it. But as we are no cragsmen we can't get down. We must go a long way round; five miles, maybe. At many points during that detour we shall, statically, be farther from the village than we were when we sat above the cliff. But only statically. In terms of progress we shall be far 'nearer' our baths and teas.

St Barnabas, Apostle   June 11

Why do we men need so much alteration? The Christian answer – that we have used our free will to become very bad – is so well known that it hardly needs to be stated. But to bring this doctrine into real life in the minds of modern men, and even of modern Christians, is very hard. When the Apostles preached, they could assume even in their Pagan hearers a real consciousness of deserving the Divine anger. The Pagan mysteries existed to allay this consciousness, and the Epicurean philosophy claimed to deliver men from the fear of eternal punishment. It was against this background that the Gospel appeared as good news. It brought news of possible healing to men who knew that they were mortally ill. But all this has changed. Christianity now has to preach the diagnosis – in itself very bad news – before it can win a hearing for the cure.

Affection

I begin with the humblest and most widely diffused of loves, the love in which our experience seems to differ least from that of the animals. Let me add at once that I do not on that account give it a lower value. Nothing in Man is either worse or better for being shared with the beasts. When we blame a man for being 'a mere animal', we mean not that he displays animal characteristics (we all do) but that he displays these, and only these, on occasions where the specifically human was demanded. (When we call him 'brutal' we usually mean that he commits cruelties impossible to most real brutes; they're not clever enough.)

The Greeks called this love *storge* (two syllables and the g is 'hard'). I shall here call it simply Affection. My Greek Lexicon defines *storge* as 'affection, especially of parents to offspring'; but also of offspring to parents. And that, I have no doubt, is the original form of the thing as well as the central meaning of the word. The image we must start with is that of a mother nursing a baby, a bitch or a cat with a basketful of puppies or kittens; all in a squeaking, nuzzling heap together; purrings, lickings, baby-talk, milk, warmth, the smell of young life.

The importance of this image is that it presents us at the very outset with a certain paradox. The Need and Need-love of the young is obvious; so is the Gift-love of the mother. She gives birth, gives suck, gives protection. On the other hand, she must give birth or die. She must give suck or suffer. That way, her Affection too is a Need-love. There is the paradox. It is a Need-love but what it needs is to give. It is a Gift-love but it needs to be needed.

Affection . . . is the humblest love. It gives itself no airs. People can be proud of being 'in love', or of friendship. Affection is modest – even furtive and shame-faced. Once when I had remarked on the affection quite often found between cat and dog, my friend replied, 'Yes. But I bet no dog would ever confess it to the other dogs.' That is at least a good caricature of much human Affection. 'Let homely faces stay at home', says Comus. Now Affection has a very homely face. So have many of those for whom we feel it. It is no proof of our refinement or perceptiveness that we love them; nor that they love us. What I have called Appreciative love is no basic element in Affection. It usually needs absence or bereavement to set us praising those to whom only Affection binds us. We take them for granted: and this taking for granted, which is an outrage in erotic love, is here right and proper up to a point. It fits the comfortable, quiet nature of the feeling. Affection would not be affection if it was loudly and frequently expressed; to produce it in public is like getting your household furniture out for a move. It did very well in its place, but it looks shabby or tawdry or grotesque in the sunshine. Affection almost slinks or seeps through our lives. It lives with humble, un-dress, private things; soft slippers, old clothes, old jokes, the thump of a sleepy dog's tail on the kitchen floor, the sound of a sewing-machine, a gollywog left on the lawn.

Affection with the Other Loves *June 14*

I am talking of Affection as it is when it exists apart from the other loves. It often does so exist; often not. As gin is not only a drink in itself but also a base for many mixed drinks, so Affection, besides being a love itself, can enter into the other loves and colour them all through and become the very medium in which from day to day they operate. They would not perhaps wear very well without it. To make a friend is not the same as to become affectionate. But when your friend has become an old friend, all those things about him which had originally nothing to do with the friendship become familiar and dear with familiarity. As for erotic love, I can imagine nothing more disagreeable than to experience it for more than a very short time without this homespun clothing of affection. That would be a most uneasy condition, either too angelic or too animal or each by turn; never quite great enough or little enough for man. There is indeed a peculiar charm, both in friendship and in Eros, about those moments when Appreciative love lies, as it were, curled up asleep, and the mere ease and ordinariness of the relationship (free as solitude, yet neither is alone) wraps us round. No need to talk. No need to make love. No needs at all except perhaps to stir the fire.

The Especial Glory of Affection   *June 15*

Affection . . . can 'rub along' with the most unpromising people. Yet oddly enough this very fact means that it can in the end make appreciations possible which, but for it, might never have existed. We may say, and not quite untruly, that we have chosen our friends and the woman we love for their various excellences – for beauty, frankness, goodness of heart, wit, intelligence, or what not. But it had to be the particular kind of wit, the particular kind of beauty, the particular kind of goodness that we like, and we have our personal tastes in these matters. That is why friends and lovers feel that they were 'made for one another'. The especial glory of Affection is that it can unite those who most emphatically, even comically, are not; people who, if they had not found themselves put down by fate in the same household or community, would have had nothing to do with each other. If Affection grows out of this – of course it often does not – their eyes begin to open. Growing fond of 'old so-and-so', at first simply because he happens to be there, I presently begin to see that there is 'something in him' after all. The moment when one first says, really meaning it, that though he is not 'my sort of man' he is a very good man 'in his own way' is one of liberation. It does not feel like that; we may feel only tolerant and indulgent. But really we have crossed a frontier. That 'in his own way' means that we are getting beyond our own idiosyncrasies, that we are learning to appreciate goodness or intelligence in themselves, not merely goodness or intelligence flavoured and served to suit our own palate.

'Dogs and cats should always be brought up together,' said someone, 'it broadens their minds so.'. . . It is Affection that creates this taste, teaching us first to notice, then to endure, then to smile at, then to enjoy, and finally to appreciate, the people who 'happen to be there'. Made for us? Thank God, no. They are themselves, odder than you could have believed and worth far more than we guessed.

Friendship *June 16*

When either Affection or Eros is one's theme, one finds a prepared audience. The importance and beauty of both have been stressed and almost exaggerated again and again. Even those who would debunk them are in conscious reaction against this laudatory tradition and, to that extent, influenced by it. But very few modern people think Friendship a love of comparable value or even a love at all. I cannot remember that any poem since *In Memoriam*, or any novel, has celebrated it. Tristan and Isolde, Antony and Cleopatra, Romeo and Juliet, have innumerable counterparts in modern literature: David

155

and Jonathan, Pylades and Orestes, Roland and Oliver, Amis and Amile, have not. To the Ancients, Friendship seemed the happiest and most fully human of all loves; the crown of life and the school of virtue. The modern world, in comparison, ignores it. We admit of course that besides a wife and family a man needs a few 'friends'. But the very tone of the admission, and the sort of acquaintanceships which those who make it would describe as 'friendships', show clearly that what they are talking about has very little to do with that *Philia* which Aristotle classified among the virtues or that *Amicitia* on which Cicero wrote a book. It is something quite marginal; not a main course in life's banquet; a diversion; something that fills up the chinks of one's time.

Friendship: the Love Valued by So Few   *June 17*

How has this come about? The first and most obvious answer is that few value it because few experience it. And the possibility of going through life without the experience is rooted in that fact which separates Friendship so sharply from both the other loves. Friendship is — in a sense not at all derogatory to it — the least *natural* of loves; the least instinctive, organic, biological, gregarious and necessary. It has least commerce with our nerves; there is nothing throaty about it; nothing that quickens the pulse or turns you red and pale. It is essentially between individuals; the moment two men are friends they have in some degree drawn apart together from the herd. Without Eros none of us would have been begotten and without Affection none of us would have been reared; but we can live and breed without Friendship. . . .

This (so to call it) 'non-natural' quality in Friendship goes far to explain why it was exalted in ancient and medieval times and has come to be made light of in our own. The deepest and most permanent thought of those ages was ascetic and world-renouncing. Nature and emotion and the body were feared as dangers to our souls, or despised as degradations of our human status. Inevitably that sort of love was most prized which seemed most independent, or even defiant, of mere Nature. Affection and Eros were too obviously connected with our nerves, too obviously shared with the brutes. You could feel these tugging at your guts and fluttering in your diaphragm. But in Friendship – in that luminous, tranquil, rational world of relationships freely chosen – you got away from all that. This alone, of all the loves, seemed to raise you to the level of gods or angels.

The Exaltation of Instinct   *June 18*

But then came Romanticism and 'tearful comedy' and the 'return to Nature' and the exaltation of Sentiment; and in their train all that great wallow of emotion which, though often criticized, has lasted ever since. Finally, the exaltation of instinct, the dark gods in the blood; whose hierophants may be incapable of male friendships. Under this new dispensation all that had once commended this love now began to work against it. It had not tearful smiles and keepsakes and baby-talk enough to please the sentimentalists. There was no blood and guts enough about it to attract the primitivists. It looked thin and etiolated; a sort of vegetarian substitute for the more organic loves.

Other causes have contributed. To those – and they are now the majority – who see human life merely as a development and complication of animal life all forms of behaviour which cannot produce certificates of an animal origin and of survival value are suspect. Friendship's certificates are not very satisfactory. Again, that outlook which values the collective above the individual necessarily disparages Friendship; it is a relation between men at their highest level of individuality. It withdraws men from collective 'togetherness' as surely as solitude itself could do; and more dangerously, for it withdraws them by twos and threes. Some forms of democratic sentiment are naturally hostile to it because it is selective and an affair of the few. To say 'These are my friends' implies 'Those are not'. For all these reasons if a man believes (as I do) that the old estimate of Friendship was the correct one, he can hardly write . . . on it except as a rehabilitation.

Invisible Cats   June 19

It has actually become necessary in our time to rebut the theory that every firm and serious friendship is really homosexual.

The dangerous word *really* is here important. To say that every Friendship is consciously and explicitly homosexual would be too obviously false; the wiseacres take refuge in the less palpable charge that it is *really* – unconsciously, cryptically, in some Pickwickian sense – homosexual. And this, though it cannot be proved, can never of course be refuted. The fact that no positive evidence of homosexuality can be discovered in the behaviour of two Friends does not disconcert the wiseacres at all: 'That', they say gravely, 'is just what we should expect.' The very lack of evidence is thus treated as evidence; the absence of smoke proves that the fire is very carefully hidden. Yes – if it exists at all. But we must first prove its existence. Otherwise we are arguing like a man who should say 'If there were an invisible cat in that chair, the chair would look empty; but the chair does look empty; therefore there is an invisible cat in it.'

A belief in invisible cats cannot perhaps be logically disproved, but it tells us a good deal about those who hold it. Those who cannot conceive Friendship as a substantive love but only as a disguise or elaboration of Eros betray the fact that they have never had a Friend. The rest of us know that though we can have erotic love and friendship for the same person yet in some ways nothing is less like a Friendship than a love affair. Lovers are always talking to one another about their love; Friends hardly ever about their Friendship. Lovers are normally face to face, absorbed in each other; Friends, side by side, absorbed in some common interest.

The Least Jealous of Loves   *June 20*

Lamb says somewhere that if, of three friends (A, B and C), A should die, then B loses not only A but 'A's part in C', while C loses not only A but 'A's part in B'. In each of my friends there is something that only some other friend can fully bring out. By myself I am not large enough to call the whole man into activity; I want other lights than my own to show all his facets. Now that Charles is dead, I shall never again see Ronald's reaction to a specifically Caroline joke. Far from having more of Ronald, having him 'to myself' now that Charles is away, I have less of Ronald. Hence true Friendship is the least jealous of loves. Two friends delight to be joined by a third, and three by a fourth, if only the newcomer is qualified to become a real friend. They can then say, as the blessed souls say in Dante, 'Here comes one who will augment our loves.' For in this love 'to divide is not to take away'. Of course the scarcity of kindred souls – not to mention practical considerations about the size of rooms and the audibility of voices – sets limits to the enlargement of the circle; but within those limits we possess each friend not less but more as the number of those with whom we share him increases. In this, Friendship exhibits a glorious 'nearness by resemblance' to Heaven itself where the very multitude of the blessed (which no man can number) increases the fruition which each has of God. For every soul, seeing Him in her own way, doubtless communicates that unique vision to all the rest. That, says an old author, is why the Seraphim in Isaiah's vision are crying 'Holy, Holy, Holy' *to one another* (Isaiah 6:3). The more we thus share the Heavenly Bread between us, the more we shall all have.

The Birth of a Friendship   *June 21*

Friendship arises out of mere Companionship when two or more of the companions discover that they have in common some insight or interest or even taste which the others do not share and which, till that moment, each believed to be his own unique treasure (or burden). The typical expression of opening Friendship would be something like, 'What? You too? I thought I was the only one.' We can imagine that among those early hunters and warriors single individuals – one in a century? one in a thousand years? – saw what others did not; saw that the deer was beautiful as well as edible, that hunting was fun as well as necessary, dreamed that his gods might be not only powerful but holy. But as long as each of these percipient persons dies without finding a kindred soul, nothing (I suspect) will come of it; art or sport or spiritual religion will not be born. It is when two such persons discover one another, when, whether with immense difficulties and semi-articulate fumblings or with what would seem to us amazing and elliptical speed, they share their vision – it is then that Friendship is born. And instantly they stand together in an immense solitude. . . .

In our own time Friendship arises in the same way. For us of course the shared activity and therefore the companionship on which Friendship supervenes will not often be a bodily one like hunting or fighting. It may be a common religion, common studies, a common profession, even a common recreation. All who share it will be our companions: but one or two or three who share something more will be our Friends. In this kind of love, as Emerson said, *Do you love me?* means *Do you see the same truth?* – Or at least, 'Do you *care about* the same truth?' The man who agrees with us that some question, little regarded by others, is of great importance can be our Friend. He need not agree with us about the answer.

Naked Personalities   *June 22*

This love (essentially) ignores not only our physical bodies but that whole embodiment which consists of our family, job, past and connections. At home, besides being Peter or Jane, we also bear a general character; husband or wife, brother or sister, chief, colleague or subordinate. Not among our Friends. It is an affair of disentangled, or stripped, minds. Eros will have naked bodies; Friendship naked personalities.

Hence (if you will not misunderstand me) the exquisite arbitrariness and irresponsibility of this love. I have no duty to be anyone's Friend and no man in the world has a duty to be mine. No claims, no shadow of necessity. Friendship is unnecessary, like philosophy, like art, like the universe itself (for God did not need to create). It has no survival value; rather it is one of those things which give value to survival. . . .

In a perfect Friendship this Appreciative love is, I think, often so great and so firmly based that each member of the circle feels, in his secret heart, humbled before all the rest. Sometimes he wonders what he is doing there among his betters. He is lucky beyond desert to be in such company. Especially when the whole group is together, each bringing out all that is best, wisest, or funniest in all the others. Those are the golden sessions; when four or five of us after a hard day's walking have come to our inn; when our slippers are on, our feet spread out towards the blaze and our drinks at our elbows; when the whole world, and something beyond the world, opens itself to our minds as we talk; and no one has any claim on or any responsibility for another, but all are freemen and equals as if we had first met an hour ago, while at the same time an Affection mellowed by the years enfolds us. Life – natural life – has no better gift to give. Who could have deserved it?

Friendship Needs Divine Protection   *June 23*

Friendship, like the other natural loves, is unable to save itself. In reality, because it is spiritual and therefore faces a subtler enemy, it must, even more wholeheartedly than they, invoke the divine protection if it hopes to remain sweet. For consider how narrow its true path is. It must not become what the people call a 'mutual admiration society'; yet if it is not full of mutual admiration, of Appreciative love, it is not Friendship at all. . . .

For a Christian, there are, strictly speaking, no chances. A secret Master of the Ceremonies has been at work. Christ, who said to the disciples, 'Ye have not chosen me, but I have chosen you', can truly say to every group of Christian friends, 'You have not chosen one another but I have chosen you for one another.' The Friendship is not a reward for our discrimination and good taste in finding one another out. It is the instrument by which God reveals to each the beauties of all the others. They are no greater than the beauties of a thousand other men; by Friendship God opens our eyes to them. They are, like all beauties, derived from Him, and then, in a good Friendship, increased by Him through the Friendship itself, so that it is His instrument for creating as well as for revealing. At this feast it is He who has spread the board and it is He who has chosen the guests. It is He, we may dare to hope, who sometimes does, and always should, preside. Let us not reckon without our Host.

Eros *June 24*

By Eros I mean of course that state which we call 'being in love'; or, if you prefer, that kind of love which lovers are 'in'. Some readers may have been surprised when . . . I described Affection as the love in which our experience seems to come closest to that of the animals. Surely, it might be asked, our sexual functions bring us equally close? That is quite true as regards human sexuality in general. But I am not going to be concerned with human sexuality simply as such. Sexuality makes part of our subject only when it becomes an ingredient in the complex state of 'being in love'. That sexual experience can occur without Eros, without being 'in love', and that Eros includes other things besides sexual activity, I take for granted. If you prefer to put it that way, I am inquiring not into the sexuality which is common to us and the beasts or even common to all men, but into one uniquely human variation of it which develops within 'love' – what I call Eros. The carnal or animally sexual element within Eros, I intend (following an old usage) to call Venus. And I mean by Venus what is sexual not in some cryptic or rarefied sense – such as a depth-psychologist might explore – but in a perfectly obvious sense; what is known to be sexual by those who experience it; what could be proved to be sexual by the simplest observations.

Eros and Obedience or Disobedience to God

Sexuality may operate without Eros or as part of Eros. Let me hasten to add that I make the distinction simply in order to limit our inquiry and without any moral implications. I am not at all subscribing to the popular idea that it is the absence or presence of Eros which makes the sexual act 'impure' or 'pure', degraded or fine, unlawful or lawful. If all who lay together without being in the state of Eros were abominable, we all come of tainted stock. The times and places in which marriage depends on Eros are in a small minority. Most of our ancestors were married off in early youth to partners chosen by their parents on grounds that had nothing to do with Eros. They went to the act with no other 'fuel', so to speak, than plain animal desire. And they did right; honest Christian husbands and wives, obeying their fathers and mothers, discharging to one another their 'marriage debt', and bringing up families in the fear of the Lord. Conversely, this act, done under the influence of a soaring and iridescent Eros which reduces the role of the senses to a minor consideration, may yet be plain adultery, may involve breaking a wife's heart, deceiving a husband, betraying a friend, polluting hospitality and deserting your children. It has not pleased God that the distinction between a sin and a duty should turn on fine feelings. This act, like any other, is justified (or not) by far more prosaic and definable criteria; by the keeping or breaking of promises, by justice or injustice, by charity or selfishness, by obedience or disobedience.

To the evolutionist Eros (the human variation) will be something that grows out of Venus, a late complication and development of the immemorial biological impulse. We must not assume, however, that this is necessarily what happens within the consciousness of the individual. There may be those who have first felt mere sexual appetite for a woman and then gone on at a later stage to 'fall in love with her'. But I doubt if this is at all common. Very often what comes first is simply a delighted preoccupation with the Beloved – a general, unspecified preoccupation with her in her totality. A man in this state really hasn't leisure to think of sex. He is too busy thinking of a person. The fact that she is a woman is far less important than the fact that she is herself. He is full of desire, but the desire may not be sexually toned. If you asked him what he wanted, the true reply would often be, 'To go on thinking of her'. He is love's contemplative. And when at a later stage the explicitly sexual element awakes, he will not feel (unless scientific theories are influencing him) that this had all along been the root of the whole matter. He is more likely to feel that the incoming tide of Eros, having demolished many sandcastles and made islands of many rocks, has now at last with a triumphant seventh wave flooded this part of his nature also – the little pool of ordinary sexuality which was there on his beach before the tide came in. Eros enters him like an invader, taking over and reorganizing, one by one, the institutions of a conquered country.

Venus Wants 'It'

George Orwell . . . preferred sexuality in its native condition, uncontaminated by Eros. In *1984* his dreadful hero, before towsing the heroine, demands a reassurance: 'You like doing this?' he asks. 'I don't mean simply me; I mean the thing in itself.' He is not satisfied till he gets the answer, 'I adore it.' This little dialogue defines the reorganization. Sexual desire, without Eros, wants *it*, the *thing in itself*; Eros wants the Beloved.

The *thing* is a sensory pleasure; that is, an event occurring within one's own body. We use a most unfortunate idiom when we say, of a lustful man prowling the streets, that he 'wants a woman'. Strictly speaking, a woman is just what he does not want. He wants a pleasure for which a woman happens to be the necessary piece of apparatus. How much he cares about the woman as such may be gauged by his attitude to her five minutes after fruition (one does not keep the carton after one has smoked the cigarettes). Now Eros makes a man really want, not a woman, but one particular woman. In some mysterious but quite indisputable fashion the lover desires the Beloved herself, not the pleasure she can give. No lover in the world ever sought the embraces of the woman he loved as the result of a calculation, however unconscious, that they would be more pleasurable than those of any other woman. If he raised the question he would, no doubt, expect that this would be so. But to raise it would be to step outside the world of Eros altogether.

•

It has been widely held in the past, and is perhaps held by many unsophisticated people today, that the spiritual danger of Eros arises almost entirely from the carnal element within it; that Eros is 'noblest' or 'purest' when Venus is reduced to the minimum. The older moral theologians certainly seem to have thought that the danger we chiefly had to guard against in marriage was that of a soul-destroying surrender to the senses. It will be noticed, however, that this is not the Scriptural approach. St Paul, dissuading his converts from marriage, says nothing about that side of the matter except to discourage prolonged abstinence from Venus (1 Corinthians 7:5). What he fears is preoccupation, the need of constantly 'pleasing' – that is, considering – one's partner, the multiple distractions of domesticity. It is marriage itself, not the marriage bed, that will be likely to hinder us from waiting uninterruptedly on God. And surely St Paul is right? If I may trust my own experience, it is (within marriage as without) the practical and prudential cares of this world, and even the smallest and most prosaic of those cares, that are the great distraction. The gnat-like cloud of petty anxieties and decisions about the conduct of the next hour have interfered with my prayers more often than any passion or appetite whatever. The great, permanent temptation of marriage is not to sensuality but (quite bluntly) to avarice.

St Peter and St Paul, Apostles   *June 29*

Peter has confessed Jesus to be the Anointed One. That flash of glory is hardly over before the dark prophecy begins – that the Son of Man must suffer and die. Then this contrast is repeated. Peter, raised for a moment by his confession, makes his false step; the crushing rebuff

'Get thee behind me' follows. Then, across that momentary ruin which Peter (as so often) becomes, the voice of the Master, turning to the crowd, generalizes the moral. All His followers must take up the cross. This avoidance of suffering, this self-preservation, is not what life is really about. Then, more definitely still, the summons to martyrdom. You must stand to your tackling. If you disown Christ here and now, He will disown you later.

I think the 'low' church milieu that I grew up in did tend to be too cosily at ease in Sion. My grandfather, I'm told, used to say that he 'looked forward to having some very interesting conversations with St Paul when he got to heaven'. Two clerical gentlemen talking at ease in a club! It never seemed to cross his mind that an encounter with St Paul might be rather an overwhelming experience even for an Evangelical clergyman of good family. But when Dante saw the great apostles in heaven they affected him like *mountains*. There's lots to be said against devotions to saints; but at least they keep on reminding us that we are very small people compared with them. How much smaller before their Master?

Angels, Tom-Cats, and the Marriage-Bed   *June 30*

We must not be totally serious about Venus. Indeed we can't be totally serious without doing violence to our humanity. It is not for nothing that every language and literature in the world is full of jokes about sex. Many of them may be dull or disgusting and nearly all of them are old. But we must insist that they embody an attitude to Venus which in the long run endangers the Christian life far less than a reverential gravity. . . .

She herself is a mocking, mischievous spirit, far more elf than deity, and makes game of us. When all external circumstances are fittest for her service she will leave one or both the lovers totally indisposed for it. When every overt act is impossible and even glances cannot be exchanged – in trains, in shops and at interminable parties – she will assail them with all her force. An hour later, when time and place agree, she will have mysteriously withdrawn; perhaps from only one of them. What a pother this must raise – what resentments, self-pities, suspicions, wounded vanities and all the current chatter about 'frustration' – in those who have deified her! But sensible lovers laugh. . . .

I can hardly help regarding it as one of God's jokes that a passion so soaring, so apparently transcendent, as Eros, should thus be linked in incongruous symbiosis with a bodily appetite which, like any other appetite, tactlessly reveals its connections with such mundane factors as weather, health, diet, circulation, and digestion. In Eros at times we seem to be flying; Venus gives us the sudden twitch that reminds us we are really captive balloons. It is a continual demonstration of the truth that we are composite creatures, rational animals, akin on one side to the angels, on the other to tom-cats. It is a bad thing not to be able to take a joke. Worse, not to take a divine joke; made, I grant you, at our expense, but also (who doubts it?) for our endless benefit.

The 'Headship' of the Christian Husband   July 1

Christian law has crowned him in the permanent relationship of marriage, bestowing – or should I say, inflicting? – a certain 'headship' on him. . . . As we could easily take the natural mystery too seriously, so we might take the Christian mystery not seriously enough. Christian writers (notably Milton) have sometimes spoken of the husband's headship with a complacency to make the blood run cold. We must go back to our Bibles. The husband is the head of the wife just in so far as he is to

169

her what Christ is to the Church. He is to love her as Christ loved the Church – read on – *and gave his life for her* (Ephesians 5:25). This headship, then, is most fully embodied not in the husband we should all wish to be but in him whose marriage is most like a crucifixion; whose wife receives most and gives least, is most unworthy of him, is – in her own mere nature – least lovable. For the Church has no beauty but what the Bridegroom gives her; he does not find, but makes her, lovely. The chrism of this terrible coronation is to be seen not in the joys of any man's marriage but in its sorrows, in the sickness and sufferings of a good wife or the faults of a bad one, in his unwearying (never paraded) care or his inexhaustible forgiveness: forgiveness, not acquiescence. As Christ sees in the flawed, proud, fanatical or lukewarm Church on earth that Bride who will one day be without spot or wrinkle, and labours to produce the latter, so the husband whose headship is Christ-like (and he is allowed no other sort) never despairs. . . .

To say this is not to say that there is any virtue or wisdom in making a marriage that involves such misery. . There is no wisdom or virtue in seeking unnecessary martyrdom or deliberately courting persecution; yet it is, none the less, the persecuted or martyred Christian in whom the pattern of the Master is most unambiguously realized. So, in these terrible marriages, once they have come about, the 'headship' of the husband, if only he can sustain it, is most Christ-like.

The sternest feminist need not grudge my sex the crown offered to it either in the Pagan or in the Christian mystery. For the one is of paper and the other of thorns. The real danger is not that husbands may grasp the latter too eagerly; but that they will allow or compel their wives to usurp it.

Eros, honoured without reservation and obeyed uncondi-
tionally, becomes a demon. And this is just how he
claims to be honoured and obeyed. Divinely indifferent
to our selfishness, he is also demoniacally rebellious to
every claim of God or Man that would oppose him. . . .
When lovers say of some act that we might blame, 'Love
made us do it', notice the tone. A man saying, 'I did it
because I was frightened', or 'I did it because I was angry',
speaks quite differently. He is putting forward an excuse
for what he feels to require excusing. But the lovers are
seldom doing quite that. Notice how tremulously,
almost how devoutly, they say the word *love*, not so
much pleading an 'extenuating circumstance' as appealing to an authority. The confession can be almost a boast.
There can be a shade of defiance in it. They 'feel like
martyrs'. In extreme cases what their words really express is a demure yet unshakable allegiance to the god of
love.

'These reasons in love's law have passed for good', says
Milton's Dalila. That is the point; *in love's law.* . . . It
seems to sanction all sorts of actions they would not
otherwise have dared. I do not mean solely, or chiefly,
acts that violate chastity. They are just as likely to be
acts of injustice or uncharity against the outer world.
They will seem like proofs of piety and zeal towards Eros.
The pair can say to one another in an almost sacrificial
spirit, 'It is for love's sake that I have neglected my
parents – left my children – cheated my partner – failed
my friend at his greatest need.' These reasons in love's
law have passed for good. The votaries may even come to
feel a particular merit in such sacrifices; what costlier
offering can be laid on love's altar than one's conscience?

The saying 'Blessed are those that have not seen and have believed' has nothing to do with our original assent to the Christian propositions. It was not addressed to a philosopher inquiring whether God exists. It was addressed to a man who already believed that, who already had long acquaintance with a particular Person, and evidence that that Person could do very odd things, and who then refused to believe one odd thing more, often predicted by that Person and vouched for by all His closest friends. It is a rebuke not to scepticism in the philosophic sense but to the psychological quality of being 'suspicious'. It says in effect, 'You should have known me better.' There are cases between man and man where we should all, in our different ways, bless those who have not seen and have believed. Our relation to those who trusted us only after we were proved innocent in court cannot be the same as our relation to those who trusted us all through.

We Must Do What Eros Cannot Do   *July 4*

The couple whose marriage will certainly be endangered ... and possibly ruined, are those who have idolized Eros. They thought he had the power and truthfulness of a god. They expected that mere feeling would do for them, and permanently, all that was necessary. When this expectation is disappointed they throw the blame on Eros or, more usually, on their partners. In reality, however, Eros, having made his gigantic promise and shown you in glimpses what its performance would be like, has 'done his stuff'. He, like a godparent, makes the vows; it is we who must keep them. It is we who must labour to bring our daily life into even closer accordance with what the glimpses have revealed. We must do the works of Eros when Eros is not present. This all good lovers know, though those who are not reflective or articulate must be able to express it only in a few conventional phrases about 'taking the rough along with the smooth', not 'expecting too much', having 'a little common sense', and the like. And all good Christian lovers know that this programme, modest as it sounds, will not be carried out except by humility, charity and divine grace; that it is indeed the whole Christian life seen from one particular angle.

Charity   *July 5*

William Morris wrote a poem called 'Love Is Enough' and someone is said to have reviewed it briefly in the words 'It isn't'. . . . The natural loves are not self-sufficient. Something else, at first vaguely described as 'decency and common sense', but later revealed as goodness, and finally as the whole Christian life in one particular relation, must come to the help of the mere feeling if the feeling is to be kept sweet.

To say this is not to belittle the natural loves but to indicate where their real glory lies. It is no disparagement to a garden to say that it will not fence and weed itself, nor prune its own fruit trees, nor roll and cut its own lawns. A garden is a good thing but that is not the sort of goodness it has. It will remain a garden, as distinct from a wilderness, only if someone does all these things to it. Its real glory is of quite a different kind. The very fact that it needs constant weeding and pruning bears witness to that glory. It teems with life. It glows with colour and smells like heaven and puts forward at every hour of a summer day beauties which man could never have created and could not even, on his own resources, have imagined. If you want to see the difference between its contribution and the gardener's, put the commonest weed it grows side by side with his hoes, rakes, shears, and packet of weed killer; you have put beauty, energy and fecundity beside dead, sterile things. Just so, our 'decency and common sense' show grey and deathlike beside the geniality of love.

Do Not Imagine You Have Come Further than You Have

July 6

For most of us the true rivalry lies between the self and the human Other, not yet between the human Other and God. It is dangerous to press upon a man the duty of getting beyond earthly love when his real difficulty lies in getting so far. And it is no doubt easy enough to love the fellow creature less and to imagine that this is happening because we are learning to love God more, when the real reason may be quite different. We may be only 'mistaking the decays of nature for the increase of Grace'. Many people do not find it really difficult to hate their wives or mothers. Mr Mauriac, in a fine scene, pictures the other disciples stunned and bewildered by this strange command, but not Judas. He laps it up easily.

The Natural Loves' Claim to Divinity

July 7

The loves prove that they are unworthy to take the place of God by the fact that they cannot even remain themselves and do what they promise to do without God's help. Why prove that some petty princeling is not the lawful Emperor when without the Emperor's support he cannot even keep his subordinate throne and make peace in his little province for half a year? Even for their own sakes the loves must submit to be second things if they are to remain the things they want to be. In this yoke lies their true freedom; they 'are taller when they bow'. For when God rules in a human heart, though He may sometimes have to remove certain of its native authorities altogether, He often continues others in their offices and, by subjecting their authority to His, gives it for the first time a firm basis. Emerson has said, 'When half-gods go, the gods arrive.' That is a very doubtful maxim. Better say, 'When God arrives (and only then) the half-gods can remain.' Left to themselves they either vanish or become demons. Only in His name can they with beauty and security 'wield their little tridents'. The rebellious slogan 'All for love' is really love's death warrant (date of execution, for the moment, left blank).

Safe Investments and Limited Liabilities   *July 8*

In words which can still bring tears to the eyes, St Augustine describes the desolation in which the death of his friend Nebridius plunged him *(Confessions* IV, 10). Then he draws a moral. This is what comes, he says, of giving one's heart to anything but God. All human beings pass away. Do not let your happiness depend on something you may lose. If love is to be a blessing, not a misery, it must be for the only Beloved who will never pass away.

Of course this is excellent sense. Don't put your goods in a leaky vessel. Don't spend too much on a house you may be turned out of. And there is no man alive who responds more naturally than I to such canny maxims. I am a safety-first creature. Of all arguments against love none makes so strong an appeal to my nature as 'Careful! This might lead you to suffering.'

To my nature, my temperament, yes. Not to my conscience. When I respond to that appeal I seem to myself to be a thousand miles away from Christ. If I am sure of anything I am sure that His teaching was never meant to confirm my congenital preference for safe investments and limited liabilities. I doubt whether there is anything in me that pleases Him less. And who could conceivably begin to love God on such a prudential ground – because the security (so to speak) is better? Who could even include it among the grounds for loving? Would you choose a wife or a Friend – if it comes to that, would you choose a dog – in this spirit? One must be outside the world of love, of all loves, before one thus calculates. Eros, lawless Eros, preferring the Beloved to happiness, is more like Love Himself than this.

No Insurances Against Heartbreak   *July 9*

Even if it were granted that insurances against heartbreak were our highest wisdom, does God Himself offer them? Apparently not. Christ comes at last to say 'Why hast thou forsaken me?'. . .

To love at all is to be vulnerable. Love anything, and your heart will certainly be wrung and possibly be broken. If you want to make sure of keeping it intact, you must give your heart to no one, not even to an animal. Wrap it carefully round with hobbies and little luxuries; avoid all entanglements; lock it up safe in the casket or coffin of your selfishness. But in that casket – safe, dark, motionless, airless – it will change. It will not be broken; it will become unbreakable, impenetrable, irredeemable. The alternative to tragedy, or at least to the risk of tragedy, is damnation. The only place outside Heaven where you can be perfectly safe from all the dangers and perturbations of love is Hell.

I believe that the most lawless and inordinate loves are less contrary to God's will than a self-invited and self-protective lovelessness. It is like hiding the talent in a napkin and for much the same reason. 'I knew thee that thou wert a hard man.' Christ did not teach and suffer that we might become, even in the natural loves, more careful of our own happiness. If a man is not uncalculating towards the earthly beloveds whom he has seen, he is none the more likely to be so towards God whom he has not. We shall draw nearer to God, not by trying to avoid the sufferings inherent in all loves, but by accepting them and offering them to Him; throwing away all defensive armour. If our hearts need to be broken, and if He chooses this as the way in which they should break, so be it.

'Hating' the People We Love   *July 10*

As so often, Our Lord's own words are both far fiercer and far more tolerable than those of the theologians. He says nothing about guarding against earthly loves for fear we might be hurt; He says something that cracks like a whip about trampling them all under foot the moment they hold us back from following Him. 'If any man come to me and hate not his father and mother and wife . . . and his own life also, he cannot be my disciple' (Luke 14:26).

But how are we to understand the word *hate*? That Love Himself should be commanding what we ordinarily mean by hatred – commanding us to cherish resentment, to gloat over another's misery, to delight in injuring him – is almost a contradiction in terms. I think Our Lord, in the sense here intended, 'hated' St Peter when he said, 'Get thee behind me.' To hate is to reject, to set one's face against, to make no concession to, the Beloved when the Beloved utters, however sweetly and however pitiably, the suggestions of the Devil. A man, said Jesus, who tries to serve two masters, will 'hate' the one and 'love' the other. It is not, surely, mere feelings of aversion and liking that are here in question. . . . In the last resort, we must turn down or disqualify our nearest and dearest when they come between us and our obedience to God.

Heaven knows, it will seem to them sufficiently like hatred. We must not act on the pity we feel; we must be blind to tears and deaf to pleadings.

 I will not say that this duty is hard; some find it too easy; some, hard almost beyond endurance. What is hard for all is to know when the occasion for such 'hating' has arisen. Our temperaments deceive us. The meek and tender – uxorious husbands, submissive wives, doting parents, dutiful children – will not easily believe that it has ever arrived. Self-assertive people, with a dash of the bully in them, will believe it too soon. That is why it is of such extreme importance so to order our loves that it is unlikely to arrive at all.

The Raising of All Loves   *July 11*

We may hope that the resurrection of the body means also the resurrection of what may be called our 'greater body'; the general fabric of our earthly life with its affections and relationships. But only on a condition; not a condition arbitrarily laid down by God, but one necessarily inherent in the character of Heaven: nothing can enter there which cannot become heavenly. 'Flesh and blood', mere nature, cannot inherit that Kingdom. Man can ascend to Heaven only because the Christ, who died and ascended to Heaven, is 'formed in him'. Must we not suppose that the same is true of a man's loves? Only those into which Love Himself has entered will ascend to Love Himself. And these can be raised with Him only if they have, in some degree and fashion, shared His death; if the natural element in them has submitted – year after year, or in some sudden agony – to transmutation. The fashion of this world passes away. The very name of nature implies the transitory. Natural loves can hope for eternity only in so far as they have allowed themselves to be taken into the eternity of Charity; have at least

178

allowed the process to begin here on earth, before the night comes when no man can work. And the process will always involve a kind of death. There is no escape. In my love for wife or friend the only eternal element is the transforming presence of Love Himself. By that presence, if at all, the other elements may hope, as our physical bodies hope, to be raised from the dead. For this only is holy in them, this only is the Lord.

Philautia: Self-Love   *July 12*

Self-renunciation is thought to be, and indeed is, very near the core of Christian ethics. When Aristotle writes in praise of a certain kind of self-love, we may feel, despite the careful distinctions which he draws between the legitimate and the illegitimate *Philautia*, that here we strike something essentially sub-Christian. It is more difficult, however, to decide what we think of St François de Sales's chapter *De la douceur envers nous-mesmes* ['Of meekness towards ourselves'], where we are forbidden to indulge resentment even against ourselves and advised to reprove even our own faults *avec des remonstrances douces et tranquilles* ['with mild and calm remonstrances'], feeling more compassion than passion. In the same spirit, Lady Julian of Norwich would have us 'loving and peaceable', not only to our 'even-Christians', but to 'ourself'. Even the New Testament bids me love my neighbour 'as myself', which would be a horrible command if the self were simply to be hated. Yet Our Lord also says that a true disciple must 'hate his own life'.

We must not explain this apparent contradiction by saying that self-love is right up to a certain point and wrong beyond that point. The question is not one of degree. There are two kinds of self-hatred which look rather alike in their earlier stages, but of which one is wrong from the beginning and the other right to the end. When Shelley speaks of self-contempt as the source of cruelty, or when a later poet says that he has no stomach for the man 'who loathes his neighbour as himself', they are referring to a very real and very un-Christian hatred of the self which may make diabolical a man whom common selfishness would have left (at least, for a while) merely animal. The hardboiled economist or psychologist of our own day, recognizing the 'ideological taint' or Freudian motive in his own make-up, does not necessarily learn Christian humility. He may end in what is called a 'low view' of all souls, including his own, which expresses itself in cynicism or cruelty, or both. Even Christians, if they accept in certain forms the doctrine of total depravity, are not always free from the danger. The logical conclusion of the process is the worship of suffering – for others as well as for the self – which we see, if I read it aright, in Mr David Lindsay's *Voyage to Arcturus*, or that extraordinary vacancy which Shakespeare depicts at the end of *Richard III*. Richard in his agony tries to turn to self-love. But he has been 'seeing through' all emotions so long that he 'sees through' even this. It becomes a mere tautology: 'Richard loves Richard; that is, I am I.'

The self can be regarded in two ways. On the one hand, it
is God's creature, an occasion of love and rejoicing; now,
indeed, hateful in condition, but to be pitied and healed.
On the other hand, it is that one self of all others which is
called *I* and *me*, and which on that ground puts forward
an irrational claim to preference. This claim is to be not
only hated, but simply killed; 'never', as George
MacDonald says, 'to be allowed a moment's respite from
eternal death.' The Christian must wage endless war
against the clamour of the *ego* as *ego*: but he loves and
approves selves as such, though not their sins. The very
self-love which he has to reject is to him a specimen of
how he ought to feel to all selves; and he may hope that
when he has truly learned (which will hardly be in this
life) to love his neighbour as himself, he may then be able
to love himself as his neighbour: that is, with charity
instead of partiality. The other kind of self-hatred, on the
contrary, hates selves as such. It begins by accepting the
special value of the particular self called *me*; then,
wounded in its pride to find that such a darling object
should be so disappointing, it seeks revenge, first upon
that self, then on all. Deeply egoistic, but now with an
inverted egoism, it uses the revealing argument, 'I don't
spare myself' – with the implication 'then *a fortiori* I
need not spare others' – and becomes like the centurion
in Tacitus, *immitior quia toleraverat* ['more relentless
because he had endured it himself'].

The wrong asceticism torments the self: the right kind
kills the selfness. We must die daily: but it is better to
love the self than to love nothing, and to pity the self
than to pity no one.

Looking Beyond Ourselves *July 15*

We should, I believe, distrust states of mind which turn our attention upon ourselves. Even at our sins we should look no longer than is necessary to know and to repent them; and our virtues or progress (if any) are certainly a dangerous object of contemplation. When the sun is vertically above a man he casts no shadow: similarly when we have come to the Divine meridian our spiritual shadow (that is, our consciousness of self) will vanish. One will thus in a sense be almost nothing: a room to be filled by God and our blessed fellow creatures, who in their turn are rooms we help to fill.

A Dislocation of the Aesthetic Life *July 16*

Until quite modern times – I think, until the time of the Romantics – nobody ever suggested that literature and the arts were an end in themselves. They 'belonged to the ornamental part of life', they provided 'innocent diversion'; or else they 'refined our manners' or 'incited us to virtue' or glorified the gods. The great music had been written for Masses, the great pictures painted to fill up a space on the wall of a noble patron's dining-room or to kindle devotion in a church; the great tragedies were produced either by religious poets in honour of Dionysius or by commercial poets to entertain Londoners on half-holidays.

It was only in the nineteenth century that we became aware of the full dignity of art. We began to 'take it seriously'. . . . But the result seems to have been a dislocation of the aesthetic life in which little is left for us but high-minded works which fewer and fewer people want to read or hear or see, and 'popular' works of which both those who make them and those who enjoy them are half ashamed. . . . By valuing too highly a real, but subordinate good, we have come near to losing that good itself.

First and Second Things *July 17*

The longer I looked into it the more I came to suspect that I was perceiving a universal law. *On cause mieux quand on ne dit pas Causons* ['One converses better when one does not say "Let us converse"']. The woman who makes a dog the centre of her life loses, in the end, not only her human usefulness and dignity but even the proper pleasure of dog-keeping. The man who makes alcohol his chief good loses not only his job but his palate and all power of enjoying the earlier (and only pleasurable) levels of intoxication. It is a glorious thing to feel for a moment or two that the whole meaning of the universe is summed up in one woman – glorious so long as other duties and pleasures keep tearing you away from her. But clear the decks and so arrange your life (it is sometimes feasible) that you will have nothing to do but contemplate her, and what happens? Of course this law has been discovered before, but it will stand re-discovery. It may be stated as follows: every preference of a small good to a great, or a partial good to a total good, involves the loss of the small or partial good for which the sacrifice was made.

Apparently the world is made that way. If Esau really got the pottage in return for his birthright, then Esau was a lucky exception. You can't get second things by putting them first; you can get second things only by putting first things first. From which it would follow that the question, What things are first? is of concern not only to philosophers but to everyone.

Is World Peace More Important than Salvation?

It is impossible . . . not to inquire what our own civilization has been putting first for the last thirty years. And the answer is plain. It has been putting itself first. To preserve civilization has been the great aim; the collapse of civilization, the great bugbear. Peace, a high standard of life, hygiene, transport, science and amusement – all these, which are what we usually mean by civilization, have been our ends. It will be replied that our concern for civilization is very natural and very necessary at a time when civilization is so imperilled. But how if the shoe is on the other foot? – how if civilization has been imperilled precisely by the fact that we have all made civilization our *summum bonum*? Perhaps it can't be preserved in that way. Perhaps civilization will never be safe until we care for something else more than we care for it.

The hypothesis has certain facts to support it. As far as peace (which is one ingredient in our idea of civilization) is concerned, I think many would now agree that a foreign policy dominated by desire for peace is one of the many roads that lead to war. And was civilization ever seriously endangered until civilization became the exclusive aim of human activity? There is much rash idealization of past ages about, and I do not wish to encourage more of it. Our ancestors were cruel, lecherous, greedy and stupid, like ourselves. But while they cared for other things more than for civilization – and they cared at different times for all sorts of things, for the will of God, for glory, for personal honour, for doctrinal purity, for justice – was civilization often in serious danger of disappearing?

At least the suggestion is worth a thought. To be sure, if it were true that civilization will never be safe till it is put second, that immediately raises the question, second to what? What is the first thing? The only reply I can offer here is that if we do not know, then the first and only truly practical thing is to set about finding out.

Progress means movement in a desired direction, and we do not all desire the same things for our species. In 'Possible Worlds' Professor Haldane pictured a future in which Man, foreseeing that Earth would soon be uninhabitable, adapted himself for migration to Venus by drastically modifying his physiology and abandoning justice, pity and happiness. The desire here is for mere survival. Now I care far more how humanity lives than how long. Progress, for me, means increasing goodness and happiness of individual lives. For the species, as for each man, mere longevity seems to me a contemptible ideal.

I therefore go even further than C.P. Snow in removing the H-bomb from the centre of the picture. Like him, I am not certain whether if it killed one-third of us (the one-third I belong to), this would be a bad thing for the remainder; like him, I don't think it will kill us all. But suppose it did? As a Christian I take it for granted that human history will some day end; and I am offering Omniscience no advice as to the best date for that consummation. I am more concerned by what the Bomb is doing already.

One meets young people who make the threat of it a reason for poisoning every pleasure and evading every duty in the present. Don't they know that, Bomb or no Bomb, all men die (many in horrible ways)?

Equality *July 20*

It is idle to say that men are of equal value. If value is taken in a worldly sense – if we mean that all men are equally useful or beautiful or good or entertaining – then it is nonsense. If it means that all are of equal value as immortal souls then I think it conceals a dangerous error.

The infinite value of each human soul is not a Christian doctrine. God did not die for man because of some value He perceived in him. The value of each human soul considered simply in itself, out of relation to God, is zero. As St Paul writes, to have died for valuable men would have been not divine but merely heroic; but God died for sinners. He loved us not because we were lovable, but because He is Love. It may be that He loves all equally – He certainly loved all to the death – and I am not certain what the expression means. If there is equality it is in His love, not in us.

Democracy   *July 21*

I am a democrat because I believe in the Fall of Man. I think most people are democrats for the opposite reason. A great deal of democratic enthusiasm descends from the ideas of people like Rousseau, who believed in democracy because they thought mankind so wise and good that everyone deserved a share in the government. The danger of defending democracy on those grounds is that they are not true. And whenever their weakness is exposed, the people who prefer tyranny make capital out of the exposure. I find that they're not true without looking further than myself. I don't deserve a share in governing a henroost, much less a nation. Nor do most people – all the people who believe advertisements, and think in catchwords and spread rumours. The real reason for democracy is just the reverse. Mankind is so fallen that no man can be trusted with unchecked power over his fellows. . . .

This introduces a view of equality rather different from that in which we have been trained. I do not think that equality is one of those things (like wisdom or happiness) which are good simply in themselves and for their own sakes. I think it is in the same class as medicine, which is good because we are ill, or clothes, which are good because we are no longer innocent. . . . When equality is treated not as a medicine or a safety-gadget but as an ideal, we begin to breed that stunted and envious sort of mind which hates all superiority.

St Mary Magdalen July 22

It is nice to be still under the care of St Mary Magdalen. . . . The allegorical sense of her great action dawned on me the other day. The precious alabaster box which one must *break* over the Holy Feet is one's *heart*. Easier said than done. And the contents become perfume only when it is broken. While they are safe inside they are more like sewage. All very alarming.

Monarchy: Our Taproot in Eden July 23

We Britons should rejoice that we have contrived to reach much legal democracy (we still need more of the economic) without losing our ceremonial monarchy. For there, right in the midst of our lives, is that which satisfies the craving for inequality, and acts as a permanent reminder that medicine is not food. Hence a man's reaction to monarchy is a kind of test. Monarchy can easily be 'debunked'; but watch the faces, mark well the accents, of the debunkers. These are the men whose taproot in Eden has been cut: whom no rumour of the polyphony, the dance, can reach – men to whom pebbles laid in a row are more beautiful than an arch. Yet even if they desire mere equality they cannot reach it. Where men are forbidden to honour a king they honour millionaires, athletes or film stars instead: even famous prostitutes or gangsters. For spiritual nature, like bodily nature, will be served; deny it food and it will gobble poison.

Monarchy and Statecraft   *July 24*

Corineus compared modern Christianity with the modern English monarchy: the forms of kingship have been retained, but the reality has been abandoned. . . . 'Why not cut the cord?' asks Corineus. 'Everything would be much easier if you would free your thought from this vestigial mythology.' To be sure: far easier. Life would be far easier for the mother of an invalid child if she put it into an Institution and adopted someone else's healthy baby instead. Life would be far easier to many a man if he abandoned the woman he has actually fallen in love with and married someone else because she is more suitable. The only defect of the healthy baby and the suitable woman is that they leave out the patient's only reason for bothering about a child or wife at all. 'Would not conversation be much more rational than dancing?' said Jane Austen's Miss Bingley. 'Much more rational,' replied Mr Bingley, 'but much less like a ball.'

In the same way, it would be much more rational to abolish the English monarchy. But how if, by doing so, you leave out the one element in our State which matters most? How if the monarchy is the channel through which all the *vital* elements of citizenship – loyalty, the consecration of secular life, the hierarchical principle, splendour, ceremony, continuity – still trickle down to irrigate the dustbowl of modern economic Statecraft?

The New Testament contains embarrassing promises that what we pray for with faith we shall receive. Mark 11:24 is the most staggering. Whatever we ask for, believing that we'll get it, we'll get. . . . How is this astonishing promise to be reconciled (a) With the observed facts? and (b) With the prayer in Gethsemane, and (as a result of that prayer) the universally accepted view that we should ask everything with a reservation ('If it be Thy will')?

As regards (a), no evasion is possible. Every war, every famine or plague, almost every deathbed, is the monument to a petition that was not granted. At this very moment thousands of people in this one island are facing as a *fait accompli* the very thing against which they have prayed night and day. . . .

But (b), though much less often mentioned, is surely an equal difficulty. How is it possible at one and the same moment to have a perfect faith – an untroubled or unhesitating faith as St James says (1:6) – that you will get what you ask and yet also prepare yourself submissively in advance for a possible refusal? If you envisage a refusal as possible, how can you have simultaneously a perfect confidence that what you ask will not be refused? If you have that confidence, how can you take refusal into account at all? . . .

As regards the first difficulty, I'm not asking why our petitions are so often refused. Anyone can see in general that this must be so. In our ignorance we ask what is not good for us or for others, or not even intrinsically possible. Or again, to grant one man's prayer involves refusing another's. There is much here which it is hard for our will to accept but nothing that is hard for our intellect to understand. The real problem is different; not why refusal is so frequent, but why the opposite result is so lavishly promised.

Shall we . . . scrap the embarrassing promises as 'venerable archaisms' which have to be 'outgrown'? Surely, even if there were no other objection, that method is too easy. If we are free to delete all inconvenient data we shall certainly have no theological difficulties; but for the same reason no solutions and no progress. The very writers of the detective stories, not to mention the scientists, know better. The troublesome fact, the apparent absurdity which can't be fitted in to any synthesis we have yet made, is precisely the one we must not ignore. . . . There is always hope if we keep an unsolved problem fairly in view; there's none if we pretend it's not there.

Screwtape on Democracy   July 26

Democracy is the word with which you must lead them by the nose. The good work which our philological experts have already done in the corruption of human language makes it unnecessary to warn you that they should never be allowed to give this word a clear and definable meaning. They won't. It will never occur to them that *democracy* is properly the name of a political system, even a system of voting, and that this has only the most remote and tenuous connection with what you are trying to sell them. Nor of course must they ever be allowed to raise Aristotle's question: whether 'democratic behaviour' means the behaviour that democracies like or the behaviour that will preserve a democracy. For if they did, it could hardly fail to occur to them that these need not be the same.

You are to use the word purely as an incantation; if you like, purely for its selling power. It is a name they venerate. And of course it is connected with the political ideal that men should be equally treated. You then make a stealthy transition in their minds from this political ideal to a factual belief that all men *are* equal. Especially the man you are working on. As a result you can use the word *democracy* to sanction in his thought the most

190

degrading (and also the least enjoyable) of all human feelings. . . . The feeling I mean is of course that which prompts a man to say *I'm as good as you*. The first and most obvious advantage is that you thus induce him to enthrone at the centre of his life a good solid, resounding lie.

Screwtape's Encouragement of Envy   *July 27*

Now, this useful phenomenon is in itself by no means new. Under the name of Envy it has been known to the humans for thousands of years. But hitherto they always regarded it as the most odious, and also the most comical, of vices. Those who were aware of feeling it felt it with shame; those who were not gave it no quarter in others. The delightful novelty of the present situation is that you can sanction it – make it respectable and even laudable – by the incantatory use of the word *democratic*.

Under the influence of this incantation those who are in any or every way inferior can labour more wholeheartedly and successfully than ever before to pull down everyone else to their own level. But that is not all. Under the same influence, those who come, or could come, nearer to a full humanity, actually draw back from it for fear of being undemocratic. I am credibly informed that young humans now sometimes suppress an incipient taste for classical music or good literature because it might prevent their Being Like Folks; that people who would really wish to be – and are offered the Grace which would enable them to be – honest, chaste, or temperate refuse it. To accept might make them Different, might offend against the Way of Life, take them out of Togetherness, impair their Integration with the Group. They might (horror of horrors!) become individuals.

Screwtape Explains the Disadvantages of War

Of course a war is entertaining. . . . But, if we are not careful, we shall see thousands turning in this tribulation to the Enemy, while tens of thousands who do not go so far as that will nevertheless have their attention diverted from themselves to values and causes which they believe to be higher than the self. I know that the Enemy disapproves many of these causes. But that is where He is so unfair. He often makes prizes of humans who have given their lives for causes He thinks bad on the monstrously sophistical ground that the humans thought them good and were following the best they knew. Consider too what undesirable deaths occur in wartime. Men are killed in places where they knew they might be killed and to which they go, if they are at all of the Enemy's party, prepared. How much better for us if *all* humans died in costly nursing homes amid doctors who lie, nurses who lie, friends who lie, as we have trained them, promising life to the dying, encouraging the belief that sickness excuses every indulgence, and even, if our workers know their job, withholding all suggestion of a priest lest it should betray to the sick man his true condition! And how disastrous for us is the continual remembrance of death which war enforces. One of our best weapons, contented worldliness, is rendered useless. In wartime not even a human can believe that he is going to live forever.

St Martha

Human Death is the result of sin and the triumph of Satan. But it is also the means of redemption from sin, God's medicine for Man and His weapon against Satan. . . .

And one can see how it might have happened. The Enemy persuades Man to rebel against God: Man, by doing so, loses power to control that other rebellion which the Enemy now raises in Man's organism (both psychical and physical) against Man's spirit: just as that organism, in its turn, loses power to maintain itself against the rebellion of the inorganic. In that way, Satan produced human Death. But when God created Man he gave him such a constitution that, if the highest part of it rebelled against Himself, it would be bound to lose control over the lower parts: i.e. in the long run to suffer Death. This provision may be regarded equally as a punitive sentence ('In the day ye eat of that fruit ye shall die'), as a mercy, and as a safety-device. It is punishment because Death – that Death of which Martha says to Christ, 'But ... Sir ... it'll *smell*' – is horror and ignominy. ... It is mercy because by willing and humble surrender to it Man undoes his act of rebellion and makes even this depraved and monstrous mode of Death an instance of that higher and mystical Death which is eternally good and a necessary ingredient in the highest life. ... It is a safety-device because, once Man has fallen, natural immortality would be the one utterly hopeless destiny for him. Added to the surrender that he must make by no external necessity of Death, free (if you call it freedom) to rivet faster and faster about himself through unending centuries the chains of his own pride and lust and of the nightmare civilizations which these build up in ever-increasing power and complication, he would progress from being merely a fallen man to being a fiend, possibly beyond all modes of redemption.

An early peasant Christian might have thought that Christ's sitting at the right hand of the Father really implied two chairs of state, in a certain spatial relation, inside a sky palace. But if the same man afterwards received a philosophical education and discovered that God has no body, parts, or passions, and therefore neither a right hand nor a palace, he would not have felt that the essentials of his belief had been altered. What had mattered to him, even in the days of his simplicity, had not been supposed details about celestial furniture. It had been the assurance that the once crucified Master was now the supreme Agent of the unimaginable Power on whom the whole universe depends. And he would recognize that in this he had never been deceived.

The critic may still ask us why the imagery – which we admit to be untrue – should be used at all. But he has not noticed that any language we attempt to substitute for it would involve imagery that is open to all the same objections. To say that God 'enters' the natural order involves just as much spatial imagery as to say that He 'comes down'; one has simply substituted horizontal (or undefined) for vertical movement. To say that He is 're-absorbed' into the Noumenal is better than to say He 'ascended' into Heaven, only if the picture of something dissolving in warm fluid, or being sucked into a throat, is less misleading than the picture of a bird, or a balloon, going up. All language, except about objects of sense, is metaphorical through and through. To call God a 'Force' (that is, something like a wind or a dynamo) is as metaphorical as to call Him a Father or a King. On such matters we can make our language more polysyllabic and duller: we cannot make it more literal.

St Ignatius Loyola . . . advised his pupils to begin their meditations with what he called a *compositio loci*. The Nativity or the Marriage at Cana, or whatever the theme might be, was to be visualized in the fullest possible detail. One of his English followers would even have us look up 'what good Authors write of those places' so as to get the topography, 'the height of the hills and the situation of the townes', correct. Now for two different reasons this is not 'addressed to my condition'.

One is that I live in an archaeological age. We can no longer, as St Ignatius could, believingly introduce the clothes, furniture, and utensils of our own age into ancient Palestine. I'd know I wasn't getting them right. I'd know that the very sky and sunlight of those latitudes were different from any my northern imagination could supply. I could no doubt pretend to myself a naïvety I don't really possess; but that would cast an unreality over the whole exercise.

The second reason is more important. St Ignatius was a great master, and I am sure he knew what his pupils needed. I conclude that they were people whose visual imagination was weak and needed to be stimulated. But the trouble with people like ourselves is the exact reverse. We can say this to one another because, in our mouths, it is not a boast but a confession. We are agreed that the power – indeed, the compulsion – to visualize is not 'Imagination' in the higher sense, not the Imagination which makes a man either a great author or a sensitive reader. Ridden on a *very* tight rein, this visualizing power can sometimes serve true Imagination; very often it merely gets in the way.

If I started with a *compositio loci* I should never reach the meditation. The picture would go on elaborating itself indefinitely and becoming every moment of less spiritual relevance.

Looking 'Along' and Looking 'At' August 1

I was standing today in the dark toolshed. The sun was shining outside and through the crack at the top of the door there came a sunbeam. From where I stood that beam of light, with the specks of dust floating in it, was the most striking thing in the place. Everything else was almost pitch black. I was seeing the beam, not seeing things by it.

Then I moved, so that the beam fell on my eyes. Instantly the whole previous picture vanished. I saw no toolshed, and (above all) no beam. Instead I saw, framed in the irregular cranny at the top of the door, green leaves moving on the branches of a tree outside and beyond that, ninety-odd million miles away, the sun. Looking along the beam, and looking at the beam are very different experiences.

But this is only a very simple example of the difference between looking at and looking along. A young man meets a girl. The whole world looks different when he sees her. Her voice reminds him of something he has been trying to remember all his life, and ten minutes' casual chat with her is more precious than all the favours that all other women in the world could grant. He is, as they say, 'in love'. Now comes a scientist and describes this young man's experience from the outside. For him it is all an affair of the young man's genes and a recognized biological stimulus. That is the difference between looking *along* the sexual impulse and looking *at* it.

Which Tells You Most about the Thing? August 2

When you have got into the habit of making this distinction you will find examples of it all day long. The mathematician sits thinking, and to him it seems that he is contemplating timeless and spaceless truths about quantity. But the cerebral physiologist, if he could look inside the mathematician's head, would find nothing timeless and spaceless there – only tiny movements in the grey matter. The savage dances in ecstasy at midnight before Nyonga and feels with every muscle that his dance is helping to bring the new green crops and the spring rain and the babies. The anthropologist, observing that savage, records that he is performing a fertility ritual of the type so-and-so. The girl cries over her broken doll and feels that she has lost a real friend; the psychologist says that her nascent maternal instinct has been temporarily lavished on a bit of shaped and coloured wax.

As soon as you have grasped this simple distinction, it raises a question. You get one experience of a thing when you look along it and another when you look at it. Which is the 'true' or 'valid' experience? Which tells you most about the thing? And you can hardly ask that question without noticing that for the last fifty years or so everyone has been taking the answer for granted. It has been assumed without discussion that if you want the true account of religion you must go, not to religious people, but to anthropologists; that if you want the true account of sexual love you must go, not to lovers, but to psychologists; that if you want to understand some 'ideology' (such as medieval chivalry or the nineteenth-century idea of a 'gentleman'), you must listen not to those who lived inside it, but to sociologists.

The 'Modern' Type of Thought   *August 3*

The people who look *at* things have had it all their own way; the people who look *along* things have simply been browbeaten. It has even come to be taken for granted that the external account of a thing somehow refutes or 'debunks' the account given from inside. 'All these moral ideals which look so transcendental and beautiful from inside,' says the wiseacre, 'are really only a mass of biological instincts and inherited taboos.' And no one plays the game the other way round by replying, 'If you will only step inside, the things that look to you like instincts and taboos will suddenly reveal their real and transcendental nature.'

That, in fact, is the whole basis of the specifically 'modern' type of thought. And is it not, you will ask, a very sensible basis? For, after all, we are often deceived by things from the inside. For example, the girl who looks so wonderful while we're in love, may really be a very plain, stupid, and disagreeable person. The savage's dance to Nyonga does not really cause the crops to grow. Having been so often deceived by looking along, are we not well advised to trust only to looking at? – in fact to discount all these inside experiences?

Well, no. There are two fatal objections to discounting them *all*. And the first is this. You discount them in order to think more accurately. But you can't think at all – and therefore, of course, can't think accurately – if you have nothing to think *about*. A physiologist, for example, can study pain and find out that it 'is' (whatever *is* means) such and such neural events. But the word *pain* would have no meaning for him unless he had 'been inside' by actually suffering. If he had never looked *along* pain he simply wouldn't know what he was looking *at*. The very subject for his inquiries from outside exists for him only because he has, at least once, been inside.

Thought Busily Working in a Vacuum   *August 4*

This case is not likely to occur, because every man has felt pain. But it is perfectly easy to go on all your life giving explanations of religion, love, morality, honour, and the like, without having been inside any of them. And if you do that, you are simply playing with counters.

You go on explaining a thing without knowing what it is. That is why a great deal of contemporary thought is, strictly speaking, thought about nothing – all the apparatus of thought busily working in a vacuum.

The other objection is this: let us go back to the toolshed. I might have discounted what I saw when looking along the beam (i.e., the leaves moving and the sun) on the ground that it was 'really only a strip of dusty light in a dark shed'. That is, I might have set up as 'true' my 'side vision' of the beam. But then that side vision is itself an instance of the activity we call seeing. And this new instance could also be looked at from outside. I could allow a scientist to tell me that what seemed to be a beam of light in a shed was 'really only an agitation of my own optic nerves'. And that would be just as good (or as bad) a bit of debunking as the previous one. The picture of the beam in the toolshed would not have to be discounted, just as the previous picture of the trees and the sun had been discounted. And then, where are you?

In other words, you can step outside one experience only by stepping inside another. Therefore, if all inside experiences are misleading, we are always misled. The cerebral physiologist may say, if he chooses, that the mathematician's thought is 'only' tiny physical movements of the grey matter. But then what about the cerebral physiologist's own thought at that very moment? A second physiologist, looking at it, could pronounce it also to be only tiny physical movements in the first physiologist's skull. Where is the rot to end?

We Must Look Both 'Along' and 'At' Everything   *August 5*

The answer is that we must never allow the rot to begin. We must, on pain of idiocy, deny from the very outset the idea that looking *at* is, by its own nature, intrinsically truer or better than looking *along*. One must look both *along* and *at* everything. In particular cases we shall find reason for regarding the one or the other vision as inferior. Thus the inside vision of rational thinking must be truer than the outside vision which sees only movements of the grey matter; for if the outside vision were the correct one all thought (including this thought itself) would be valueless, and this is self-contradictory. You cannot have a proof that no proofs matter. On the other hand, the inside vision of the savage's dance to Nyonga may be found deceptive because we find reason to believe that crops and babies are not really affected by it. In fact, we must take each case on its merits. But we must start with no prejudice for or against either kind of looking. We do not know in advance whether the lover or the psychologist is giving the more correct account of love, or whether both accounts are equally correct in different ways, or whether both are equally wrong. We just have to find out. But the period of browbeating has got to end.

The Transfiguration of the Lord   August 6

The Transfiguration or 'Metamorphosis' of Jesus is . . . no doubt an anticipatory glimpse of something to come. He is seen conversing with two of the ancient dead. The change which His own human form had undergone is described as one to luminosity, to 'shining whiteness'. A similar whiteness characterizes His appearance at the beginning of the Book of Revelation. One rather curious detail is that this shining or whiteness affected His clothes as much as His body. St Mark indeed mentions the clothes more explicitly than the face, and adds, with his inimitable naïvety, that 'no laundry could do anything like it'. Taken by itself this episode bears all the marks of a 'vision': that is, of an experience which, though it may be divinely sent and may reveal great truth, yet is not, objectively speaking, the experience it seems to be. But if the theory of 'vision' (or holy hallucination) will not cover the Resurrection appearances, it would be only a multiplying of hypotheses to introduce it here. We do not know to what phase or feature of the New Creation this episode points. It may reveal some special glorifying of Christ's manhood at some phase of its history (since history it apparently has), or it may reveal the glory which that manhood always has in its New Creation: it may even reveal a glory which all risen men will inherit.

Using a Crucifix   *August 7*

A particular toy or a particular ikon may be itself a work of art, but that is logically accidental; its artistic merits will not make it a better toy or a better ikon. They may make it a worse one. For its purpose is, not to fix attention upon itself, but to stimulate and liberate certain activities in the child or the worshipper. The teddy bear exists in order that the child may endow it with imaginary life and personality and enter into a quasi-social relationship with it. That is what 'playing with it' means. The better this activity succeeds the less the actual appearance of the object will matter. Too close or prolonged attention to its changeless and expressionless face impedes the play. A crucifix exists in order to direct the worshipper's thought and affections to the Passion. It had better not have any excellences, subtleties, or originalities which will fix attention upon itself. Hence devout people may, for this purpose, prefer the crudest and emptiest ikon. The emptier, the more permeable; and they want, as it were, to pass through the material image and go beyond.

The Crucifixion as an Aid to Devotion   *August 8*

There is indeed one mental image which does not lure
me away into trivial elaborations. I mean the Crucifixion
itself; not seen in terms of all the pictures and crucifixes,
but as we must suppose it to have been in its raw, historical reality. But even this is of less spiritual value than one
might expect. Compunction, compassion, gratitude – all
the fruitful emotions – are strangled. Sheer physical
horror leaves no room for them. Nightmare. Even so, the
image ought to be periodically faced. But no one could
live with it. It did not become a frequent motive of
Christian art until the generations which had seen real
crucifixions were all dead. As for many hymns and
sermons on the subject – endlessly harping on blood, as if
that were all that mattered – they must be the work
either of people so far above me that they can't reach me,
or else of people with no imagination at all. (Some might
be cut off from me by both these gulfs.)

Yet mental images play an important part in my
prayers. I doubt if any act of will or thought or emotion
occurs in me without them. But they seem to help me
most when they are most fugitive and fragmentary – rising
and bursting like bubbles in champagne or wheeling like
rooks in a windy sky: contradicting one another (in logic)
as the crowded metaphors of a swift poet may do. Fix on
any one, and it goes dead. You must do as Blake would do
with a joy; kiss it as it flies. And then, in their total effect,
they do mediate to me something very important.

Our Holy Obligation   *August 9*

When I first became a Christian . . . I thought that I could
do it on my own, by retiring to my rooms and reading
theology, and I wouldn't go to the churches and gospel
halls; and then later I found that it was the only way of

flying your flag; and, of course, I found that this meant being a target. It is extraordinary how inconvenient to your family it becomes for you to get up early to go to church. It doesn't matter so much if you get up early for anything else, but if you get up early to go to church it's very selfish of you and you upset the house. If there is anything in the teaching of the New Testament which is in the nature of a command, it is that you are obliged to take the Sacrament, and you can't do it without going to church.

A Fixed Form of Service   *August 10*

The advantage of a fixed form of service is that we know what is coming. *Ex tempore* public prayer has this difficulty: we don't know whether we can mentally join in it until we've heard it – it might be phoney or heretical. We are therefore called upon to carry on a *critical* and a *devotional* activity at the same moment: two things hardly compatible. In a fixed form we ought to have 'gone through the motions' before in our private prayers; the rigid form really sets our devotions *free.* I also find the more rigid it is, the easier it is to keep one's thoughts from straying. Also it prevents getting too completely eaten up by whatever happens to be the preoccupation of the moment (i.e. war, an election, or what not). The *permanent* shape of Christianity shows through.

The Proper Pleasure of Ritual   *August 11*

This will be understood by any one who really understands the meaning of the Middle English word *solempne.* This means something different, but not quite different, from modern English *solemn.* Like *solemn* it implies the opposite of what is familiar, free and easy, or ordinary. But unlike *solemn* it does not suggest gloom, oppression, or austerity. The ball in the first act of *Romeo and Juliet* was a 'solemnity'. The feast at the beginning of *Gawain and the Green Knight* is very much of a solemnity. A great mass by Mozart or Beethoven is as much a solemnity in its hilarious *gloria* as in its poignant *crucifixus est*. Feasts are, in this sense, *more* solemn than fasts. Easter is *solempne*, Good Friday is not. The *solempne* is the festal which is also the stately and the ceremonial, the proper occasion for *pomp* – and the very fact that *pompous* is now used only in a bad sense measures the degree to which we have lost the old idea of 'solemnity'. To recover it you must think of a court ball, or a coronation, or a victory march, as these things appear to people who *enjoy* them; in an age when everyone puts on his oldest clothes to be happy in, you must re-awake the simpler state of mind in which people put on gold and scarlet to be happy in. Above all, you must be rid of the hideous idea, fruit of a widespread inferiority complex, that pomp, on the proper occasions, has any connection with vanity or self-conceit. A celebrant approaching the altar, a princess led out by a king to dance a minuet, a general officer on a ceremonial parade, a major domo preceding the boar's head at a Christmas feast – all these wear unusual clothes and move with calculated dignity. This does not mean that they are vain, but that they are obedient; they are obeying the *hoc age* which presides over every solemnity. The modern habit of doing ceremonial things unceremoniously is no proof of humility; rather it proves the offender's inability to forget himself in the rite, and his readiness to spoil for everyone else the proper pleasure of ritual.

I think our business as laymen is to take what we are given and make the best of it. And I think we should find this a great deal easier if what we were given was always and everywhere the same.

To judge from their practice, very few Anglican clergymen take this view. It looks as if they believed people can be lured to go to church by incessant brightenings, lightenings, lengthenings, abridgements, simplifications, and complications of the service. And it is probably true that a new, keen vicar will usually be able to form within his parish a minority who are in favour of his innovations. The majority, I believe, never are. Those who remain – many give up churchgoing altogether – merely endure.

Is this simply because the majority are hidebound? I think not. They have a good reason for their conservatism. Novelty, simply as such, can have only an entertainment value. And they don't go to church to be entertained. They go to *use* the service, or, if you prefer, to *enact* it. Every service is a structure of acts and words through which we receive a sacrament, or repent, or supplicate, or adore. And it enables us to do these things best – if you like, it 'works' best – when, through long familiarity, we don't have to think about it. As long as you notice, and have to count, the steps, you are not yet dancing but only learning to dance. A good shoe is a shoe you don't notice. Good reading becomes possible when you need not consciously think about eyes, or light, or print, or spelling. The perfect church service would be one we were almost unaware of; our attention would have been on God.

The Liturgical Fidget

Novelty may fix our attention not even on the service but on the celebrant. You know what I mean. Try as one may to exclude it, the question 'What on earth is he up to now?' will intrude. It lays one's devotion waste. There is really some excuse for the man who said, 'I wish they'd remember that the charge to Peter was Feed my sheep; not Try experiments on my rats, or even, Teach my performing dogs new tricks.'

Thus my whole liturgiological position really boils down to an entreaty for permanence and uniformity. I can make do with almost any kind of service whatever, if only it will stay put. But if each form is snatched away just when I am beginning to feel at home in it, then I can never make any progress in the art of worship. You give me no chance to acquire the trained habit – *habito dell 'arte.*

It may well be that some variations which seem to me merely matters of taste really involve grave doctrinal differences. But surely not all? For if grave doctrinal differences are really as numerous as variations in practice, then we shall have to conclude that no such thing as the Church of England exists. And anyway, the Liturgical Fidget is not a purely Anglican phenomenon; I have heard Roman Catholics complain of it too.

Membership in the Body of Christ

No Christian and, indeed, no historian could accept the epigram which defines religion as 'what a man does with his solitude'. It was one of the Wesleys, I think, who said that the New Testament knows nothing of solitary religion. We are forbidden to neglect the assembling of ourselves together. Christianity is already institutional in the earliest of its documents. The Church is the Bride of Christ. We are members of one another.

In our own age the idea that religion belongs to our private life – that it is, in fact, an occupation for the individual's hour of leisure – is at once paradoxical, dangerous, and natural. It is paradoxical because this exaltation of the individual in the religious field springs up in an age when collectivism is ruthlessly defeating the individual in every other field. . . . There is a crowd of busybodies, self-appointed masters of ceremonies, whose life is devoted to destroying solitude wherever solitude still exists. They call it 'taking the young people out of themselves', or 'waking them up', or 'overcoming their apathy'. If an Augustine, a Vaughan, a Traherne or a Wordsworth should be born in the modern world, the leaders of a Youth Organization would soon cure him. If a really good home, such as the home of Alcinous and Arete in the *Odyssey* or the Rostovs in *War and Peace* or any of Charlotte M. Yonge's families, existed today, it would be denounced as *bourgeois* and every engine of destruction would be levelled against it. And even where the planners fail and someone is left physically by himself, the wireless has seen to it that he will be – in a sense not intended by Scipio – never less alone than when alone. We live, in fact, in a world starved for solitude, silence, and privacy: and therefore starved for meditation and true friendship.

The Intrusion of Collectivism   *August 15*

That religion should be relegated to solitude in such an age is, then, paradoxical. But it is also dangerous for two reasons. In the first place, when the modern world says to us aloud, 'You may be religious when you are alone', it adds under its breath, 'and I will see to it that you never are alone.' To make Christianity a private affair while banishing all privacy is to relegate it to the rainbow's end or the Greek Calends. That is one of the enemy's stratagems. In the second place, there is the danger that real Christians who know that Christianity is not a solitary affair may react against that error by simply transporting into our spiritual life that same collectivism which has already conquered our secular life. That is the enemy's other stratagem. Like a good chess player he is always trying to manoeuvre you into a position where you can save your castle only by losing your bishop. In order to avoid the trap we must insist that though the private conception of Christianity is an error it is a profoundly natural one, and is clumsily attempting to guard a great truth. Behind it is the obvious feeling that our modern collectivism is an outrage upon human nature and that from this, as from all other evils, God will be our shield and buckler.

The Purpose of the Secular Community   *August 16*

As personal and private life is lower than participation in the Body of Christ, so the collective life is lower than the personal and private life and has no value save in its service. The secular community, since it exists for our natural good and not for our supernatural, has no higher end than to facilitate and safeguard the family, and friendship, and solitude. To be happy at home, said Johnson, is the end of all human endeavour. As long as we are thinking only of natural values we must say that the sun looks down on nothing half so good as a household laughing together over a meal, or two friends talking over a pint of beer, or a man alone reading a book that interests him; and that all economics, politics, laws, armies, and institutions, save in so far as they prolong and multiply such scenes, are a mere ploughing the sand and sowing the ocean, a meaningless vanity and vexation of spirit. Collective activities are, of course, necessary; but this is the end to which they are necessary. Great sacrifices of this private happiness by those who have it may be necessary in order that it may be more widely distributed. All may have to be a little hungry in order that none may starve. But do not let us mistake necessary evils for good. The mistake is easily made. Fruit has to be tinned if it is to be transported, and has to lose thereby some of its good qualities. But one meets people who have learned actually to prefer the tinned fruit to the fresh. A sick society must think much about politics, as a sick man must think much about his digestion: to ignore the subject may be fatal cowardice for the one as for the other. But if either comes to regard it as the natural food of the mind – if either forgets that we think of such things only in order to be able to think of something else – then what was undertaken for the sake of health has become itself a new and deadly disease.

Our Only Safeguard Against Collectivism   *August 17*

There is, in fact, a fatal tendency in all human activities for the means to encroach upon the very ends which they were intended to serve. Thus money comes to hinder the exchange of commodities, and rules of art to hamper genius, and examinations to prevent young men from becoming learned. It does not, unfortunately, always follow that the encroaching means can be dispensed with. I think it probable that the collectivism of our life is necessary and will increase; and I think that our only safeguard against its deathly properties is in a Christian life; for we were promised that we could handle serpents and drink deadly things and yet live. That is the truth behind the erroneous definition of religion with which we started. Where it went wrong was in opposing to the collective mass mere solitude. The Christian is called, not to individualism but to membership in the mystical body. A consideration of the differences between the secular collective and the mystical body is therefore the first step to understanding how Christianity without being individualistic can yet counteract collectivism.

The Biblical Meaning of 'Members'   *August 18*

At the outset we are hampered by a difficulty of language. The very word *membership* is of Christian origin, but it has been taken over by the world and emptied of all meaning. In any book on logic you may see the expression 'members of a class'. It must be most emphatically stated that the items or particulars included in a homogeneous class are almost the reverse of what St Paul meant by *members*. By *members* ($\mu\acute{\epsilon}\lambda\eta$) he meant what we should call *organs*, things essentially different from, and complementary to, one another: things differing not only in structure and function but also in dignity. Thus, in a club, the committee as a whole, and the servants as a whole, may both properly be regarded as 'members'; what we should call the members of the club are merely units. A row of identically dressed and identically trained soldiers set side by side, or a number of citizens listed as voters in a constituency, are not members of anything in the Pauline sense. I am afraid that when we describe a man as 'a member of the Church' we usually mean nothing Pauline: we mean only that he is a unit – that he is one more specimen of the same kind of thing as X and Y and Z. How true membership in a body differs from inclusion in a collective may be seen in the structure of a family. The grandfather, the parents, the grown-up son, the child, the dog, and the cat are true members (in the organic sense) precisely because they are not members or units of a homogeneous class. They are not interchangeable. Each person is almost a species in himself. The mother is not

210

simply a different person from the daughter, she is a different kind of person. The grown-up brother is not simply one unit in the class children, he is a separate estate of the realm. The father and grandfather are almost as different as the cat and the dog. If you subtract any one member you have not simply reduced the family in number, you have inflicted an injury on its structure. Its unity is a unity of unlikes, almost of incommensurables.

Differences in Kind   *August 19*

A dim perception of the richness inherent in this kind of unity is one reason why we enjoy a book like *The Wind in the Willows*; a trio such as Rat, Mole, and Badger symbolizes the extreme differentiation of persons in harmonious union which we know intuitively to be our true refuge both from solitude and from the collective. The affection between such oddly matched couples as Dick Swiveller and the Marchioness, or Mr Pickwick and Sam Weller, pleases in the same way. That is why the modern notion that children should call their parents by their Christian names is so perverse. For this is an effort to ignore the difference in kind which makes for real organic unity. They are trying to inoculate the child with the preposterous view that one's mother is simply a fellow citizen like anyone else, to make it ignorant of what all men know and insensible to what all men feel. They are trying to drag the featureless repetitions of the collective into the fuller and more concrete world of the family.

A convict has a number instead of a name. That is the collective idea carried to its extreme.

211

The society into which the Christian is called at baptism is not a collective but a Body. It is in fact that Body of which the family is an image on the natural level. If anyone came to it with the misconception that membership of the Church was membership in a debased modern sense – a massing together of persons as if they were pennies or counters – he would be corrected at the threshold by the discovery that the Head of this Body is so unlike the inferior members that they share no predicate with Him save by analogy. We are summoned from the outset to combine as creatures with our Creator, as mortals with immortal, as redeemed sinners with sinless Redeemer. His presence, the interaction between Him and us, must always be the overwhelmingly dominant factor in the life we are to lead within the Body; and any conception of Christian fellowship which does not mean primarily fellowship with Him is out of court. After that it seems almost trivial to trace further down the diversity of operations to the unity of the Spirit. But it is very plainly there. There are priests divided from the laity, catechumens divided from those who are in full fellowship. There is authority of husbands over wives and parents over children. There is, in forms too subtle for official embodiment, a continual interchange of complementary ministrations. We are all constantly teaching and learning, forgiving and being forgiven, representing Christ to man when we intercede, and man to Christ when others intercede for us. The sacrifice of selfish privacy which is daily demanded of us is daily repaid a hundredfold in the true growth of personality which the life of the Body encourages. Those who are members of one another become as diverse as the hand and the ear. That is why the worldlings are so monotonously alike compared with the almost fantastic variety of the saints. Obedience is the road to freedom, humility the road to pleasure, unity the road to personality.

You have often heard that, though in the world we hold different stations, yet we are all equal in the sight of God. There are of course senses in which this is true. God is no accepter of persons: His love for us is not measured by our social rank or our intellectual talents. But I believe there is a sense in which this maxim is the reverse of the truth. I am going to venture to say that artificial equality is necessary in the life of the State, but that in the Church we strip off this disguise, we recover our real inequalities, and are thereby refreshed and quickened. . . .

I believe the authority of parent over child, husband over wife, learned over simple, to have been as much a part of the original plan as the authority of man over beast. I believe that if we had not fallen Filmer would be right, and patriarchal monarchy would be the sole lawful government. But since we have learned sin, we have found, as Lord Acton says, that 'all power corrupts, and absolute power corrupts absolutely'. The only remedy has been to take away the powers and substitute a legal fiction of equality. . . .

Equality is a quantitative term and therefore love often knows nothing of it. Authority exercised with humility, and obedience accepted with delight are the very lines along which our spirits live. Even in the life of the affections, much more in the Body of Christ, we step outside that world which says 'I am as good as you'. It is like turning from a march to a dance. It is like taking off our clothes. We become, as Chesterton said, taller when we bow; we become lowlier when we instruct. It delights me that there should be moments in the services of my own Church when the priest stands and I kneel. As democracy becomes more complete in the outer world and opportunities for reverence are successively removed, the refreshment, the cleansing, and invigorating returns to inequality, which the Church offers us, become more and more necessary.

A rejection, or in Scripture's strong language, a cruci-fixion of the natural self is the passport to everlasting life. Nothing that has not died will be resurrected. That is just how Christianity cuts across the antithesis between indi-vidualism and collectivism. There lies the maddening ambiguity of our faith as it must appear to outsiders. It sets its face relentlessly against our natural individual-ism; on the other hand, it gives back to those who abandon individualism an eternal possession of their own personal being, even of their bodies. As mere biological entities, each with its separate will to live and to expand, we are apparently of no account; we are cross-fodder. But as organs in the Body of Christ, as stones and pillars in the temple, we are assured of our eternal self-identity and shall live to remember the galaxies as an old tale.

This may be put in another way. Personality is eternal and inviolable. But then, personality is not a datum from which we start. The individualism in which we all begin is only a parody or shadow of it. True personality lies ahead – how far ahead, for most of us, I dare not say. And the key to it does not lie in ourselves. It will not be attained by development from within outwards. It will come to us when we occupy those places in the structure of the eternal cosmos for which we were designed or invented. As a colour first reveals its true quality when placed by an excellent artist in its pre-elected spot be-tween certain others, as a spice reveals its true flavour when inserted just where and when a good cook wishes among the other ingredients, as the dog becomes really doggy only when he has taken his place in the household of man, so we shall then first be true persons when we have suffered ourselves to be fitted into our places.

Starting with the doctrine that every individuality is 'of infinite value' we then picture God as a kind of employment committee whose business it is to find suitable careers for all souls, square holes for square pegs. In fact, however, the value of the individual does not lie in him. He is capable of receiving value. He receives it by union with Christ. There is no question of finding for him a place in the living temple which will do justice to his inherent value and give scope to his natural idiosyncrasy. The place was there first. The man was created for it. He will not be himself till he is there. We shall be true and everlasting and really divine persons only in Heaven. . . .

To say this is to repeat what everyone here admits already – that we are saved by grace, that in our flesh dwells no good thing, that we are, through and through, creatures not creators, derived beings, living not of ourselves but from Christ. If I seem to have complicated a simple matter, you will, I hope, forgive me. I have been anxious to bring out two points. I have wanted to try to expel that quite un-Christian worship of the human individual simply as such which is so rampant in modern thought side by side with our collectivism; for one error begets the opposite error and, far from neutralizing, they aggravate each other. I mean the pestilent notion (one sees it in literary criticism) that each of us starts with a treasure called 'Personality' locked up inside him, and that to expand and express this, to guard it from interference, to be 'original', is the main end of life. This is Pelagian, or worse, and it defeats even itself. No man who values originality will ever be original. But try to tell the truth as you see it, try to do any bit of work as well as it can be done for the work's sake, and what men call originality will come unsought. Even on that level, the submission of the individual to the function is already beginning to bring true Personality to birth. And secondly, I have wanted to show that Christianity is not, in the long run, concerned either with individuals or communities. Neither the individual nor the community as popular thought understands them can inherit eternal life: neither the natural self, nor the collective mass, but a new creature.

St Bartholomew, Apostle August 24

Surely God saves different souls in different ways? To preach instantaneous conversion and eternal security as if they must be the experiences of all who are saved, seems to me very dangerous: the very way to drive some into presumption and others into despair. How very different were the callings of the disciples. I don't agree that if anyone were completely a new creature, you and I would necessarily recognize him as such. It takes holiness to detect holiness.

Modern Criticism August 25

What are the key words of modern criticism? *Creative*, with its opposite *derivative*; *spontaneity*, with its opposite *convention*; *freedom*, contrasted with *rules*. Great authors are innovators, pioneers, explorers; bad authors bunch in schools and follow models. Or again, great authors are always 'breaking fetters' and 'bursting bonds'. They have personality, they 'are themselves'. I do not know whether we often think out the implication of such language into a consistent philosophy; but we certainly have a general picture of bad work flowing from conformity and discipleship, and of good work bursting out from certain centres of explosive force – apparently self-originating force – which we call men of genius.

Now the New Testament has nothing at all to tell us of

literature. I know that there are some who like to think of Our Lord Himself as a poet and cite the parables to support their view. I admit freely that to believe in the Incarnation at all is to believe that every mode of human excellence is implicit in His historical human character: poethood, of course, included. But if all had been developed, the limitations of a single human life would have been transcended and He would not have been a man; therefore all excellences save the spiritual remained in varying degrees implicit.

Becoming Clean Mirrors   *August 26*

In the New Testament the art of life itself is an art of imitation: can we, believing this, believe that literature, which must derive from real life, is to aim at being 'creative', 'original', and 'spontaneous'? 'Originality' in the New Testament is quite plainly the prerogative of God alone; even within the triune being of God it seems to be confined to the Father. The duty and happiness of every other being is placed in being derivative, in reflecting like a mirror. Nothing could be more foreign to the tone of Scripture than the language of those who describe a saint as a 'moral genius' or a 'spiritual genius' thus insinuating that his virtue or spirituality is 'creative' or 'original'. If I have read the New Testament aright, it leaves no room for 'creativeness' even in a modified or metaphorical sense. Our whole destiny seems to lie in the opposite direction, in being as little as possible ourselves, in acquiring a fragrance that is not our own but borrowed, in becoming clean mirrors filled with the image of a face that is not ours. I am not here supporting the doctrine of total depravity, and I do not say that the New Testament supports it; I am saying only that the highest good of a creature must be creaturely – that is, derivative or reflective – good. In other words, as St

Augustine makes plain (*De Civ. Dei* xii, cap. I), pride does not only go before a fall but is a fall – a fall of the creature's attention from what is better, God, to what is worse, itself.

Two Attitudes Towards the Self   *August 27*

The unbeliever may take his own temperament and experience, just as they happen to stand, and consider them worth communicating simply because they are facts or, worse still, because they are his. To the Christian his own temperament and experience, as mere fact, and as merely his, are of no value or importance whatsoever: he will deal with them, if at all, only because they are the medium through which, or the position from which, something universally profitable appeared to him. We can imagine two men seated in different parts of a church or theatre. Both, when they come out, may tell us their experiences, and both may use the first person. But the one is interested in his seat only because it was his – 'I was most uncomfortable', he will say. 'You would hardly believe what a draught comes in from the door in that corner. And the people! I had to speak pretty sharply to the woman in front of me.' The other will tell us what could be seen from his seat, choosing to describe this because this is what he knows, and because every seat must give the best view of something. 'Do you know,' he will begin, 'the moulding on those pillars goes on round at the back. It looks, too, as if the design on the back were the older of the two.' Here we have the expressionist and the Christian attitudes towards the self or temperament. Thus St Augustine and Rousseau both write *Confessions*; but to the one his own temperament is a kind of absolute (*au moins je suis autre*), to the other it is 'a narrow house too narrow for Thee to enter – oh make it wide. It is in ruins – oh rebuild it'. . . .

The Christian writer may be self-taught or original . . . but if his talents are such that he can produce good work by writing in an established form and dealing with experiences common to all his race, he will do so just as gladly. I even think he will do so more gladly. It is to him an argument not of strength but of weakness that he should respond fully to the vision only 'in his own way'. And always, of every idea and of every method he will ask not 'Is it mine?', but 'Is it good?'

St Augustine of Hippo   August 28

Everyone has noticed how hard it is to turn our thoughts to God when everything is going well with us. We 'have all we want' is a terrible saying when 'all' does not include God. We find God an interruption. As St Augustine says somewhere, 'God wants to give us something, but cannot, because our hands are full – there's nowhere for Him to put it.' Or as a friend of mine said, 'We regard God as an airman regards his parachute; it's there for emergencies but he hopes he'll never have to use it.' Now God, who has made us, knows what we are and that our happiness lies in Him. Yet we will not seek it in Him as long as He leaves us any other resort where it can even plausibly be looked for. While what we call 'our own life' remains agreeable we will not surrender it to Him. What then can God do in our interests but make 'our own life' less agreeable to us, and take away the plausible sources of false happiness? It is just here, where God's providence seems at first to be most cruel, that the Divine humility, the stooping down of the Highest, most deserves praise.

My own professional work, though conditioned by taste
and talents, is immediately motivated by the need for
earning my living. And on earning one's living I was
relieved to note that Christianity, in spite of its revolutionary and apocalyptic elements, can be delight-
fully humdrum. The Baptist did not give the tax gather-
ers and soldiers lectures on the immediate necessity of
turning the economic and military system of the ancient
world upside down; he told them to obey the moral law –
as they had presumably learned it from their mothers and
nurses – and sent them back to their jobs. St Paul advised
the Thessalonians to stick to their work (1 Thessalonians
4:11) and not to become busybodies (2 Thessalonians
3:11). The need for money is therefore *simpliciter* an
innocent, though by no means a splendid, motive for any
occupation. The Ephesians are warned to work pro-
fessionally at something that is 'good' (Ephesians 4:28). I
hoped that 'good' here did not mean much more than
'harmless', and I was certain it did not imply anything
very elevated. Provided, then, that there was a demand
for culture, and that culture was not actually deleterious,
I concluded I was justified in making my living by
supplying that demand – and that all others in my position (dons, schoolmasters, professional authors, critics,
reviewers) were similarly justified; especially if, like me,
they had few or no talents for any other career – if their
'vocation' to a cultural profession consisted in the brute
fact of not being fit for anything else.

But is culture even harmless? It certainly can be harmful and often is. If a Christian found himself in the position of one inaugurating a new society *in vacuo* he might well decide not to introduce something whose abuse is so easy and whose use is, at any rate, not necessary. But that is not our position. The abuse of culture is already there, and will continue whether Christians cease to be cultured or not. It is therefore probably better that the ranks of the 'culture sellers' should include some Christians – as an antidote. It may even be the duty of some Christians to be culture sellers. Not that I have yet said anything to show that even the lawful use of culture stands very high. The lawful use might be no more than innocent pleasure; but if the abuse is common, the task of resisting that abuse might be not only lawful but obligatory. . . . I must add that when I speak of 'resisting the abuse of culture' I do not mean that a Christian should take money for supplying one thing (culture) and use the opportunity thus gained to supply a quite different thing (homilectics and apologetics). That is stealing. The mere presence of Christians in the ranks of the culture sellers will inevitably provide an antidote. . . .

When I ask what culture has done to me personally, the most obviously true answer is that it has given me quite an enormous amount of pleasure. I have no doubt at all that pleasure is in itself a good and pain in itself an evil; if not, then the whole Christian tradition about heaven and hell and the Passion of Our Lord seems to have no meaning. Pleasure, then, is good; a 'sinful' pleasure means a good offered, and accepted, under conditions which involve a bréach of the moral law. The pleasures of culture are not intrinsically bound up with such conditions. . . . Often, as Newman saw, they are an excellent diversion from guilty pleasures. We may, therefore, enjoy them ourselves, and lawfully, even charitably, teach others to enjoy them.

My general case may be stated . . . that culture is a store-house of the best (sub-Christian) values. These values are in themselves of the soul, not the spirit. But God created the soul. Its values may be expected, therefore, to contain some reflection or antepast of the spiritual values. They will save no man. They resemble the regenerate life only as affection resembles charity, or honour resembles virtue, or the moon the sun. But though 'like is not the same', it is better than unlike. Imitation may pass into initiation. For some it is a good beginning. For others it is not; culture is not everyone's road into Jerusalem, and for some it is a road out.

There is another way in which it may predispose to conversion. The difficulty of converting an uneducated man nowadays lies in his complacency. Popularized science, the conventions or 'unconventions' of his immediate circle, party programmes, etc., enclose him in a tiny windowless universe which he mistakes for the only possible universe. There are no distant horizons, no mysteries. He thinks everything has been settled. A cultured person, on the other hand, is almost compelled to be aware that reality is very odd and that the ultimate truth, whatever it may be, *must* have the characteristics of strangeness – *must* be something that would seem remote and fantastic to the uncultured. . . . On these grounds I conclude that culture has a distinct part to play in bringing certain souls to Christ. Not all souls – there is a shorter, and safer, way which has always been followed by thousands of simple affectional natures who begin, where we hope to end, with devotion to the person of Christ.

Sunlight at Second Hand September 1

Has it any part to play in the life of the converted? I think
so, and in two ways. (a) If all the cultural values, on the
way up to Christianity, were dim antepasts and ectypes
of the truth, we can recognize them as such still. And
since we must rest and play, where can we do so better
than here – in the suburbs of Jerusalem? It is lawful to
rest our eyes in moonlight – especially now that we
know where it comes from, that it is only sunlight at
second hand. (b) Whether the purely contemplative life
is, or is not, desirable for any, it is certainly not the
vocation of all. Most men must glorify God by doing to
His glory something which is not *per se* an act of
glorifying but which becomes so by being offered. If, as I
now hope, cultural activities are innocent and even useful, then they also (like the sweeping of the room in
Herbert's poem) can be done to the Lord. The work of a
charwoman and the work of a poet become spiritual in
the same way and on the same condition.

Two Kinds of Good and Bad September 2

Is there a kind of good which is not good? Is there any
good that is not pleasing to God or any bad which is not
hateful to Him? If you press me along these lines I end in
doubts. But I will not get rid of those doubts by falsifying
the little light I already have. That little light seems to
compel me to say that there are two kinds of good and
bad. The first, such as virtue and vice or love and hatred,
besides being good or bad themselves make the possessor
good or bad. The second do not. They include such things
as physical beauty or ugliness, the possession or lack of a
sense of humour, strength or weakness, pleasure or pain.
But the two most relevant for us are . . . conjugal *eros* (as
distinct from *agape*, which, of course, is a good of the

first class) and physical cleanliness. Surely we have all met people who said, indeed, that the latter was *next* to godliness, but whose unconscious attitude made it a *part* of godliness, and no small part? And surely we agree that any good of this second class, however good on its own level, becomes an enemy when it thus assumes demonic pretensions and erects itself into a quasi-spiritual value. As M. de Rougemount has recently told us, the conjugal *eros* 'ceases to be a devil only when it ceases to be a god'. My whole contention is that in literature, in addition to the spiritual good and evil which it carries, there is also a good and evil of this second class, a properly cultural or literary good and evil, which must not be allowed to masquerade as good and evil of the first class. . . . I enjoyed my breakfast this morning, and I think that was a good thing and do not think it was condemned by God. But I do not think myself a good man for enjoying it.

St Gregory the Great   *September 3*

The glory of God, and, as our only means to glorifying Him, the salvation of human souls, is the real business of life. What, then, is the value of culture? It is, of course, no new question; but as a living question it was new to me. . . .

I found the famous saying, attributed to Gregory, that our use of secular culture was comparable to the action of the Israelites in going down to the Philistines to have their knives sharpened. This seems to me a most satisfactory argument as far as it goes, and very relevant to modern conditions. If we are to convert our heathen neighbours, we must understand their culture. We must 'beat them at their own game'. But of course, while this would justify Christian culture (at least for some Christians whose vocation lay in that direction) at the moment, it would come very far short of the claims made for culture in our modern tradition. On the Gregorian view culture is a weapon; and a weapon is essentially a thing we lay aside as soon as we safely can.

Do All to the Glory of God   *September 4*

Religion cannot occupy the whole of life in the sense of excluding all our natural activities. For, of course, in some sense, it must occupy the whole of life. There is no question of a compromise between the claims of God and the claims of culture, or politics, or anything else. God's claim is infinite and inexorable. You can refuse it: or you can begin to try to grant it. There is no middle way. Yet in spite of this it is clear that Christianity does not exclude any of the ordinary human activities. St Paul tells people to get on with their jobs. He even assumes that Christians may go to dinner parties, and, what is more, dinner parties given by pagans. Our Lord attends a wedding and provides miraculous wine. Under the aegis of His Church, and in the most Christian ages, learning and the arts flourish. The solution of this paradox is, of course, well known to you. 'Whether ye eat or drink or whatsoever ye do, do all to the glory of God.'

All our merely natural activities will be accepted, if they are offered to God, even the humblest: and all of them, even the noblest, will be sinful if they are not. Christianity does not simply replace our natural life and substitute a new one: it is rather a new organization which exploits, to its own supernatural ends, these natural materials.

Our Need of Knowledge September 5

If all the world were Christian, it might not matter if all the world were uneducated. But, as it is, a cultural life will exist outside the Church whether it exists inside or not. To be ignorant and simple now – not to be able to meet the enemies on their own ground – would be to throw down our weapons, and to betray our uneducated brethren who have, under God, no defence but us against the intellectual attacks of the heathen. Good philosophy must exist, if for no other reason, because bad philosophy needs to be answered. The cool intellect must work not only against cool intellect on the other side, but against the muddy heathen mysticisms which deny intellect altogether. Most of all, perhaps, we need intimate knowledge of the past. Not that the past has any magic about it, but because we cannot study the future, and yet need something to set against the present, to remind us that the basic assumptions have been quite different in different periods and that much which seems certain to the uneducated is merely temporary fashion. A man who has lived in many places is not likely to be deceived by the local errors of his native village: the scholar has lived in many times and is therefore in some degree immune from the great cataract of nonsense that pours from the press and the microphone of his own age.

Theology: the Science of God September 6

In a way I quite understand why some people are put off by Theology. I remember once when I had been giving a talk to the R.A.F., an old, hardbitten officer got up and said, 'I've no use for all that stuff. But, mind you, I'm a religious man too. I *know* there's a God. I've *felt* Him: out alone in the desert at night: the tremendous mystery. And that's just why I don't believe all your neat little

dogmas and formulas about Him. To anyone who's met the real thing they all seem so petty and pedantic and unreal!'

Now in a sense I quite agreed with that man. I think he had probably had a real experience of God in the desert. And when he turned from that experience to the Christian creeds, I think he really was turning from something real to something less real. In the same way, if a man has once looked at the Atlantic from the beach, and then goes and looks at a map of the Atlantic, he also will be turning from something real to something less real: turning from real waves to a bit of coloured paper. But here comes the point. The map is admittedly only coloured paper, but there are two things you have to remember about it. In the first place, it is based on what hundreds and thousands of people have found by sailing the real Atlantic. In that way it has behind it masses of experience just as real as the one you could have from the beach; only, while yours would be a single isolated glimpse, the map fits all those different experiences together. In the second place, if you want to go anywhere, the map is absolutely necessary. As long as you are content with walks on the beach, your own glimpses are far more fun than looking at a map. But the map is going to be more use than walks on the beach if you want to get to America.

Don't Go to Sea without a Map   *September 7*

Theology is like a map. Merely learning and thinking about the Christian doctrines, if you stop there, is less real and less exciting than the sort of thing my friend got in the desert. Doctrines are not God: they are only a kind of map. But that map is based on the experience of hundreds of people who really were in touch with God – experiences compared with which any thrills or pious feelings you and I are likely to get on our own are very elementary and very confused. And secondly, if you want to get any further, you must use the map. You see, what happened to that man in the desert may have been real, and was certainly exciting, but nothing comes of it. It leads nowhere. There is nothing to do about it. In fact, that is just why a vague religion – all about feeling God in nature, and so on – is so attractive. It is all thrills and no work; like watching the waves from the beach. But you will not get to Newfoundland by studying the Atlantic that way, and you will not get eternal life by simply feeling the presence of God in flowers or music. Neither will you get anywhere by looking at maps without going to sea. Nor will you be very safe if you go to sea without a map.

In other words, Theology is practical: especially now. In the old days, when there was less education and discussion, perhaps it was possible to get on with a very few simple ideas about God. But it is not so now. Everyone reads, everyone hears things discussed. Consequently, if you do not listen to Theology, that will not mean that you have no ideas about God. It will mean that you have a lot of wrong ones – bad, muddled, out-of-date ideas. For a great many of the ideas about God which are trotted out as novelties today are simply the ones which real Theologians tried centuries ago and rejected. To believe in the popular religion of modern England is retrogression – like believing the earth is flat.

The Creation   *September 8*

I won't admit without a struggle that when I speak of God 'uttering' or 'inventing' the creatures I am 'watering down the concept of creation'. I am trying to give it, by remote analogies, some sort of content. I know that to create is defined as 'to make out of nothing', *ex nihilo*. But I take that to mean '*not* out of any pre-existing material'.

228

It can't mean that God makes what God has not thought of, or that He gives His creatures any powers or beauties which He Himself does not possess. Why, we think that even human work comes nearest to creation when the maker has 'got it all out of his own head'.

Nor am I suggesting a theory of 'emanations'. The differentia of an 'emanation' – literally an overflowing, a trickling out – would be that it suggests something involuntary. But my words – 'uttering' and 'inventing' – are meant to suggest an act.

This act, as it is for God, must always remain totally inconceivable to man. For we – even our poets and musicians and inventors – never, in the ultimate sense, *make*. We only build. We always have materials to build from. All we can know about the act of creation must be derived from what we can gather about the relation of the creatures to their Creator.

Divine Omnipotence   *September 9*

Omnipotence means 'power to do all, or everything'. And we are told in Scripture that 'with God all things are possible'. It is common enough, in argument with an unbeliever, to be told that God, if He existed and were good, would do this or that; and then, if we point out that the proposed action is impossible, to be met with the retort, 'But I thought God was supposed to be able to do anything.' This raises the whole question of impossibility.

In ordinary usage the word *impossible* generally implies a suppressed clause beginning with the word *unless*. Thus it is impossible for me to see the street from where I sit writing at this moment; that is, it is impossible to see the street *unless* I go up to the top floor where I shall be high enough to overlook the intervening building. If I had broken my leg I should say 'But it is impossible to go up

229

to the top floor' – meaning, however, that it is impossible *unless* some friends turn up who will carry me. Now let us advance to a different plane of impossibility, by saying, 'It is, at any rate, impossible to see the street *so long as* I remain where I am and the intervening building remains where it is.' Someone might add 'unless the nature of space, or of vision, were different from what it is'. I do not know what the best philosophers and scientists would say to this, but I should have to reply 'I don't know whether space and vision *could possibly* have been of such a nature as you suggest.' Now it is clear that the words *could possibly* here refer to some absolute kind of possibility or impossibility which is different from the relative possibilities and impossibilities we have been considering. I cannot say whether seeing round corners is, in this new sense, possible or not, because I do not know whether it is self-contradictory or not. But I know very well that if it is self-contradictory it is absolutely impossible. The absolutely impossible may also be called the intrinsically impossible because it carries its impossibility within itself.

Omnipotence and Nonsense September 10

Omnipotence means power to do all that is intrinsically possible, not to do the intrinsically impossible. You may attribute miracles to Him, but not nonsense. This is no limit to His power. If you choose to say 'God can give a creature free will and at the same time withhold free will from it', you have not succeeded in saying *anything* about God: meaningless combinations of words do not suddenly acquire meaning simply because we prefix to them the two other words 'God can'. It remains true that all *things* are possible with God: the intrinsic impossibilities are not things but nonentities. It is no more possible for God than for the weakest of His creatures to carry out both of two mutually exclusive alternatives; not because His power meets an obstacle, but because nonsense remains nonsense even when we talk it about God.

The Context of Freedom *September 11*

There is no reason to suppose that self-consciousness, the recognition of a creature by itself as a 'self', can exist except in contrast with an 'other', a something which is not the self. It is against an environment, and preferably a social environment, an environment of other selves, that the awareness of Myself stands out. This would raise a difficulty about the consciousness of God if we were mere theists: being Christians, we learn from the doctrine of the Blessed Trinity that something analogous to 'society' exists within the Divine being from all eternity – that God is Love, not merely in the sense of being the Platonic form of love, but because, within Him, the concrete reciprocities of love exist before all worlds and are thence derived to the creatures.

Again, the freedom of a creature must mean freedom to choose: and choice implies the existence of things to choose between. A creature with no environment would have no choices to make: so that freedom, like self-consciousness (if they are not, indeed, the same thing), again demands the presence to the self of something other than the self.

Competition or Courtesy

If the fixed nature of matter prevents it from being always, and in all its dispositions, equally agreeable even to a single soul, much less is it possible for the matter of the universe at any moment to be distributed so that it is equally convenient and pleasurable to each member of a society. If a man travelling in one direction is having a journey down hill, a man going in the opposite direction must be going up hill. If even a pebble lies where I want it to lie, it cannot, except by a coincidence, be where you want it to lie. And this is very far from being an evil: on the contrary, it furnishes occasion for all those acts of courtesy, respect, and unselfishness by which love and good humour and modesty express themselves. But it certainly leaves the way open to a great evil, that of competition and hostility. And if souls are free, they cannot be prevented from dealing with the problem by competition instead of by courtesy. And once they have advanced to actual hostility, they can then exploit the fixed nature of matter to hurt one another. The permanent nature of wood which enables us to use it as a beam also enables us to use it for hitting our neighbour on the head. The permanent nature of matter in general means that when human beings fight, the victory ordinarily goes to those who have superior weapons, skill, and number, even if their cause is unjust.

Fixed Laws and Man's Choice

That God can and does, on occasions, modify the behaviour of matter and produce what we call miracles, is part of the Christian faith; but the very conception of a common, and therefore, stable, world, demands that these occasions should be extremely rare. In a game of chess you can make certain arbitrary concessions to your opponent, which stand to the ordinary rules of the game as miracles stand to the laws of nature. You can deprive yourself of a castle, or allow the other man sometimes to take back a move made inadvertently. But if you conceded everything that at any moment happened to suit him – if all his moves were revocable and if all your pieces disappeared whenever their position on the board was not to his liking – then you could not have a game at all. So it is with the life of souls in a world: fixed laws, consequences unfolding by causal necessity, the whole natural order, are at once the limits within which their common life is confined and also the sole condition under which any such life is possible. Try to exclude the possibility of suffering which the order of nature and the existence of free wills involve, and you find that you have excluded life itself.

Possible Worlds *September 14*

With every advance in our thought the unity of the creative act, and the impossibility of tinkering with the creation as though this or that element of it could have been removed, will become more apparent. Perhaps this is not the 'best of all possible' universes, but the only possible one. Possible worlds can mean only 'worlds that God could have made, but didn't'. The idea of that which God 'could have' done involves a too anthropomorphic conception of God's freedom. Whatever human freedom means, Divine freedom cannot mean indeterminacy between alternatives and choice of one of them. Perfect goodness can never debate about the end to be attained, and perfect wisdom cannot debate about the means most suited to achieve it. The freedom of God consists in the fact that no cause other than Himself produces His acts and no external obstacle impedes them – that His own goodness is the root from which they all grow and His own omnipotence the air in which they all flower. . . .

I shall not attempt to prove that to create was better than not to create: I am aware of no human scales in which such a portentous question can be weighed. Some comparison between one state of being and another can be made, but the attempt to compare being and not being ends in mere words. 'It would be better for me not to exist' – in what sense 'for me'? How should I, if I did not exist, profit by not existing?

God Intends to Give Us What We Need

We are bidden to 'put on Christ', to become like God. That is, whether we like it or not, God intends to give us what we need, not what we now think we want. Once more, we are embarrassed by the intolerable compliment, by too much love, not too little.

Yet perhaps even this view falls short of the truth. It is not simply that God has arbitrarily made us such that He is our only good. Rather God is the only good of all creatures: and by necessity, each must find its good in that kind and degree of the fruition of God which is proper to its nature. The kind and degree may vary with the creature's nature: but that there ever could be any other good, is an atheistic dream. George MacDonald, in a passage I cannot now find, represents God as saying to men 'You must be strong with my strength and blessed with my blessedness, *for I have no other to give you.*' That is the conclusion of the whole matter. God gives what He has, not what He has not: He gives the happiness that there is, not the happiness that is not. To be God – to be like God and to share His goodness in creaturely response – to be miserable – these are the only three alternatives. If we will not learn to eat the only food that the universe grows – the only food that any possible universe ever can grow – then we must starve eternally.

Some people think they can imagine a creature which was free but had no possibility of going wrong; I cannot. If a thing is free to be good it is also free to be bad. And free will is what has made evil possible. Why, then, did God give them free will? Because free will, though it makes evil possible, is also the only thing that makes possible any love or goodness or joy worth having. A world of automata – of creatures that worked like machines – would hardly be worth creating. The happiness which God designs for His higher creatures is the happiness of being freely, voluntarily united to Him and to each other in an ecstasy of love and delight, compared with which the most rapturous love between a man and a woman on this earth is mere milk and water. And for that they must be free.

How did the Dark Power go wrong? Here, no doubt, we ask a question to which human beings cannot give an answer with any certainty. A reasonable (and traditional) guess, based on our own experiences of going wrong, can, however, be offered. The moment you have a self at all, there is a possibility of putting yourself first – wanting to be the centre – wanting to be God, in fact. That was the sin of Satan: and that was the sin he taught the human race. Some people think the fall of man had something to do with sex, but that is a mistake. (The story in the Book of Genesis rather suggests that some corruption in our sexual nature followed the fall and was its result, not its cause.) What Satan put into the heads of our remote ancestors was the idea that they could 'be like gods' – could set up on their own as if they had created themselves – be their own masters – invent some sort of happiness for themselves outside God, apart from God. And out of that hopeless attempt has come nearly all that we call human history – money, poverty, ambition, war, prostitution, classes, empires, slavery – the long terrible story of man trying to find something other than God which will make him happy.

Satan and St Michael   *September 18*

The commonest question is whether I really 'believe in the Devil'.

Now if by 'the Devil' you mean a power opposite to God and, like God, self-existent from all eternity, the answer is certainly 'No'. There is no uncreated being except God. God has no opposite. No being could attain a 'perfect badness' opposite to the perfect goodness of God; for when you have taken away every kind of good thing (intelligence, will, memory, energy, and existence itself) there would be none of him left.

The proper question is whether I believe in devils. I do. That is to say, I believe in angels and I believe that some of these, by the abuse of their free will, have become enemies to God and, as a corollary, to us. These we may call devils. They do not differ in nature from good angels, but their nature is depraved. *Devil* is the opposite of *angel* only as Bad Man is the opposite of Good Man. Satan, the leader or dictator of devils, is the opposite not of God but of Michael.

The Case Against Dualism _

If Dualism is true, then the bad Power must be a being who likes badness for its own sake. But in reality we have no experience of anyone liking badness just because it is bad. The nearest we can get to it is in cruelty. But in real life people are cruel for one of two reasons – either because they are sadists, that is, because they have a sensual perversion which makes cruelty a cause of sensual pleasure to them, or else for the sake of something they are going to get out of it – money, or power, or safety. But pleasure, money, power, and safety are all, as far as they go, good things. The badness consists in pursuing them by the wrong method, or in the wrong way, or too much. I do not mean, of course, that the people who do this are not desperately wicked. I do mean that wickedness, when you examine it, turns out to be the pursuit of some good in the wrong way. You can be good for the mere sake of goodness: you cannot be bad for the mere sake of badness. You can do a kind action when you are not feeling kind and when it gives you no pleasure, simply because kindness is right; but no one ever did a cruel action simply because cruelty is wrong – only because cruelty was pleasant or useful to him. In other words badness cannot succeed even in being bad in the same way in which goodness is good. Goodness is, so to speak, itself: badness is only spoiled goodness. And there must be something good first before it can be spoiled.

Satanic Blindness

Satan is the best-drawn of Milton's characters. The reason is not hard to find. Of the major characters whom Milton attempted he is incomparably the easiest to draw. Set a hundred poets to tell the same story and in ninety of the resulting poems Satan will be the best character. In all but a few writers the 'good' characters are the least successful, and everyone who has ever tried to make even the humblest story ought to know why. To make a character worse than oneself it is only necessary to release imaginatively from control some of the bad passions which, in real life, are always straining at the leash; the Satan, the Iago, the Becky Sharp, within each of us, is always there and only too ready, the moment the leash is slipped, to come out and have in our books that holiday we try to deny them in our lives. But if you try to draw a character better than yourself, all you can do is to take the best moments you have had and to imagine them prolonged and more consistently embodied in action. But the real high virtues which we do not possess at all, we cannot depict except in a purely external fashion. We do not really know what it feels like to be a man much better than ourselves. His whole inner landscape is one we have never seen, and when we guess it we blunder. It is in their 'good' characters that novelists make, unawares, the most shocking self-revelations. Heaven understands Hell and Hell does not understand Heaven, and all of us, in our measure, share the Satanic, or at least the Napoleonic, blindness. To project ourselves into a wicked character, we have only to stop doing something, and something that we are already tired of doing: to project ourselves into a good one we have to do what we cannot and become what we are not. . . . The Satan in Milton enables him to draw the character well just as the Satan in us enables us to receive it.

Sin

Is it still God speaking when a liar or a blasphemer speaks? In one sense, almost Yes. Apart from God he could not speak at all; there are no words not derived from the Word; no acts not derived from Him who is

Actus purus. And indeed the only way in which I can make real to myself what theology teaches about the heinousness of sin is to remember that every sin is the distortion of an energy breathed into us – an energy which, if not thus distorted, would have blossomed into one of those holy acts whereof 'God did it' and 'I did it' are both true descriptions. We poison the wine as He decants it into us; murder a melody He would play with us as the instrument. We caricature the self-portrait He would paint. Hence all sin, whatever else it is, is sacrilege.

The Fall   *September 22*

They wanted, as we say, to 'call their souls their own'. But that means to live a lie, for our souls are not, in fact, our own. They wanted some corner in the universe of which they could say to God, 'This is our business, not yours.' But there is no such corner. They wanted to be nouns, but they were, and eternally must be, mere adjectives. We have no idea in what particular act, or series of acts, the self-contradictory, impossible wish found expression. For all I can see, it might have concerned the literal eating of a fruit, but the question is of no consequence.

This act of self-will on the part of the creature, which constitutes an utter falseness to its true creaturely position, is the only sin that can be conceived as the Fall. For the difficulty about the first sin is that it must be very heinous, or its consequences would not be so terrible, and yet it must be something which a being free from the temptations of fallen man could conceivably have committed. The turning from God to self fulfils both conditions. It is a sin possible even to Paradisal man, because the mere existence of a self – the mere fact that we call it 'me' – includes, from the first, the danger of self-idolatry.

Since I am I, I must make an act of self-surrender, however small or however easy, in living to God rather than to myself. This is, if you like, the 'weak spot' in the very nature of creation, the risk which God apparently thinks worth taking. But the sin was very heinous, because the self which Paradisal man had to surrender contained no natural recalcitrancy to being surrendered. His *data*, so to speak, were a psycho-physical organism wholly subject to the will and a will wholly disposed, though not compelled, to turn to God. The self-surrender which he practised before the Fall meant no struggle but only the delicious overcoming of an infinitesimal self-adherence which delighted to be overcome – of which we see a dim analogy in the rapturous mutual self-surrenders of lovers even now. He had, therefore, no *temptation* (in our sense) to choose the self – no passion or inclination obstinately inclining that way – nothing but the bare fact that the self was *him*self.

The Loss of Man's Original Nature   *September 23*

Up to that moment the human spirit had been in full control of the human organism. It doubtless expected that it would retain this control when it had ceased to obey God. But its authority over the organism was a delegated authority which it lost when it ceased to be God's delegate. Having cut itself off, as far as it could, from the source of its being, it had cut itself off from the source of power. For when we say of created things that A rules B this must mean that God rules B through A. I doubt whether it would have been intrinsically possible for God to continue to rule the organism *through* the human spirit when the human spirit was in revolt against Him. At any rate He did not. He began to rule the organism in a more external way, not by the laws of spirit, but by those of nature. Thus the organs, no longer

governed by man's will, fell under the control of ordinary
biochemical laws and suffered whatever the inter-work-
ings of those laws might bring about in the way of pain,
senility and death. And desires began to come up into the
mind of man, not as his reason chose, but just as the
biochemical and environmental facts happened to cause
them. And the mind itself fell under the psychological
laws of association and the like which God had made to
rule the psychology of the higher anthropoids. And the
will, caught in the tidal wave of mere nature, had no
resource but to force back some of the new thoughts and
desires by main strength, and these uneasy rebels became
the subconscious as we now know it. The process was
not, I conceive, comparable to mere deterioration as it
may now occur in a human individual; it was a loss of
status as a *species*. What man lost by the Fall was his
original specific nature. 'Dust thou art, and unto dust
shalt thou return.'

Our Rebel Wills and Pain   *September 24*

The proper good of a creature is to surrender itself to its
Creator – to enact intellectually, volitionally, and
emotionally, that relationship which is given in the mere
fact of its being a creature. When it does so, it is good and
happy. Lest we should think this a hardship, this kind of
good begins on a level far above the creatures, for God
Himself, as Son, from all eternity renders back to God as
Father by filial obedience the being which the Father by
paternal love eternally generates in the Son. This is the
pattern which man was made to imitate – which Paradisal man did imitate – and wherever the will conferred by
the Creator is thus perfectly offered back in delighted and
delighting obedience by the creature, there, most undoubtedly, is Heaven, and there the Holy Ghost proceeds.
In the world as we now know it, the problem is how to

recover this self-surrender. We are not merely imperfect creatures who must be improved: we are, as Newman said, rebels who must lay down our arms. The first answer, then, to the question why our cure should be painful, is that to render back the will which we have so long claimed for our own, is in itself, wherever and however it is done, a grievous pain.

God's Megaphone *September 25*

The human spirit will not even begin to try to surrender self-will as long as all seems to be well with it. Now error and sin both have this property, that the deeper they are the less their victim suspects their existence; they are masked evil. Pain is unmasked, unmistakable evil; every man knows that something is wrong when he is being hurt. . . . And pain is not only immediately recognizable evil, but evil impossible to ignore. We can rest contentedly in our sins and in our stupidities; and anyone who has watched gluttons shovelling down the most exquisite foods as if they did not know what they were eating, will admit that we can ignore even pleasure. But pain insists upon being attended to. God whispers to us in our pleasures, speaks in our conscience, but shouts in our pains: it is His megaphone to rouse a deaf world.

Pain as an Opportunity for Amendment *September 26*

When our ancestors referred to pains and sorrows as God's 'vengeance' upon sin they were not necessarily attributing evil passions to God; they may have been recognizing the good element in the idea of retribution.

Until the evil man finds evil unmistakably present in his existence, in the form of pain, he is enclosed in illusion. Once pain has roused him, he knows that he is in some way or other 'up against' the real universe: he either rebels (with the possibility of a clearer issue and deeper repentance at some later stage) or else makes some attempt at an adjustment, which, if pursued, will lead him to religion. It is true that neither effect is so certain now as it was in ages when the existence of God (or even of the gods) was more widely known, but even in our own days we see it operating. Even atheists rebel and express, like Hardy and Housman, their rage against God although (or because) He does not, on their view, exist: and other atheists, like Mr Huxley, are driven by suffering to raise the whole problem of existence and to find some way of coming to terms with it which, if not Christian, is almost infinitely superior to fatuous contentment with a profane life. No doubt Pain as God's megaphone is a terrible instrument; it may lead to final and unrepented rebellion. But it gives the only opportunity the bad man can have for amendment. It removes the veil; it plants the flag of truth within the fortress of a rebel soul.

Divine Humility   *September 27*

We are perplexed to see misfortune falling upon decent, inoffensive, worthy people – on capable, hardworking mothers of families or diligent, thrifty, little tradespeople, on those who have worked so hard, and so honestly, for their modest stock of happiness and now seem to be entering on the enjoyment of it with the fullest right. How can I say with sufficient tenderness what here needs to be said? It does not matter that I know I must become, in the eyes of every hostile reader, as it were personally responsible for all the sufferings I try to explain – just as, to this day, everyone talks as if St

Augustine *wanted* unbaptized infants to go to Hell. But it matters enormously if I alienate anyone from the truth. Let me implore the reader to try to believe, if only for the moment, that God, who made these deserving people, may really be right when He thinks that their modest prosperity and the happiness of their children are not enough to make them blessed: that all this must fall from them in the end, and that if they have not learned to know Him they will be wretched. And therefore He troubles them, warning them in advance of an insufficiency that one day they will have to discover. The life to themselves and their families stands between them and the recognition of their need; He makes that life less sweet to them. I call this a Divine humility because it is a poor thing to strike our colours to God when the ship is going down under us; a poor thing to come to Him as a last resort, to offer up 'our own' when it is no longer worth keeping.

The Necessity of Tribulation   *September 28*

I am progressing along the path of life in my ordinary contentedly fallen and godless condition, absorbed in a merry meeting with my friends for the morrow or a bit of work that tickles my vanity today, a holiday or a new book, when suddenly a stab of abdominal pain that threatens serious disease, or a headline in the newspapers that threatens us all with destruction, sends this whole pack of cards tumbling down. At first I am overwhelmed, and all my little happinesses look like broken toys. Then, slowly and reluctantly, bit by bit, I try to bring myself into the frame of mind that I should be in at all times. I remind myself that all these toys were never intended to possess my heart, that my true good is in another world and my only real treasure is Christ. And perhaps, by God's grace, I succeed, and for a day or two become a creature consciously dependent on God and drawing its strength from the right sources. But the moment the threat is withdrawn, my whole nature leaps back to the toys: I am even anxious, God forgive me, to banish from my mind the only thing that supported me under the threat because it is now associated with the misery of those few days. Thus the terrible necessity of tribulation is only too clear. God has had me for but forty-eight hours and then only by dint of taking everything else away from me. Let Him but sheathe that sword for a moment and I behave like a puppy when the hated bath is over – I shake myself as dry as I can and race off to reacquire my comfortable dirtiness, if not in the nearest manure heap, at least in the nearest flower bed. And that is why tribulations cannot cease until God either sees us remade or sees that our remaking is now hopeless.

St Michael and All Angels   September 29

All angels, both the 'good' ones and the bad or 'fallen' ones which we call devils, are equally 'Supernatural' in relation to *this* spatio-temporal Nature: i.e. they are out-side it and have powers and a mode of existence which it could not provide. But the good angels lead a life which is Supernatural in another sense as well. That is to say, they have, of their own free will, offered back to God in love the 'natures' He gave them at their creation. All creatures of course live from God in the sense that He made them and at every moment maintains them in existence. But there is a further and higher kind of 'life from God' which can be given only to a creature who voluntarily surrenders himself to it. This life the good angels have and the bad angels have not: and it is absolutely Super-natural because no creature in any world can have it by the mere fact of being the sort of creature it is.

I do not maintain that God's creation of Nature can be proved as rigorously as God's existence, but it seems to me overwhelmingly probable, so probable that no one who approached the question with an open mind would very seriously entertain any other hypothesis. In fact one seldom meets people who have grasped the existence of a supernatural God and yet deny that He is the Creator. All the evidence we have points in that direction, and difficulties spring up on every side if we try to believe otherwise. No philosophical theory which I have yet come across is a radical improvement on the words of Genesis, that 'In the beginning God made Heaven and Earth'. I say 'radical' improvement, because the story in Genesis – as St Jerome said long ago – is told in the manner 'of a popular poet', or as we should say, in the form of folk tale. But if you compare it with the creation legends of other peoples – with all these delightful absurdities in which giants to be cut up and floods to be dried up are made to exist *before* creation – the depth and originality of this Hebrew folk tale will soon be apparent. The idea of *creation* in the rigorous sense of the word is there fully grasped.

The Law of Human Nature *October 1*

Everyone has heard people quarrelling. Sometimes it sounds funny and sometimes it sounds merely unpleasant; but however it sounds, I believe we can learn something very important from listening to the kind of things they say. They say things like this: 'How'd you like it if anyone did the same to you?' – 'That's my seat, I was there first' – 'Leave him alone, he isn't doing you any harm' – 'Why should you shove in first?' – 'Give me a bit of your orange, I gave you a bit of mine' – 'Come on, you promised.' People say things like that every day, educated people as well as uneducated, and children as well as grown-ups.

Now what interests me about all these remarks is that the man who makes them is not merely saying that the other man's behaviour does not happen to please him. He is appealing to some kind of standard of behaviour which he expects the other man to know about. And the other man very seldom replies: 'To hell with your standard.' Nearly always he tries to make out that what he has been doing does not really go against the standard, or that if it does there is some special excuse. . . . It looks, in fact, very much as if both parties had in mind some kind of Law or Rule of fair play or decent behaviour or morality or whatever you like to call it, about which they really agreed. And they have. If they had not, they might, of course, fight like animals, but they could not *quarrel* in the human sense of the word. Quarrelling means trying to show that the other man is in the wrong. And there would be no sense in trying to do that unless you and he had some sort of agreement as to what Right and Wrong are; just as there would be no sense in saying that a footballer had committed a foul unless there was some agreement about the rules of football.

Right and Wrong   *October 2*

The most remarkable thing is this. Whenever you find a man who says he does not believe in a real Right and Wrong, you will find the same man going back on this a moment later. He may break his promise to you, but if you try breaking one to him he will be complaining 'It's not fair' before you can say Jack Robinson. A nation may say treaties do not matter; but then, next minute, they spoil their case by saying that the particular treaty they want to break was an unfair one. But if treaties do not matter, and if there is no such thing as Right and Wrong – in other words, if there is no Law of Nature – what is the difference between a fair treaty and an unfair one? Have they not let the cat out of the bag and shown that, whatever they say, they really know the Law of Nature just like anyone else?

It seems, then, we are forced to believe in a real Right and Wrong. People may be sometimes mistaken about them, just as people sometimes get their sums wrong; but they are not a matter of mere taste and opinion any more than the multiplication table.

The Moral Law and Instinct   *October 3*

Supposing you hear a cry for help from a man in danger. You will probably feel two desires – one a desire to give help (due to your herd instinct), the other a desire to keep out of danger (due to the instinct for self-preservation). But you will find inside you, in addition to these two impulses, a third thing which tells you that you ought to follow the impulse to help, and suppress the impulse to run away. Now this thing that judges between two instincts, that decides which should be encouraged, cannot itself be either of them. You might as well say that the sheet of music which tells you, at a given moment, to play one note on the piano and not another, is itself one of the notes on the keyboard. The Moral Law tells us the tune we have to play: our instincts are merely the keys.

Another way of seeing that the Moral Law is not simply one of our instincts is this. If two instincts are in conflict, and there is nothing in a creature's mind except those two instincts, obviously the stronger of the two must win. But at those moments when we are most conscious of the Moral Law, it usually seems to be telling us to side with the weaker of the two impulses. You probably *want* to be safe much more than you want to help the man who is drowning: but the Moral Law tells you to help him all the same. And surely it often tells us to try to make the right impulse stronger than it naturally is? I mean, we often feel it our duty to stimulate the herd instinct, by waking up our imaginations and arousing our pity and so on, so as to get up enough steam for doing the right thing. But clearly we are not acting *from* instinct when we set about making an instinct stronger than it is. The thing that says to you, 'Your herd instinct is asleep. Wake it up', cannot itself *be* the herd instinct. The thing that tells you which note on the piano needs to be played louder cannot itself be that note.

St Francis of Assisi   October 4

Man has held three views of his body. First there is that of those ascetic Pagans who called it the prison or the 'tomb' of the soul, and of Christians like Fisher to whom it was a 'sack of dung', food for worms, filthy, shameful, a source of nothing but temptation to bad men and humiliation to good ones. Then there are the Neo-Pagans (they seldom know Greek), the nudists and the sufferers from Dark Gods, to whom the body is glorious. But thirdly we have the view which St Francis expressed by calling his body 'Brother Ass'. All three may be – I am not sure – defensible; but give me St Francis for my money.

Ass is exquisitely right because no one in his senses can either revere or hate a donkey. It is a useful, sturdy, lazy, obstinate, patient, lovable and infuriating beast; deserving now the stick and now a carrot; both pathetically and absurdly beautiful. So the body.

The Chinese . . . speak of a great thing (the greatest thing) called the *Tao*. It is the reality beyond all predicates, the abyss that was before the Creator Himself. It is Nature, it is the Way, the Road. It is the Way in which the universe goes on, the Way in which things everlastingly emerge, stilly and tranquilly, into space and time. It is also the Way which every man should tread in imitation of that cosmic and supercosmic progression, conforming all activities to that great exemplar. 'In ritual', say the Analects, 'it is harmony with Nature that is prized.' The ancient Jews likewise praise the Law as being 'true'.

This conception in all its forms, Platonic, Aristotelian, Stoic, Christian, and Oriental alike, I shall henceforth refer to for brevity simply as 'the *Tao*'. . . . It is the doctrine of objective value, the belief that certain attitudes are really true, and others really false, to the kind of thing the universe is and the kind of things we are. Those who know the *Tao* can hold that to call children delightful or old men venerable is not simply to record a psychological fact about our own parental or filial emotions at the moment, but to recognize a quality which demands a certain response from us whether we make it or not. . . . And because our approvals and disapprovals are thus recognitions of objective value or responses to an objective order, therefore emotional states can be in harmony with reason (when we feel liking for what ought to be approved) or out of harmony with reason (when we perceive that liking is due but cannot feel it). No emotion is, in itself, a judgement: in that sense all emotions and sentiments are alogical. But they can be reasonable or unreasonable as they conform to Reason or fail to conform. The heart never takes the place of the head: but it can, and should, obey it.

The Sole Source of All Value Judgements

This thing which I have called for convenience the *Tao*, and which others may call Natural Law or Traditional Morality or the First Principles of Practical Reason or the First Platitudes, is not one among a series of possible systems of value. It is the sole source of all value judgements. If it is rejected, all value is rejected. If any value is retained, it is retained. The effort to refute it and raise a new system of value in its place is self-contradictory. There never has been, and never will be, a radically new judgement of value in the history of the world. What purport to be new systems, or (as they now call them) 'ideologies', all consist of fragments from the *Tao* itself, arbitrarily wrenched from their context in the whole and then swollen to madness in their isolation, yet still owing to the *Tao* and to it alone such validity as they possess. If my duty to my parents is a superstition, then so is my duty to my country or my race. If the pursuit of scientific knowledge is a real value, then so is conjugal fidelity. The rebellion of new ideologies against the *Tao* is a rebellion of the branches against the tree: if the rebels could succeed they would find that they had destroyed themselves. The human mind has no more power of inventing a new value than of imagining a new primary colour, or, indeed, of creating a new sun and a new sky for it to move in.

Does the Moral Law Become Stagnant?

The modern mind has two lines of defence. . . . The second claims that to tie ourselves to an immutable moral code is to cut off all progress and acquiesce in 'stagnation'. . . .

Let us strip it of the illegitimate emotional power it

derives from the word 'stagnation' with its suggestion of puddles and mantled pools. If water stands too long it stinks. To infer thence that whatever stands long must be unwholesome is to be the victim of metaphor. Space does not stink because it has preserved its three dimensions from the beginning. The square on the hypotenuse has not gone mouldy by continuing to equal the sum of the squares on the other two sides. Love is not dishonoured by constancy, and when we wash our hands we are seeking stagnation and 'putting the clock back', artificially restoring our hands to the *status quo* in which they began the day and resisting the natural trend of events which would increase their dirtiness steadily from our birth to our death. For the emotive term 'stagnant' let us substitute the descriptive term 'permanent'. Does a permanent moral standard preclude progress? On the contrary, except on the supposition of a changeless standard, progress is impossible. If good is a fixed point, it is at least possible that we should get nearer and nearer to it; but if the terminus is as mobile as the train, how can the train progress towards it? Our ideas of the good may change, but they cannot change either for the better or the worse if there is no absolute and immutable good to which they can approximate or from which they can recede. We can go on getting a sum more and more nearly right only if the one perfectly right answer is 'stagnant'.

At the Back of the Moral Law – a Person
October 8

Christianity tells people to repent and promises them forgiveness. It therefore has nothing (as far as I know) to say to people who do not know they have done anything to repent of and who do not feel that they need any forgiveness. It is after you have realized that there is a real Moral Law, and a Power behind the law, and that you have broken that law and put yourself wrong with that Power – it is after all this, and not a moment sooner, that Christianity begins to talk. When you know you are sick, you will listen to the doctor. When you have realized that our position is nearly desperate you will begin to understand what the Christians are talking about. They offer an explanation of how we got into our present state of both hating goodness and loving it. They offer an explanation of how God can be this impersonal mind at the back of the Moral Law and yet also a Person. They tell you how the demands of this law, which you and I cannot meet, have been met on our behalf, how God Himself becomes a man to save man from the disapproval of God. . . . I quite agree that the Christian religion is, in the long run, a thing of unspeakable comfort. But it does not begin in comfort; it begins in the dismay I have been describing, and it is no use at all trying to go on to that comfort without first going through that dismay. In religion, as in war and everything else, comfort is the one thing you cannot get by looking for it. If you look for truth, you may find comfort in the end: if you look for comfort you will not get either comfort or truth – only soft soap and wishful thinking to begin with and, in the end, despair.

Atheism   *October 9*

My argument against God was that the universe seemed so cruel and unjust. But how had I got this idea of *just* and *unjust*? A man does not call a line crooked unless he has some idea of a straight line. What was I comparing this universe with when I called it unjust? If the whole show was bad and senseless from A to Z, so to speak, why did I, who was supposed to be part of the show, find myself in such violent reaction against it? A man feels wet when he falls into water, because man is not a water animal: a

253

fish would not feel wet. Of course I could have given up my idea of justice by saying it was nothing but a private idea of my own. But if I did that, then my argument against God collapsed too – for the argument depended on saying that the world was really unjust, not simply that it did not happen to please my private fancies. Thus in the very act of trying to prove that God did not exist – in other words, that the whole of reality was senseless – I found I was forced to assume that one part of reality – namely my idea of justice – was full of sense. Consequently atheism turns out to be too simple. If the whole universe has no meaning, we should never have found out that it has no meaning: just as, if there were no light in the universe and therefore no creatures with eyes, we should never know it was dark. *Dark* would be without meaning.

Universal Evolutionism   *October 10*

By universal evolutionism I mean the belief that the very formula of universal process is from imperfect to perfect, from small beginnings to great endings, from the rudimentary to the elaborate, the belief which makes people find it natural to think that morality springs from savage taboos, adult sentiment from infantile sexual maladjustments, thought from instinct, mind from matter, organic from inorganic, cosmos from chaos. This is perhaps the deepest habit of mind in the contemporary world. It seems to me immensely unplausible, because it makes the general course of nature so very unlike those parts of nature we can observe. You remember the old puzzle as to whether the owl came from the egg or the egg from the owl. The modern acquiescence in universal evolutionism is a kind of optical illusion, produced by attending exclusively to the owl's emergence from the egg. We are taught from childhood to notice how the perfect oak grows from the acorn and to forget that the acorn itself was dropped by a perfect oak. We are reminded constantly that the adult human being was an embryo, never that the life of the embryo came from two adult human beings. We love to notice that the express engine of today is the descendant of the 'Rocket'; we do not equally remember that the 'Rocket' springs not from some even more rudimentary engine, but from something much more perfect and complicated than itself – namely, a man of genius. The obviousness or naturalness which most people seem to find in the idea of emergent evolution thus seems to be a pure hallucination.

The Life Force   *October 11*

One reason why many people find Creative Evolution so attractive is that it gives one much of the emotional comfort of believing in God and none of the less pleasant consequences. When you are feeling fit and the sun is shining and you do not want to believe that the whole universe is a mere mechanical dance of atoms, it is nice to be able to think of this great mysterious Force rolling on through the centuries and carrying you on its crest. If, on the other hand, you want to do something rather shabby, the Life Force, being only a blind force, with no morals and no mind, will never interfere with you like that troublesome God we learned about when we were children. The Life Force is a sort of tame God. You can switch it on when you want, but it will not bother you. All the thrills of religion and none of the cost. Is the Life Force the greatest achievement of wishful thinking the world has yet seen?

You must really re-educate yourself: must work hard and consistently to eradicate from your mind the whole type of thought in which we have all been brought up. . . . It is technically called *Monism*; but perhaps the unlearned reader will understand me best if I call it *Everythingism*. I mean by this the belief that 'everything', or 'the whole show', must be self-existent, must be more important than every particular thing, and must contain all particular things in such a way that they cannot be really very different from one another – that they must be not merely 'at one', but one. Thus the Everythingist, if he starts from God, becomes a Pantheist; there must be nothing that is not God. If he starts from Nature he becomes a Naturalist; there must be nothing that is not Nature. He thinks that everything is in the long run 'merely' a precursor or a development or a relic or an instance or a disguise, of everything else. This philosophy I believe to be profoundly untrue. One of the moderns has said that reality is 'incorrigibly plural'. I think he is right. All things come from One. All things are related – related in different and complicated ways. But all things are not one. The word 'everything' should mean simply the total (a total to be reached, if we knew enough, by enumeration) of all the things that exist at a given moment. It must not be given a mental capital letter; must not (under the influence of picture thinking) be turned into a sort of pool in which particular things sink or even a cake in which they are the currants. Real things are sharp and knobbly and complicated and different. Everythingism is congenial to our minds because it is the natural philosophy of a totalitarian, mass-producing, conscripted age. That is why we must be perpetually on our guard against it.

It is no good asking for a simple religion. After all, real things are not simple. They look simple, but they are not. The table I am sitting at looks simple: but ask a scientist to tell you what it is really made of – all about the atoms and how the light waves rebound from them and hit my eye and what they do to the optic nerve and what it does to my brain – and, of course, you find that what we call 'seeing a table' lands you in mysteries and complications which you can hardly get to the end of. A child saying a child's prayer looks simple. And if you are content to stop there, well and good. But if you are not – and the modern world usually is not – if you want to go on and ask what is really happening – then you must be prepared for something difficult. If we ask for something more than simplicity, it is silly then to complain that the something more is not simple.

Very often, however, this silly procedure is adopted by people who are not silly, but who, consciously or unconsciously, want to destroy Christianity. Such people put up a version of Christianity suitable for a child of six and make that the object of their attack. When you try to explain the Christian doctrine as it is really held by an instructed adult, they then complain that you are making their heads turn round and that it is all too complicated and that if there really were a God they are sure He would have made 'religion' simple, because simplicity is so beautiful, etc. You must be on your guard against these people for they will change their ground every minute and only waste your time. Notice, too, their idea of God 'making religion simple': as if 'religion' were something God invented, and not His statement to us of certain quite unalterable facts about His own nature.

Besides being complicated, reality, in my experience, is usually odd. It is not neat, not obvious, not what you expect. For instance, when you have grasped that the earth and the other planets all go round the sun, you would naturally expect that all the planets were made to match – all at equal distances from each other, say, or distances that regularly increased, or all the same size, or else getting bigger or smaller as you go further from the sun. In fact, you find no rhyme or reason (that we can see) about either the sizes or the distances; and some of them have one moon, one has four, one has two, some have none, and one has a ring.

Reality, in fact, is usually something you could not have guessed. That is one of the reasons I believe Christianity. It is a religion you could not have guessed. If it offered us just the kind of universe we had always expected, I should feel we were making it up. But, in fact, it is not the sort of thing anyone would have made up. It has just that queer twist about it that real things have. So let us leave behind all these boys' philosophies – these over-simple answers. The problem is not simple and the answer is not going to be simple either.

Holy War   *October 15*

One of the things that surprised me when I first read the New Testament seriously was that it talked so much about a Dark Power in the universe – a mighty evil spirit who was held to be the Power behind death and disease, and sin. The difference is that Christianity thinks this Dark Power was created by God, and was good when he was created, and went wrong. Christianity agrees with Dualism that this universe is at war. But it does not think this is a war between independent powers. It thinks it is a civil war, a rebellion, and that we are living in a part of the universe occupied by the rebel.

Enemy-occupied territory – that is what this world is. Christianity is the story of how the rightful king has landed, you might say landed in disguise, and is calling us all to take part in a great campaign of sabotage. When you go to church you are really listening in to the secret wireless from our friends: that is why the enemy is so anxious to prevent us from going. He does it by playing on our conceit and laziness and intellectual snobbery. I know someone will ask me, 'Do you really mean, at this time of day, to re-introduce our old friend the devil – hoofs and horns and all?' Well, what the time of day has to do with it I do not know. And I am not particular about the hoofs and horns. But in other respects my answer is 'Yes, I do'. I do not claim to know anything about his personal appearance. If anybody really wants to know him better I would say to that person, 'Don't worry. If you really want to, you will. Whether you'll like it when you do is another question.'

Screwtape's Policy on Appearances   *October 16*

Our policy, for the moment, is to conceal ourselves. Of course this has not always been so. We are really faced with a cruel dilemma. When the humans disbelieve in our existence we lose all the pleasing results of direct terrorism and we make no magicians. On the other hand, when they believe in us, we cannot make them materialists and sceptics. At least, not yet. I have great hopes that we shall learn in due time how to emotionalize and mythologize their science to such an extent that what is, in effect, a belief in us (though not under that name), will creep in while the human mind remains closed to belief in the Enemy. The 'Life Force', the worship of sex, and some aspects of Psychoanalysis, may here prove useful. If once we can produce our perfect work – the Materialist Magician, the man, not using, but veritably worshipping, what he vaguely calls 'Forces' while denying the existence of 'spirits' – then the end of the war will be in sight. But in the meantime we must obey our orders. I do not think you will have much difficulty in keeping the patient in the dark. The fact that 'devils' are predominantly *comic* figures in the modern imagination will help you. If any faint suspicion of your existence begins to arise in his mind, suggest to him a picture of something in red tights, and persuade him that since he cannot believe in that (it is an old textbook method of confusing them) he therefore cannot believe in you.

The Price of Free Will   *October 17*

Christians, then, believe that an evil power has made himself for the present the Prince of this World. And, of course, that raises problems. Is this state of affairs in accordance with God's will or not? If it is, He is a strange God, you will say: and if it is not, how can anything happen contrary to the will of a being with absolute power? . . .

God created things which had free will. That means creatures which can go either wrong or right. Some people think they can imagine a creature which was free but had no possibility of going wrong; I cannot. If a thing is free to be good it is also free to be bad. . . . Of course God knew what would happen if they used their freedom the wrong way: apparently He thought it worth the risk. Perhaps we feel inclined to disagree with Him. But there is a difficulty about disagreeing with God. He is the source from which all your reasoning power comes: you could not be right and He wrong any more than a stream can rise higher than its own source. When you are arguing against Him you are arguing against the very power that makes you able to argue at all: it is like cutting off the branch you are sitting on. If God thinks this state of war in the universe a price worth paying for free will – that is, for making a live world in which creatures can do real good or harm and something of real importance can happen, instead of a toy world which only moves when He pulls the strings – then we may take it it is worth paying.

St Luke, Evangelist   October 18

Surely there's no difficulty about the prayer in Gethsemane on the ground that if the disciples were asleep they couldn't have heard it and therefore couldn't have recorded it? The words they did record would hardly have taken three seconds to utter. He was only 'a stone's throw' away. The silence of night was around them. And we may be sure He prayed aloud. People did everything aloud in those days. . . .

There is a rather amusing instance of the same thing in Acts 24. The Jews had got down a professional orator called Tertullos to conduct the prosecution of St Paul. The speech as recorded by St Luke takes eighty-four words in the Greek, if I've counted correctly. Eighty-four words are impossibly short for a Greek advocate on a full-dress occasion. Presumably, then, they are a précis? But of those eighty-odd words forty are taken up with preliminary compliments to the bench – stuff which, in a précis on that tiny scale, ought not to have come in at all. It is easy to guess what has happened. St Luke, though an excellent narrator, was no good as a reporter. He starts off by trying to memorize, or to get down, the whole speech verbatim. And he succeeds in reproducing a certain amount of the exordium. (The style unmistakable. Only a practising *rhetor* ever talks that way.) But he is soon defeated. The whole of the rest of the speech has to be represented by a ludicrously inadequate abstract. But he doesn't tell us what has happened, and thus seems to attribute to Tertullos a performance which would have spelled professional ruin.

God's Answer to a Fallen World   *October 19*

What did God do? First of all He left us conscience, the sense of right and wrong: and all through history there have been people trying (some of them very hard) to obey it. None of them ever quite succeeded. Secondly, He sent the human race what I call good dreams: I mean those queer stories scattered all through the heathen religions about a god who dies and comes to life again and, by his death, has somehow given new life to men. Thirdly, He selected one particular people and spent several centuries hammering into their heads the sort of God He was – that there was only one of Him and that He cared about right conduct. Those people were the Jews, and the Old Testament gives an account of the hammering process.

Then comes the real shock. Among these Jews there suddenly turns up a man who goes about talking as if He was God. He claims to forgive sins. He says He has always existed. He says He is coming to judge the world at the end of time. Now let us get this clear. Among Pantheists, like the Indians, anyone might say that he was a part of God, or one with God: there would be nothing very odd about it. But this man, since He was a Jew, could not mean that kind of God. God, in their language, meant the Being outside the world Who had made it and was infinitely different from anything else. And when you have grasped that, you will see that what this man said was, quite simply, the most shocking thing that has ever been uttered by human lips.

An Extraordinary Claim

One part of the claim tends to slip past us unnoticed because we have heard it so often that we no longer see what it amounts to. I mean the claim to forgive sins: any sins. Now unless the speaker is God, this is really so preposterous as to be comic. We can all understand how a man forgives offences against himself. You tread on my toe and I forgive you, you steal my money and I forgive you. But what should we make of a man, himself un-robbed and untrodden on, who announced that he forgave you for treading on other men's toes and stealing other men's money? Asinine fatuity is the kindest description we should give of his conduct. Yet this is what Jesus did. He told people that their sins were forgiven, and never waited to consult all the other people whom their sins had undoubtedly injured. He unhesitatingly behaved as if He was the party chiefly concerned, the person chiefly offended in all offences. This makes sense only if He really was the God whose laws are broken and whose love is wounded in every sin. In the mouth of any speaker who is not God, these words would imply what I can only regard as a silliness and conceit unrivalled by any other character in history.

The Shocking Alternative

Christ says that He is 'humble and meek' and we believe Him; not noticing that, if He were merely a man, humility and meekness are the very last characteristics we could attribute to some of His sayings.

I am trying here to prevent anyone saying the really foolish thing that people often say about Him: 'I'm ready to accept Jesus as a great moral teacher, but I don't accept His claim to be God.' That is the one thing we must not say. A man who was merely a man and said the sort of things Jesus said would not be a great moral teacher. He would either be a lunatic – on a level with the man who says he is a poached egg – or else he would be the Devil of Hell. You must make your choice. Either this man was, and is, the Son of God: or else a madman or something worse. You can shut Him up for a fool, you can spit at Him and kill Him as a demon; or you can fall at His feet and call Him Lord and God. But let us not come with any patronizing nonsense about His being a great human teacher. He has not left that open to us. He did not intend to.

The Teaching of Our Lord   *October 22*

We might have expected, we may think we should have preferred, an unrefracted light giving us ultimate truth in systematic form – something we could have tabulated and memorized and relied on like the multiplication table. One can respect, and at moments envy, both the Fundamentalist's view of the Bible and the Roman Catholic's view of the Church. But there is one argument which we should beware of using for either position: God must have done what is best, this is best, therefore God has done this. For we are mortals and do not know what is best for us, and it is dangerous to prescribe what God must have done – especially when we cannot, for the life of us, see that He has after all done it.

We may observe that the teaching of Our Lord Himself, in which there is no imperfection, is not given us in that cut-and-dried, foolproof, systematic fashion we might have expected or desired. He wrote no book. We have only reported sayings, most of them uttered in answers to questions, shaped in some degree by their context. And when we have collected them all we cannot reduce them to a system. He preaches but He does not lecture. He used paradox, proverb, exaggeration, parable, irony; even

(I mean no irreverence) the 'wisecrack'. He utters maxims which, like popular proverbs, if rigorously taken, may seem to contradict one another. His teaching therefore cannot be grasped by the intellect alone, cannot be 'got up' as if it were a 'subject'. If we try to do that with it, we shall find Him the most elusive of teachers. He hardly ever gave a straight answer to a straight question. He will not be, in the way we want, 'pinned down'. The attempt is (again, I mean no irreverence) like trying to bottle a sunbeam.

The Perfect Penitent   *October 23*

God has landed on this enemy-occupied world in human form. And now, what was the purpose of it all? What did He come to do? Well, to teach, of course; but as soon as you look into the New Testament or any other Christian writing you will find they are constantly talking about something different – about His death and His coming to life again. It is obvious that Christians think the chief point of the story lies here. They think the main thing He came to earth to do was to suffer and be killed.

Now before I became a Christian I was under the impression that the first thing Christians had to believe was one particular theory as to what the point of this dying was. According to that theory God wanted to punish men for having deserted and joined the Great Rebel, but Christ volunteered to be punished instead, and so God let us off. . . . What I came to see later on was that neither this theory nor any other is Christianity. The central Christian belief is that Christ's death has somehow put us right with God and given us a fresh start. Theories as to how it did this are another matter. A good many different theories have been held as to how it works; what all Christians are agreed on is that it does work. I will tell you what I think it is like. All sensible people

265

know that if you are tired and hungry a meal will do you good. But the modern theory of nourishment – about the vitamins and proteins – is a different thing. People ate their dinners and felt better long before the theory of vitamins was ever heard of: and if the theory of vitamins is some day abandoned they will go on eating their dinners just the same. Theories about Christ's death are not Christianity: they are explanations about how it works.

The Perfect Sacrifice October 24

The death of Christ is just that point in history at which something absolutely unimaginable from outside shows through into our own world. And if we cannot picture even the atoms of which our own world is built, of course we are not going to be able to picture this. Indeed, if we found that we could fully understand it, that very fact would show it was not what it professes to be – the inconceivable, the uncreated, the thing from beyond nature, striking down into nature like lightning. You may ask what good will it be to us if we do not understand it. But that is easily answered. A man can eat his dinner without understanding exactly how food nourishes him. A man can accept what Christ has done without knowing how it works: indeed, he certainly would not know how it works until he has accepted it.

We are told that Christ was killed for us, that His death has washed out our sins, and that by dying He disabled death itself. That is the formula. That is Christianity. That is what has to be believed. Any theories we build up as to how Christ's death did all this are, in my view, quite secondary: mere plans or diagrams to be left alone if they do not help us, and, even if they do help us, not to be confused with the thing itself.

The perfect surrender and humiliation were undergone by Christ: perfect because He was God, surrender and humiliation because He was man. Now the Christian belief is that if we somehow share the humility and suffering of Christ we shall also share in His conquest of death and find a new life after we have died and in it become perfect, and perfectly happy, creatures. This means something much more than our trying to follow His teaching. People often ask when the next step in evolution – the step to something beyond man – will happen. But on the Christian view, it has happened already. In Christ a new kind of man appeared: and the new kind of life which began in Him is to be put into us. How is this to be done? . . .

There are three things that spread the Christ-life to us: baptism, belief, and that mysterious action which different Christians call by different names – Holy Communion, the Mass, the Lord's Supper. At least, those are the three ordinary methods. I am not saying there may not be special cases where it is spread without one or more of these. I have not time to go into special cases, and I do not know enough. If you are trying in a few minutes to tell a man how to get to Edinburgh you will tell him the trains: he can, it is true, get there by boat or by a plane, but you will hardly bring that in. . . . Anyone who professes to teach you Christian doctrine will, in fact, tell you to use all three, and that is enough for our present purpose.

Do not think I am setting up baptism and belief and the Holy Communion as things that will do instead of your own attempts to copy Christ. Your natural life is derived from your parents; that does not mean it will stay there if you do nothing about it. You can lose it by neglect, or you can drive it away by committing suicide. You have to feed it and look after it: but always remember you are not making it, you are only keeping up a life you got from someone else. In the same way a Christian can lose the Christ-life which has been put into him, and he has to make efforts to keep it. But even the best Christian that ever lived is not acting on his own steam – he is only nourishing or protecting a life he could never have acquired by his own efforts. And that has practical consequences. As long as the natural life is in your body, it will do a lot towards repairing that body. Cut it, and up to a point it will heal, as a dead body would not. A live body is not one that never gets hurt, but one that can to some extent repair itself. In the same way a Christian is not a man who never goes wrong, but a man who is enabled to repent and pick himself up and begin over again after each stumble – because the Christ-life is inside him, repairing him all the time, enabling him to repeat (in some degree) the kind of voluntary death which Christ Himself carried out.

Believing on Authority *October 27*

We have to take reality as it comes to us: there is no good jabbering about what it ought to be like or what we should have expected it to be like. But though I cannot see why it should be so, I can tell you why I believe it is so. I have explained why I have to believe that Jesus was (and is) God. And it seems plain as a matter of history that He taught His followers that the new life was communicated in this way. In other words, I believe it on His authority. Do not be scared by the word authority. Believing things on authority only means believing them because you have been told them by someone you think trustworthy. Ninety-nine per cent of the things you believe are believed on authority. I believe there is such a place as New York. I have not seen it myself. I could not prove by abstract reasoning that there must be such a place. I believe it because reliable people have told me so. The ordinary man believes in the Solar System, atoms, evolution, and the circulation of the blood on authority – because the scientists say so. Every historical statement in the world is believed on authority. None of us has seen the Norman Conquest or the defeat of the Armada. None of us could prove them by pure logic as you prove a thing in mathematics. We believe them simply because people who did see them have left writings that tell us about them: in fact, on authority. A man who jibbed at authority in other things as some people do in religion would have to be content to know nothing all his life.

St Simon and St Jude, Apostles   October 28

About Lucius' argument that the evangelists would have put the doctrine of the atonement into the Gospel if they had had the slightest excuse, and, since they didn't, therefore Our Lord didn't teach it: surely, since we know from the Epistles that the Apostles (who had actually known Him) *did* teach this doctrine in His name *immediately* after His death, it is clear that He *did* teach it: or else, that they allowed themselves a very free hand. But if people shortly after His death were so very free in interpreting His doctrine, why should people who wrote much later (when such freedom would be more excusable from lapse of memory in an honest writer, and more likely to escape detection in a dishonest one) become so very much more accurate? The accounts of a thing don't usually get more and more accurate as time goes on. Anyway, if you take the sacrificial idea out of Christianity you deprive both Judaism and Paganism of all significance.

Christ Acts Through His Church   *October 29*

When Christians say the Christ-life is in them, they do not mean simply something mental or moral. When they speak of being 'in Christ' or of Christ being 'in them', this is not simply a way of saying that they are thinking about Christ or copying Him. They mean that Christ is actually operating through them; that the whole mass of Christians are the physical organism through which Christ acts – that we are His fingers and muscles, the cells of His Body. And perhaps that explains one or two things. It explains why this new life is spread not only by purely mental acts like belief, but by bodily acts like baptism and Holy Communion. It is not merely the spreading of an idea; it is more like evolution – a biological or superbiological fact. There is no good trying to be more spiritual than God. God never meant man to be a purely spiritual creature. That is why He uses material things like bread and wine to put the new life into us. We may think this rather crude and unspiritual. God does not: He invented eating. He likes matter. He invented it.

If anything whatever is common to all believers, and
even to many unbelievers, it is the sense that in the
gospels they have met a personality. There are characters
whom we know to be historical but of whom we do not
feel that we have any personal knowledge – knowledge
by acquaintance; such are Alexander, Attila, or William
of Orange. There are others who make no claim to
historical reality but whom, none the less, we know as
we know real people: Falstaff, Uncle Toby, Mr Pickwick.
But there are only three characters who, claiming the
first sort of reality, also actually have the second. And
surely everyone knows who they are: Plato's Socrates,
the Jesus of the gospels, and Boswell's Johnson. Our
acquaintance with them shows itself in a dozen ways.
When we look into the Apocryphal gospels, we find
ourselves constantly saying of this or that *logion*, 'No.
It's a fine saying, but not His. That wasn't how He talked'
– just as we do with all pseudo-Johnsoniana. We are not
in the least perturbed by the contrasts within each
character: the union in Socrates of silly and scabrous
titters about Greek pederasty with the highest mystical
fervour and homeliest good sense; in Johnson, of profound gravity and melancholy with that love of fun and
nonsense which Boswell never understood though Fanny
Burney did; in Jesus, of peasant shrewdness, intolerable
severity, and irresistible tenderness. So strong is the
flavour of the personality that, even while He says things
which, on any other assumption than that of Divine Incarnation in the fullest sense, would be appallingly arrogant, yet we – and many unbelievers – accept Him at His
own valuation when He says 'I am meek and lowly of
heart'. Even those passages in the New Testament which
superficially, and in intention, are most concerned with
the Divine, and least with the Human Nature, bring us
face to face with the personality. I am not sure that they
don't do this more than any others. 'We beheld His glory,
the glory as of the only begotten of the Father, full of

graciousness and reality . . . which we have looked upon and our hands have handled.'

We Must Choose   *October 31*

Why is God landing in this enemy-occupied world in disguise and starting a sort of secret society to undermine the Devil? Why is He not landing in force, invading it? Is it that He is not strong enough? Well, Christians think He is going to land in force; we do not know when. But we can guess why He is delaying. He wants to give us the chance of joining His side freely. I do not suppose you and I would have thought much of a Frenchman who waited till the Allies were marching into Germany and then announced he was on our side. God will invade. But I wonder whether people who ask God to interfere openly and directly in our world quite realize what it will be like when He does. When that happens, it is the end of the world. When the author walks on to the stage the play is over. God is going to invade, all right: but what is the good of saying you are on His side then, when you see the whole natural universe melting away like a dream and something else – something it never entered your head to conceive – comes crashing in; something so beautiful to some of us and so terrible to others that none of us will have any choice left? For this time it will be God without disguise; something so overwhelming that it will strike either irresistible love or irresistible horror into every creature. It will be too late then to choose your side. There is no use saying you choose to lie down when it has become impossible to stand up. That will not be the time for choosing: it will be the time when we discover which side we really have chosen, whether we realized it before or not. Now, today, this moment, is our chance to choose the right side. God is holding back to give us that chance. It will not last for ever. We must take it or leave it.

All Saints   *November 1*

If you can ask for the prayers of the living, why should
you not ask for the prayers of the dead? There is clearly
also a great danger. In some popular practice we see it
leading off into an infinitely silly picture of Heaven as an
earthly court where applicants will be wise to pull the
right wires, discover the best 'channels', and attach
themselves to the most influential pressure groups. But I
have nothing to do with all this. . . . The consoling thing
is that while Christendom is divided about the
rationality, and even the lawfulness, of praying *to* the
saints, we are all agreed about praying *with* them. 'With
angels and archangels and all the company of heaven'. . . .
One always accepted this *with* theoretically. But it is
quite different when one brings it into consciousness at
an appropriate moment and wills the association of one's
own little twitter with the voice of the great saints and
(we hope) of our own dear dead. They may drown some of
its uglier qualities and set off any tiny value it has.

Commemoration of All Souls   *November 2*

Of course I pray for the dead. The action is so
spontaneous, so all but inevitable, that only the most
compulsive theological case against it would deter me.
And I hardly know how the rest of my prayers would
survive if those for the dead were forbidden. At our age
the majority of those we love best are dead. What sort of
intercourse with God could I have if what I love best
were unmentionable to Him?

On the traditional Protestant view, all the dead are
damned or saved. If they are damned, prayer for them is
useless. If they are saved, it is equally useless. God has
already done all for them. What more should we ask?

But don't we believe that God has already done and is

already doing all that He can for the living? What more should we ask? Yet we are told to ask.

'Yes,' it will be answered, 'but the living are still on the road. Further trials, developments, possibilities of error, await them. But the saved have been made perfect. They have finished the course. To pray for them presupposes that progress and difficulty are still possible. In fact, you are bringing in something like Purgatory.'

Well, I suppose I am. Though even in Heaven some perpetual increase of beatitude, reached by a continually more ecstatic self-surrender, without the possibility of failure but not perhaps without its own ardours and exertions – for delight also has its severities and steep ascents, as lovers know – might be supposed.

Making and Begetting   *November 3*

The point in Christianity which gives us the greatest shock is the statement that by attaching ourselves to Christ, we can 'become Sons of God'. One asks 'Aren't we Sons of God already? Surely the Fatherhood of God is one of the main Christian ideas?' Well, in a certain sense, no doubt we are sons of God already. I mean, God has brought us into existence and loves us and looks after us, and in that way is like a father. But when the Bible talks of our 'becoming' Sons of God, obviously it must mean something different. And that brings us up against the very centre of theology.

One of the creeds says that Christ is the Son of God 'begotten, not created'; and it adds 'begotten by his Father before all worlds'. Will you please get it quite clear that this has nothing to do with the fact that when Christ was born on earth as a man, that man was the son of a virgin? We are not now thinking about the Virgin Birth. We are thinking about something that happened before Nature was created at all, before time began. 'Before all worlds' Christ is begotten, not created. What does it mean? . . .

To beget is to become the father of: to create is to make. And the difference is this. When you beget, you beget something of the same kind as yourself. A man begets human babies, a beaver begets little beavers and a bird begets eggs which turn into little birds. But when you make, you make something of a different kind from yourself. A bird makes a nest, a beaver builds a dam, a man makes a wireless set – or he may make something more like himself than a wireless set: say, a statue. If he is a clever enough carver he may make a statue which is very like a man indeed. But, of course, it is not a real man; it only looks like one. It cannot breathe or think. It is not alive.

Biological Life and Spiritual Life   *November 4*

What man, in his natural condition, has not got, is spiritual life – the higher and different sort of life that exists in God. We use the same word *life* for both: but if you thought that both must therefore be the same sort of thing, that would be like thinking that the 'greatness' of space and the 'greatness' of God were the same sort of greatness. In reality, the difference between biological life and spiritual life is so important that I am going to give them two distinct names. The biological sort which comes to us through Nature, and which (like everything else in Nature) is always tending to run down and decay so that it can only be kept up by incessant subsidies from Nature in the form of air, water, food, etc., is *Bios*. The spiritual life which is in God from all eternity, and which made the whole natural universe, is *Zoe*. *Bios* has, to be sure, a certain shadowy or symbolic resemblance to *Zoe*: but only the sort of resemblance there is between a photo and a place, or a statue and a man. A man who changed

275

from having *Bios* to having *Zoe* would have gone through as big a change as a statue which changed from being a carved stone to being a real man.

And that is precisely what Christianity is about. This world is a great sculptor's shop. We are the statues and there is a rumour going round the shop that some of us are some day going to come to life.

Beyond Personality   *November 5*

A good many people nowadays say, 'I believe in a God, but not in a personal God.' They feel that the mysterious something which is behind all other things must be more than a person. Now the Christians quite agree. But the Christians are the only people who offer any idea of what a being that is beyond personality could be like. All the other people, though they say that God is beyond personality, really think of Him as something impersonal: that is, as something less than personal. If you are looking for something super-personal, something more than a person, then it is not a question of choosing between the Christian idea and the other ideas. The Christian idea is the only one on the market.

Again, some people think that after this life, or perhaps after several lives, human souls will be 'absorbed' into God. But when they try to explain what they mean, they seem to be thinking of our being absorbed into God as one material thing is absorbed into another. They say it is like a drop of water slipping into the sea. But of course that is the end of the drop. If that is what happens to us, then being absorbed is the same as ceasing to exist. It is only the Christians who have any idea of how human souls can be taken into the life of God and yet remain themselves – in fact, be very much more themselves than they were before.

People already knew about God in a vague way. Then
came a man who claimed to be God; and yet he was not
the sort of man you could dismiss as a lunatic. He made
them believe Him. They met Him again after they had
seen Him killed. And then, after they had been formed
into a little society or community, they found God
somehow inside them as well: directing them, making
them able to do things they could not do before. And
when they worked it all out they found they had arrived
at the Christian definition of the three-personal God. . . .

When you come to knowing God, the initiative lies on
His side. If He does not show Himself, nothing you can
do will enable you to find Him. And, in fact, He shows
much more of Himself to some people than to others –
not because He has favourites, but because it is impossible for Him to show Himself to a man whose whole
mind and character are in the wrong condition. Just as
sunlight, though it has no favourites, cannot be reflected
in a dusty mirror as clearly as in a clean one . . . God can
show Himself as He really is only to real men. And that
means not simply to men who are individually good, but
to men who are united together in a body, loving one
another, helping one another, showing Him to one
another. For that is what God meant humanity to be like;
like players in one band, or organs in one body.

Our 'Unveiling' Before God   *November 7*

We are always completely, and therefore equally, known
to God. That is our destiny whether we like it or not. But
though this knowledge never varies, the quality of our
being known can. A school of thought holds that 'freedom is willed necessity'. Never mind if they are right or
not. I want this idea only as an analogy. Ordinarily, to be

known by God is to be, for this purpose, in the category of things. We are like earthworms, cabbages, and nebulae, objects of divine knowledge. But when we (a) become aware of the fact – the present fact, not the generalization – and (b) assent with all our will to be so known, then we treat ourselves, in relation to God, not as things but as persons. We have unveiled. Not that any veil could have baffled this sight. The change is in us. The passive changes to the active. Instead of merely being known, we show, we tell, we offer ourselves to view.

To put ourselves thus on a personal footing with God could, in itself and without warrant, be nothing but presumption and illusion. But we are taught that it is not; that it is God who gives us that footing. For it is by the Holy Spirit that we cry 'Father'. By unveiling, by confessing our sins and 'making known' our requests, we assume the high rank of persons before Him. And He, descending, becomes a Person to us.

Time and Beyond Time   *November 8*

Our life comes to us moment by moment. One moment disappears before the next comes along: and there is room for very little in each. That is what time is like. And of course you and I tend to take it for granted that this time series – this arrangement of past, present and future – is not simply the way life comes to us but the way all things really exist. We tend to assume that the whole universe and God Himself are always moving on from past to future just as we do. . . .

Almost certainly God is not in time. His life does not consist of moments following one another. If a million people are praying to Him at ten-thirty tonight, He need not listen to them all in that one little snippet which we call ten-thirty. Ten-thirty – and every other moment from the beginning of the world – is always the Present for Him. If you like to put it that way, He has all eternity in which to listen to the split second of prayer put up by a pilot as his plane crashes in flames.

That is difficult, I know. Let me try to give something, not the same, but a bit like it. Suppose I am writing a novel. I write 'Mary laid down her work; next moment came a knock at the door!' For Mary who has to live in the imaginary time of my story there is no interval between putting down the work and hearing the knock. But I, who am Mary's maker, do not live in that imaginary time at all. Between writing the first half of that sentence and the second, I might sit down for three hours and think steadily about Mary. I could think about Mary as if she were the only character in the book and for as long as I pleased, and the hours I spent in doing so would not appear in Mary's time (the time inside the story) at all.

The Infinite Attention of God   *November 9*

God is not hurried along in the time stream of this universe any more than an author is hurried along in the imaginary time of his own novel. He has infinite attention to spare for each one of us. He does not have to deal with us in the mass. You are as much alone with Him as if you were the only being He had ever created. When Christ died, He died for you individually just as much as if you had been the only man in the world.

The way in which my illustration breaks down is this. In it the author gets out of one time series (that of the novel) only by going into another time series (the real one). But God, I believe, does not live in a time series at all. His life is not dribbled out moment by moment like ours: with Him it is, so to speak, still 1920 and already 1960. For His life is Himself.

If you picture time as a straight line along which we have to travel, then you must picture God as the whole page on which the line is drawn. We come to the parts of the line one by one: we have to leave A behind before we get to B, and cannot reach C until we leave B behind. God, from above or outside or all round, contains the whole line, and sees it all.

We Confuse Ourselves about Time   *November 10*

Before I became a Christian one of my objections was as follows. The Christians said that the eternal God who is everywhere and keeps the whole universe going, once became a human being. Well then, said I, how did the whole universe keep going while He was a baby, or while He was asleep? How could He at the same time be God who knows everything and also a man asking his disciples 'Who touched me?' You will notice that the sting lay in the *time* words: '*While* He was a baby' – 'How could He *at the same time*?' In other words I was assuming that Christ's life as God was in time, and that His life as the man Jesus in Palestine was a shorter period taken out of that time – just as my service in the army was a shorter period taken out of my total life. And that is how most of us perhaps tend to think about it. We picture God living through a period when His human life was still in the future: then coming to a period when it was present: then going on to a period when He could look back on it as something in the past. But probably these ideas correspond to nothing in the actual facts. You cannot fit Christ's earthly life in Palestine into any time-relations with His life as God beyond all space and time. It is really, I suggest, a timeless truth about God that human nature, and the human experience of weakness and sleep and ignorance, are somehow included in His whole divine life. This human life in God is from our point of view a particular period in the history of our world (from the year A.D. One till the Crucifixion). We therefore imagine it is also a period in the history of God's own existence. But God has no history. He is too completely and utterly real to have one. For, of course, to have a history means losing part of your reality (because it had already slipped away into the past) and not yet having another part (because it is still in the future): in fact having nothing but the tiny little present, which has gone before you can speak about it. God forbid we should think God was like that. Even we may hope not to be always rationed in that way.

The Eternal 'Now'   *November 11*

Everyone who believes in God at all believes that He knows what you and I are going to do tomorrow. But if He knows I am going to do so-and-so, how can I be free to do otherwise? Well, here once again, the difficulty comes from thinking that God is progressing along the time line like us: the only difference being that He can see ahead and we cannot. Well, if that were true, if God *foresaw* our acts, it would be very hard to understand how we could be free not to do them. But suppose God is outside and above the time line. In that case, what we call 'tomorrow' is visible to Him in just the same way as what we call 'today'. All the days are 'Now' for Him. He does not remember you doing things yesterday; He simply sees you doing them, because, though you have lost yesterday, He has not. He does not 'foresee' you doing things tomorrow; He simply sees you doing them: because, though tomorrow is not yet there for you, it is for Him. You never supposed that your actions at this moment were any less free because God knows what you are doing. Well, He knows your tomorrow's actions in just the same way – because He is already in tomorrow and can simply watch you. In a sense, He does not know your action till you have done it: but then the moment at which you have done it is already 'Now' for Him.

When we are praying about the result, say, of a battle or a medical consultation the thought will often cross our minds that (if only we knew it) the event is already decided one way or the other. I believe this to be no good reason for ceasing our prayers. The event certainly has been decided — in a sense it was decided 'before all worlds'. But one of the things taken into account in deciding it, and therefore one of the things that really cause it to happen, may be this very prayer that we are now offering. Thus, shocking as it may sound, I conclude that we can at noon become part causes of an event occurring at ten o'clock. (Some scientists would find this easier than popular thought does.) The imagination will, no doubt, try to play all sort of tricks on us at this point. It will ask, 'Then if I stop praying can God go back and alter what has already happened?' No. The event has already happened and one of its causes has been the fact that you are asking such questions instead of praying. It will ask, 'Then if I begin to pray can God go back and alter what has already happened?' No. The event has already happened and one of its causes is your present prayer. Thus something does really depend on my choice. My free act contributes to the cosmic shape. That contribution is made in eternity 'before all worlds'; but my consciousness of contributing reaches me at a particular point in the time series.

Some years ago I got up one morning intending to have my hair cut in preparation for a visit to London, and the first letter I opened made it clear I need not go to London. So I decided to put the haircut off too. But then there began the most unaccountable little nagging in my mind, almost like a voice saying, 'Get it cut all the same. Go and get it cut.' In the end I could stand it no longer. I went. Now my barber at that time was a fellow Christian and a man of many troubles whom my brother and I had sometimes been able to help. The moment I opened his shop door he said, 'Oh, I was praying you might come today.' And in fact if I had come a day or so later I should have been of no use to him.

It awed me; it awes me still. But of course one cannot rigorously prove a causal connection between the barber's prayer and my visit. It might be telepathy. It might be accident. . . .

The question then arises, 'What sort of evidence *would* prove the efficacy of prayer?' The thing we pray for may happen, but how can you ever know it was not going to happen anyway? Even if the thing were indisputably miraculous it would not follow that the miracle had occurred because of your prayers. The answer surely is that a compulsive empirical proof such as we have in the sciences can never be attained.

Some things are proved by the unbroken uniformity of our experiences. The law of gravitation is established by the fact that, in our experience, all bodies without exception obey it. Now even if all the things that people prayed for happened, which they do not, this would not prove what Christians mean by the efficacy of prayer. For prayer is request. The essence of request, as distinct from compulsion, is that it may or may not be granted. And if an infinitely wise Being listens to the requests of finite and foolish creatures, of course He will sometimes grant and sometimes refuse them.

Prayer is Not a 'Gimmick'

There are, no doubt, passages in the New Testament which may seem at first sight to promise an invariable granting of our prayers. But that cannot be what they really mean. For in the very heart of the story we meet a glaring instance to the contrary. In Gethsemane the holiest of all petitioners prayed three times that a certain cup might pass from Him. It did not. After that the idea that prayer is recommended to us as a sort of infallible gimmick may be dismissed.

Other things are proved not simply by experience but by those artificially contrived experiences which we call experiments. Could this be done about prayer? I will pass over the objection that no Christian could take part in such a project, because he has been forbidden it: 'You must not try experiments on God, your Master.' Forbidden or not, is the thing even possible?

I have seen it suggested that a team of people – the more the better – should agree to pray as hard as they knew how, over a period of six weeks, for all the patients in Hospital A and none of those in Hospital B. Then you would tot up the results and see if A had more cures and fewer deaths. . . .

The trouble is that I do not see how any real prayer could go on under such conditions. 'Words without thoughts never to heaven go', says the King in *Hamlet*. Simply to say prayers is not to pray; otherwise a team of properly trained parrots would serve as well as men for our experiment. You cannot pray for the recovery of the sick unless the end you have in view is their recovery. But you can have no motive for desiring the recovery of all the patients in one hospital and none of those in another. You are not doing it in order that suffering should be relieved; you are doing it to find out what happens. The real purpose and the nominal purpose of your prayers are at variance.

We make requests of our fellow creatures as well as of God: we ask for the salt, we ask for a rise in pay, we ask a friend to feed the cat while we are on our holidays, we ask a woman to marry us. Sometimes we get what we ask for and sometimes not. But when we do, it is not nearly so easy as one might suppose to prove with scientific certainty a causal connection between the asking and the getting.

Your neighbour may be a humane person who would not have let your cat starve even if you had forgotten to make any arrangement. Your employer is never so likely to grant your request for a rise as when he is aware that you could get better money from a rival firm and is quite possibly intending to secure you by a rise in any case. As for the lady who consents to marry you – are you sure she had not decided to do so already? Your proposal, you know, might have been the result, not the cause, of her decision. A certain important conversation might never have taken place unless she had intended that it should.

Thus in some measure the same doubt that hangs about the causal efficacy of our prayers to God hangs also about our prayers to man. Whatever we get we might have been going to get anyway. But only, as I say, in some measure. Our friend, boss, and wife may tell us that they acted because we asked; and we may know them so well as to feel sure, first that they are saying what they believe to be true, and secondly that they understand their own motives well enough to be right. But notice that when this happens our assurance has not been gained by the methods of science. We do not try the control experiment of refusing the rise or breaking off the engagement and then making our request again under fresh conditions. Our assurance is quite different in kind from scientific knowledge. It is born out of our personal relation to the other parties; not from knowing things about them but from knowing *them*.

Does Prayer Work? November 16

Our assurance – if we reach an assurance – that God always hears and sometimes grants our prayers, and that apparent grantings are not merely fortuitous, can only come in the same sort of way. There can be no question of tabulating successes and failures and trying to decide whether the successes are too numerous to be accounted for by chance. Those who best know a man best know whether, when he did what they asked, he did it because they asked. I think those who best know God will best know whether He sent me to the barber's shop because the barber prayed.

For up till now we have been tackling the whole question in the wrong way and on the wrong level. The very question 'Does prayer work?' puts us in the wrong frame of mind from the outset. 'Work': as if it were magic, or a machine – something that functions automatically. Prayer is either a sheer illusion or a personal contact between embryonic, incomplete persons (ourselves) and the utterly concrete Person. Prayer in the sense of petition, asking for things, is a small part of it; confession and penitence are its threshold, adoration its sanctuary, the presence and vision and enjoyment of God its bread and wine. In it God shows Himself to us. That He answers prayers is a corollary – not necessarily the most important one – from that revelation. What He does is learned from what He is.

Divine Abdication November 17

'God', said Pascal, 'instituted prayer in order to lend to His creatures the dignity of causality.' But not only prayer; whenever we act at all He lends us that dignity. It is not really stranger, nor less strange, that my prayers should affect the course of events than that my other actions should do so. They have not advised or changed God's mind – that is, His over-all purpose. But that purpose will be realized in different ways according to the actions, including the prayers, of His creatures.

For He seems to do nothing of Himself which He can possibly delegate to His creatures. He commands us to do slowly and blunderingly what He could do perfectly and in the twinkling of an eye. He allows us to neglect what He would have us do, or to fail. Perhaps we do not fully realize the problem, so to call it, of enabling finite free wills to co-exist with Omnipotence. It seems to involve at every moment almost a sort of divine abdication. We are not mere recipients or spectators. We are either privileged to share in the game or compelled to collaborate in the work, 'to wield our little tridents'. Is this amazing process simply Creation going on before our eyes? This is how (no light matter) God makes something – indeed, makes gods – out of nothing.

One Continuous Act of God   *November 18*

What I have offered can be, at the very best, only a mental model or symbol. All that we say on such subjects must be merely analogical and parabolic. The reality is doubtless not comprehensible by our faculties. But we can at any rate try to expel bad analogies and bad parables. Prayer is not a machine. It is not magic. It is not advice offered to God. Our act, when we pray, must not, any more than all our other acts, be separated from the continuous act of God Himself, in which alone all finite causes operate.

It would be even worse to think of those who get what they pray for as a sort of court favourites, people who have influence with the throne. The refused prayer of Christ in Gethsemane is answer enough to that. And I dare not leave out the hard saying which I once heard from an experienced Christian: 'I have seen many striking answers to prayer and more than one that I thought miraculous. But they usually come at the beginning: before conversion, or soon after it. As the Christian life proceeds, they tend to be rarer. The refusals, too, are not only more frequent; they become more unmistakable, more emphatic.'

Does God then forsake just those who serve Him best? Well, He who served Him best of all said, near His tortured death, 'Why hast thou forsaken me?' When God becomes man, that Man, of all others, is least comforted by God, at His greatest need. There is a mystery here which, even if I had the power, I might not have the courage to explore. Meanwhile, little people like you and me, if our prayers are sometimes granted, beyond all hope and probability, had better not draw hasty conclusions to our own advantage. If we were stronger, we might be less tenderly treated. If we were braver, we might be sent, with far less help, to defend far more desperate posts in the great battle.

Harking Back   *November 19*

I am beginning to feel that we need a preliminary act of submission not only towards possible future afflictions but also towards possible future blessings. I know it sounds fantastic; but think it over. It seems to me that we often, almost sulkily, reject the good that God offers us because, at that moment, we expected some other good. Do you know what I mean? On every level of our life – in our religious experience, in our gastronomic, erotic, aesthetic, and social experience – we are always harking back to some occasion which seemed to us to reach perfection, setting that up as a norm, and depreciating all other occasions by comparison. But these other occasions, I now suspect, are often full of their own new blessing, if only we would lay ourselves open to it. God shows us a new facet of the glory, and we refuse to look at it because we're still looking for the old one. And of course we don't get that. You can't, at the twentieth reading, get again the experience of reading *Lycidas* for the first time. But what you do get can be in its own way as good.

Encore! *November 20*

Many religious people lament that the first fervours of their conversion have died away. They think – sometimes rightly, but not, I believe, always – that their sins account for this. They may even try by pitiful efforts of will to revive what now seem to have been the golden days. But were those fervours – the operative word is *those* – ever intended to last?

It would be rash to say that there is any prayer which God *never* grants. But the strongest candidate is the prayer we might express in the single word *encore*. And how should the Infinite repeat Himself? All space and time are too little for Him to utter Himself in them *once*.

And the joke, or tragedy, of it all is that these golden moments in the past, which are so tormenting if we erect them into a norm, are entirely nourishing, wholesome, and enchanting if we are content to accept them for what they are, for memories. Properly bedded down in a past which we do not miserably try to conjure back, they will send up exquisite growths. Leave the bulbs alone, and the new flowers will come up. Grub them up and hope, by fondling and sniffing, to get last year's blooms, and you will get nothing. 'Unless a seed die . . .'

The moment of prayer is for me – or involves for me as its condition – the awareness, the re-awakened awareness, that this 'real world' and 'real self' are very far from being rockbottom realities. I cannot, in the flesh, leave the stage, either to go behind the scenes or to take my seat in the pit; but I can remember that these regions exist. And I also remember that my apparent self – this clown or hero or super – under his greasepaint is a real person with an off-stage life. The dramatic person could not tread the stage unless he concealed a real person: unless the real and unknown I existed, I would not even make mistakes about the imagined me. And in prayer this real I struggles to speak, for once, from his real being, and to address, for once, not the other actors, but – what shall I call Him? The Author, for He invented us all? The Producer, for He controls all? Or the Audience, for He watches, and will judge, the performance?

The attempt is not to escape from space and time and from my creaturely situation as a subject facing objects. It is more modest: to re-awaken the awareness of that situation. If that can be done, there is no need to go anywhere else. This situation itself is, at every moment, a possible theophany. Here is the holy ground; the Bush is burning now.

Of course this attempt may be attended with almost every degree of success or failure. The prayer preceding all prayers is 'May it be the real I who speaks. May it be the real Thou that I speak to.' Infinitely various are the levels from which we pray. Emotional intensity is in itself no proof of spiritual depth. If we pray in terror we shall pray earnestly; it only proves that terror is an earnest emotion. Only God Himself can let the bucket down to the depths in us. And, on the other side, He must constantly work as the iconoclast. Every idea of Him we form, He must in mercy shatter. The most blessed result of prayer would be to rise thinking 'But I never knew before. I never dreamed . . .' I suppose it was at such a moment that Thomas Aquinas said of all his own theology, 'It reminds me of straw.'

St Cecilia, Patroness of Church Music

November 22

There are two musical situations on which I think we can be confident that a blessing rests. One is where a priest or an organist, himself a man of trained and delicate taste, humbly and charitably sacrifices his own (aesthetically right) desires and gives the people humbler and coarser fare than he would wish, in a belief (even, as it may be, the erroneous belief) that he can thus bring them to God. The other is where the stupid and unmusical layman humbly and patiently, and above all silently, listens to music which he cannot, or cannot fully, appreciate, in the belief that it somehow glorifies God, and that if it does not edify him this must be his own defect. Neither such a High Brow nor such a Low Brow can be far out of the way. To both, Church Music will have been a means of grace; not the music they have liked, but the music they have disliked. They have both offered, sacrificed, their taste in the fullest sense. But where the opposite situation arises, where the musician is filled with the pride of skill or the virus of emulation and looks with contempt on the unappreciative congregation, or where the unmusical, complacently entrenched in their own ignorance and conservatism, look with the restless and resentful hostility of an inferiority complex on all who would try to improve their taste — there, we may be sure, all that both offer is unblessed and the spirit that moves them is not the Holy Ghost.

It seems to me that we must define rather carefully the way, or ways, in which music can glorify God. There is ... a sense in which all natural agents, even inanimate ones, glorify God continually by revealing the powers He has given them. And in that sense we, as natural agents, do the same. On that level our wicked actions, in so far as they exhibit our skill and strength, may be said to glorify God, as well as our good actions. An excellently performed piece of music, as a natural operation which reveals in a very high degree the peculiar powers given to man, will thus always glorify God whatever the intention of the performers may be. But that is a kind of glorifying which we share with 'the dragons and great deeps', with the 'frosts and snows'. What is looked for in us, as men, is another kind of glorifying, which depends on intention. How easy or how hard it may be for a whole choir to preserve that intention through all the discussions and decisions, all the corrections and disappointments, all the temptations to pride, rivalry and ambition, which precede the performance of a great work, I (naturally) do not know. But it is on the intention that all depends. When it succeeds, I think the performers are the most enviable of men; privileged while mortals to honour God like angels and, for a few golden moments, to see spirit and flesh, delight and labour, skill and worship, the natural and the supernatural, all fused into that unity they would have had before the Fall.

'Can't you lead a good life without believing in Christianity?' This is the question on which I have been asked to write, and straight away, before I begin trying to answer it, I have a comment to make. The question sounds as if it were asked by a person who said to himself, 'I don't care whether Christianity is in fact true or not. I'm not interested in finding out whether the real universe is more like what the Christians say than what the Materialists say. All I'm interested in is leading a good life. I'm going to choose beliefs not because I think them true but because I find them helpful.' Now frankly, I find it hard to sympathize with this state of mind. One of the things that distinguishes man from the other animals is that he wants to know things, wants to find out what reality is like, simply for the sake of knowing. When that desire is completely quenched in anyone, I think he has become something less than human. As a matter of fact, I don't believe any of you have really lost that desire. More probably, foolish preachers, by always telling you how much Christianity will help you and how good it is for society, have actually led you to forget that Christianity is not a patent medicine. Christianity claims to give an account of *facts* – to tell you what the real universe is like. Its account of the universe may be true, or it may not, and once the question is really before you, then your natural inquisitiveness must make you want to know the answer. If Christianity is untrue, then no honest man will want to believe it, however helpful it might be: if it is true, every honest man will want to believe it, even if it gives him no help at all.

The Christian and the Materialist   *November 25*

There are quite a lot of things which these two men could agree in doing for their fellow citizens. Both would approve of efficient sewers and hospitals and a healthy diet. But sooner or later the difference of their beliefs would produce differences in their practical proposals. Both, for example, might be very keen about education: but the kinds of education they wanted people to have would obviously be very different. Again, where the Materialist would simply ask about a proposed action, 'Will it increase the happiness of the majority?', the Christian might have to say, 'Even if it does increase the happiness of the majority, we can't do it. It is unjust.' And all the time, one great difference would run through their whole policy. To the Materialist things like nations, classes, civilizations must be more important than individuals, because the individuals live only seventy-odd years each and the group may last for centuries. But to the Christian, individuals are more important, for they live eternally; and races, civilizations and the like, are in comparison the creatures of a day. The Christian and the Materialist hold different beliefs about the universe. They can't both be right. The one who is wrong will act in a way which simply doesn't fit the real universe. Consequently, with the best will in the world, he will be helping his fellow creatures to their destruction.

The Question Before Each of Us   *November 26*

The question before each of us is not 'Can *someone* lead a good life without Christianity?' The question is, 'Can *I*?' We all know there have been good men who were not Christians; men like Socrates and Confucius who had never heard of it, or men like J.S. Mill who quite honestly couldn't believe it. Supposing Christianity to be true, these men were in a state of honest ignorance or honest error. If their intentions were as good as I suppose them to have been (for of course I can't read their secret hearts) I hope and believe that the skill and mercy of God will remedy the evils which their ignorance, left to itself, would naturally produce both for them and for those whom they influenced. But the man who asks me, 'Can't I lead a good life without believing in Christianity?' is clearly not in the same position. If he hadn't heard of Christianity he would not be asking this question. If, having heard of it, and having seriously considered it, he had decided that it was untrue, then once more he would not be asking the question. The man who asks this question has heard of Christianity and is by no means certain that it may not be true. He is really asking, 'Need I bother about it? Mayn't I just evade the issue, just let sleeping dogs lie, and get on with being "good"? Aren't good intentions enough to keep me safe and blameless without knocking at that dreadful door and making sure whether there is, or isn't someone inside?'

To such a man it might be enough to reply that he is really asking to be allowed to get on with being 'good' before he has done his best to discover what *good* means. . . . We need not inquire whether God will punish him for his cowardice and laziness; they will punish themselves. The man is shirking.

The Shirker   *November 27*

The man who remains an unbeliever for such reasons is not in a state of honest error. He is in a state of dishonest error, and that dishonesty will spread through all his thoughts and actions: a certain shiftiness, a vague worry in the background, a blunting of his whole mental edge, will result. He has lost his intellectual virginity. Honest rejection of Christ, however mistaken, will be forgiven

and healed – 'Whosoever shall speak a word against the
Son of Man, it shall be forgiven him.' But to *evade* the
Son of Man, to look the other way, to pretend you haven't
noticed, to become suddenly absorbed in something on
the other side of the street, to leave the receiver off the
telephone because it might be He who was ringing up, to
leave unopened certain letters in a strange handwriting
because they might be from Him – this is a different
matter. You may not be certain yet whether you ought to
be a Christian; but you do know you ought to be a Man,
not an ostrich, hiding its head in the sand.

But still – for intellectual honour has sunk very low in
our age – I hear someone whimpering on with his question, 'Will it help me? Will it make me happy? Do you
really think I'd be better if I became a Christian?' Well, if
you must have it, my answer is 'Yes'. But I don't like
giving an answer at all at this stage. Here is a door,
behind which, according to some people, the secret of the
universe is waiting for you. Either that's true, or it isn't.
And if it isn't, then what the door really conceals is
simply the greatest fraud, the most colossal 'sell' on record. Isn't it obviously the job of every man (that is a man
and not a rabbit) to try to find out which, and then to
devote his full energies either to serving this tremendous
secret or to exposing and destroying this gigantic
humbug? Faced with such an issue, can you really remain
wholly absorbed in your own blessed 'moral development'?

The Rabbit Must Disappear   *November 28*

All right, Christianity will do you good – a great deal
more good than you ever wanted or expected. And the
first bit of good it will do you is to hammer into your
head (you won't enjoy *that*!) the fact that what you have
hitherto called 'good' – all that about 'leading a decent

life' and 'being kind' – isn't quite the magnificent and all-important affair you supposed. It will teach you that in fact you can't be 'good' (not for twenty-four hours) on your own moral efforts. And then it will teach you that even if you were, you still wouldn't have achieved the purpose for which you were created. Mere *morality* is not the end of life. You were made for something quite different from that.... The people who keep on asking if they can't lead a decent life without Christ, don't know what life is about; if they did they would know that 'a decent life' is mere machinery compared with the thing we men are really made for. Morality is indispensable: but the Divine Life, which gives itself to us and which calls us to be gods, intends for us something in which morality will be swallowed up. We are to be re-made. All the rabbit in us is to disappear – the worried, conscientious, ethical rabbit as well as the cowardly and sensual rabbit. We shall bleed and squeal as the handfuls of fur come out; and then, surprisingly, we shall find underneath it all a thing we have never yet imagined: a real Man, an ageless god, a son of God, strong, radiant, wise, beautiful, and drenched in joy.

Morality – Not an End in Itself   *November 29*

I think all Christians would agree with me if I said that though Christianity seems at first to be all about morality, all about duties and rules and guilt and virtue, yet it leads you on, out of all that, into something beyond. One has a glimpse of a country where they do not talk of those things, except perhaps as a joke. Everyone there is filled full with what we should call goodness as a mirror is filled with light. But they do not call it goodness. They do not call it anything. They are not thinking of it. They are too busy looking at the source from which it comes. But this is near the stage where the road passes over the rim of our world. No one's eyes can see very far beyond that: lots of people's eyes can see further than mine.

St Andrew, Apostle   *November 30*

If you read history you will find that the Christians who did most for the present world were just those who thought most of the next. The Apostles themselves, who set on foot the conversion of the Roman Empire, the great men who built up the Middle Ages, the English Evangelicals who abolished the Slave Trade, all left their mark on earth, precisely because their minds were occupied with Heaven. It is since Christians have largely ceased to think of the other world that they have become so ineffective in this. Aim at Heaven and you will get earth 'thrown in': aim at earth and you will get neither. It seems a strange rule, but something like it can be seen at work in other matters. Health is a great blessing, but the moment you make health one of your main, direct objects you start becoming a crank and imagining there is something wrong with you. You are only likely to get health provided you want other things more – food, games, work, fun, open air. In the same way, we shall never save civilization as long as civilization is our main object. We must learn to want something else even more.

Advent   *December 1*

Imagine yourself as a living house. God comes in to rebuild that house. At first, perhaps, you can understand what He is doing. He is getting the drains right and stopping the leaks in the roof and so on: you knew that those jobs needed doing and so you are not surprised. But presently He starts knocking the house about in a way that hurts abominably and does not seem to make sense. What on earth is He up to? The explanation is that He is building quite a different house from the one you thought of – throwing out a new wing here, putting on an extra floor there, running up towers, making courtyards. You thought you were going to be made into a decent little cottage: but He is building a palace. He intends to come and live in it Himself.

The Way Things Work Now   *December 2*

The Son of God became a man to enable men to become sons of God. We do not know – anyway, *I* do not know – how things would have worked if the human race had never rebelled against God and joined the enemy. Perhaps every man would have been 'in Christ', would have shared the life of the Son of God, from the moment he was born. Perhaps the *Bios* or natural life would have been drawn up into the *Zoe*, the uncreated life, at once and as a matter of course. But that is guesswork. You and I are concerned with the way things work now.

And the present state of things is this. The two kinds of life are now not only different (they would always have been that) but actually opposed. The natural life in each of us is something self-centred, something that wants to be petted and admired, to take advantage of other lives, to exploit the whole universe. And especially it wants to be left to itself: to keep well away from anything better or stronger or higher than it, anything that might make it feel small. It is afraid of the light and air of the spiritual world, just as people who have been brought up to be dirty are afraid of a bath. And in a sense it is quite right. It knows that if the spiritual life gets hold of it, all its self-centredness and self-will are going to be killed, and it is ready to fight tooth and nail to avoid that.

Obstinate Toy Soldiers *December 3*

Did you ever think, when you were a child, what fun it would be if your toys could come to life? Well, suppose you could really have brought them to life. Imagine turning a tin soldier into a real little man. It would involve turning the tin into flesh. And suppose the tin soldier did not like it. He is not interested in flesh; all he sees is that the tin is being spoilt. He thinks you are killing him. He will do everything he can to prevent you. He will not be made into a man if he can help it.

What you would have done about that tin soldier I do not know. But what God did about us was this. The Second Person in God, the Son, became human Himself: was born into the world as an actual man – a real man of a particular height, with hair of a particular colour, speaking a particular language, weighing so many stone. The Eternal Being, who knows everything and who created the whole universe, became not only a man but (before that) a baby, and before that a foetus inside a Woman's body. If you want to get the hang of it, think how you would like to become a slug or a crab.

The First Real Man *December 4*

The result of this was that you now had one man who really was what all men were intended to be: one man in whom the created life, derived from His Mother, allowed itself to be completely and perfectly turned into the begotten life. The natural human creature in Him was taken up fully into the divine Son. Thus in one instance humanity had, so to speak, arrived: had passed into the life of Christ. And because the whole difficulty for us is that the natural life has to be, in a sense, 'killed', He chose an earthly career which involved the killing of His human desires at every turn – poverty, misunderstanding

from His own family, betrayal by one of His intimate friends, being jeered at and manhandled by the police, and execution by torture. And then, after being thus killed – killed every day in a sense – the human creature in Him, because it was united to the divine Son, came to life again. The Man in Christ rose again: not only the God. That is the whole point. For the first time we saw a real man. One tin soldier – real tin, just like the rest – had come fully and splendidly alive.

God So Loved the *World* . . . December 5

We come to the point where my illustration about the tin soldier breaks down. In the case of real toy soldiers or statues, if one came to life, it would obviously make no difference to the rest. They are all separate. But human beings are not. They look separate because you see them walking about separately. But then, we are so made that we can see only the present moment. If we could see the past, then of course it would look different. For there was a time when every man was part of his mother, and (earlier still) part of his father as well: and when they were part of his grandparents. If you could see humanity spread out in time, as God sees it, it would not look like a lot of separate things dotted about. It would look like one single growing thing – rather like a very complicated tree. Every individual would appear connected with every other. And not only that. Individuals are not really separate from God any more than from one another. Every man, woman, and child all over the world is feeling and breathing at this moment only because God, so to speak, is 'keeping him going'.

Consequently, when Christ becomes man it is not really as if you could become one particular tin soldier. It is as if something which is always affecting the whole human mass begins, at one point, to affect that whole

301

human mass in a new way. From that point the effect spreads through all mankind. It makes a difference to people who lived before Christ as well as to people who lived after Him. It makes a difference to people who have never heard of Him. It is like dropping into a glass of water one drop of something which gives a new taste or a new colour to the whole lot.

Each Must Accept or Reject Salvation   *December 6*

What, then, is the difference which He has made to the whole human mass? It is just this; that the business of becoming a son of God, of being turned from a created thing into a begotten thing, of passing over from the temporary biological life into timeless 'spiritual' life, has been done for us. Humanity is already 'saved' in principle. We individuals have to appropriate that salvation. But the really tough work – the bit we could not have done for ourselves – has been done for us. We have not got to try to climb up into spiritual life by our own efforts; it has already come down into the human race. If we will only lay ourselves open to the one Man in whom it was fully present, and who, in spite of being God, is also a real man, He will do it in us and for us. Remember what I said about 'good infection'. One of our own race has this new life: if we get close to Him we shall catch it from Him.

Of course, you can express this in all sorts of different ways. You can say that Christ died for our sins. You may say that the Father has forgiven us because Christ has done for us what we ought to have done. You may say that we are washed in the blood of the Lamb. You may say that Christ has defeated death. They are all true. If any of them does not appeal to you, leave it alone and get on with the formula that does. And, whatever you do, do not start quarrelling with other people because they use a different formula from yours.

Do Not Dictate to God a 'Formula' for Conversion

Everyone who accepts the teaching of St Paul must have a belief in 'sanctification'. But I should myself be very chary of describing such operations of the Holy Ghost as 'experiences' if by experiences we mean things necessarily discoverable by introspection. And I should be still more chary of mapping out a series of such experiences as an indispensable norm (or syllabus!) for all Christians. I think the ways in which God saves us are probably infinitely various and admit varying degrees of consciousness in the patient. Anything which sets him saying 'Now – Stage II ought soon to be coming along – is this it?' I think bad and likely to lead some to presumption and others to despair. We must leave God to dress the wound and not keep on taking peeps under the bandage for ourselves.

Neither Totalitarians Nor Individualists

December 8

Christianity thinks of human individuals not as mere members of a group or items in a list, but as organs in a body – different from one another and each contributing what no other could. When you find yourself wanting to turn your children, or pupils, or even your neighbours, into people exactly like yourself, remember that God probably never meant them to be that. You and they are different organs, intended to do different things. On the other hand, when you are tempted not to bother about someone else's troubles because they are 'no business of yours', remember that though he is different from you he is part of the same organism as you. If you forget that he belongs to the same organism as yourself you will become an Individualist. If you forget that he is a different

303

organ from you, if you want to suppress differences and make people all alike, you will become a Totalitarian. But a Christian must not be either a Totalitarian or an Individualist.

I feel a strong desire to tell you – and I expect you feel a strong desire to tell me – which of these two errors is the worse. That is the Devil getting at us. He always sends errors into the world in pairs – pairs of opposites. And he always encourages us to spend a lot of time thinking which is the worse. You see why, of course? He relies on your extra dislike of the one error to draw you gradually into the opposite one. But do not let us be fooled. We have to keep our eyes on the goal and go straight through between both errors. We have no other concern than that with either of them.

Dressing Up as Christ   *December 9*

If you are interested enough to have read thus far you are probably interested enough to make a shot at saying your prayers: and, whatever else you say, you will probably say the Lord's Prayer. Its very first words are *Our Father*. Do you now see what those words mean? They mean quite frankly, that you are putting yourself in the place of a son of God. To put it bluntly, you are *dressing up as Christ*. If you like, you are pretending. Because, of course, the moment you realize what the words mean, you realize that you are not a son of God. You are not being like the Son of God, whose will and interests are at one with those of the Father: you are a bundle of self-centred fears, hopes, greeds, jealousies, and self-conceit, all doomed to death. So that, in a way, this dressing up as Christ is a piece of outrageous cheek. But the odd thing is that He has ordered us to do it. . . .

There are two kinds of pretending. There is a bad kind, where the pretence is there instead of the real thing; as when a man pretends he is going to help you instead of really helping you. But there is also a good kind, where the pretence leads up to the real thing. When you are not feeling particularly friendly but know you ought to be, the best thing you can do, very often, is to put on a friendly manner and behave as if you were a nicer person than you actually are. And in a few minutes, as we have all noticed, you will be really feeling friendlier than you were. Very often the only way to get a quality in reality is to start behaving as if you had it already.

Pretence into Reality   *December 10*

The moment you realize 'Here I am, dressing up as Christ', it is extremely likely that you will see at once some way in which at that very moment the pretence could be made less of a pretence and more of a reality. You will find several things going on in your mind which would not be going on there if you were really a son of God. Well, stop them. Or you may realize that, instead of saying your prayers, you ought to be downstairs writing a letter, or helping your wife to wash up. Well, go and do it.

You see what is happening. The Christ Himself, the Son of God who is man (just like you) and God (just like His Father) is actually at your side and is already at that moment beginning to turn your pretence into a reality. This is not merely a fancy way of saying that your conscience is telling you what to do. If you simply ask your conscience, you get one result: if you remember that you are dressing up as Christ, you get a different one. There are lots of things which your conscience might not call definitely wrong (especially things in your mind) but which you will see at once you cannot go on doing if you are seriously trying to be like Christ. For you are no longer thinking simply about right and wrong; you are trying to catch the good infection from a Person. It is more like painting a portrait than like obeying a set of rules. And the odd thing is that while in one way it is much harder than keeping rules, in another way it is far easier.

The real Son of God is at your side. He is beginning to turn you into the same kind of thing as Himself. He is beginning, so to speak, to 'inject' His kind of life and thought, His *Zoe*, into you.

Instruments of Divine Grace   *December 11*

You may say 'I've never had the sense of being helped by an invisible Christ, but I often have been helped by other human beings.' That is rather like the woman in the first war who said that if there were a bread shortage it would not bother her house because they always ate toast. If there is no bread there will be no toast. If there were no help from Christ, there would be no help from other human beings. He works on us in all sorts of ways: not only through what we think our 'religious life'. He works through Nature, through our own bodies, through books, sometimes through experiences which seem (at the time) *anti*-Christian. When a young man who has been going to church in a routine way honestly realizes that he does not believe in Christianity and stops going – provided he does it for honesty's sake and not just to annoy his parents – the spirit of Christ is probably nearer to him then than it ever was before. But above all, He works on us through each other.

Men are mirrors, or 'carriers' of Christ to other men. Sometimes unconscious carriers. This 'good infection' can be carried by those who have not got it themselves. People who were not Christians themselves helped me to Christianity. But usually it is those who know Him that bring Him to others. That is why the Church, the whole body of Christians showing Him to one another, is so important.

A House Built on Sand   *December 12*

Do not forget this. At first it is natural for a baby to take
its mother's milk without knowing its mother. It is
equally natural for us to see the man who helps us without seeing Christ behind him. But we must not remain
babies. We must go on to recognize the real Giver. It is
madness not to. Because, if we do not, we shall be relying
on human beings. And that is going to let us down. The
best of them will make mistakes; all of them will die. We
must be thankful to all the people who have helped us,
we must honour them and love them. But never, never
pin your whole faith on any human being: not if he is the
best and wisest in the whole world. There are lots of nice
things you can do with sand; but do not try building a
house on it.

The Everlasting Man   *December 13*

And now we begin to see what it is that the New Testament is always talking about. It talks about Christians
'being born again'; it talks about them 'putting on
Christ'; about Christ 'being formed in us'; about our
coming to 'have the mind of Christ'.

Put right out of your head the idea that these are only
fancy ways of saying that Christians are to read what
Christ said and try to carry it out – as a man may read
what Plato or Marx said and try to carry it out. They
mean something much more than that. They mean that a
real Person, Christ, here and now, in that very room
where you are saying your prayers, is doing things to you.
It is not a question of a good man who died two thousand
years ago. It is a living Man, still as much a man as you,
and still as much God as He was when He created the
world, really coming and interfering with your very self;
killing the old natural self in you and replacing it with

the kind of self He has. At first, only for moments. Then for longer periods. Finally, if all goes well, turning you permanently into a different sort of thing; into a new little Christ, a being which, in its own small way, has the same kind of life as God; which shares in His power, joy, knowledge and eternity.

St John of the Cross   December 14

About the higher level – the crags up which the mystics vanish out of my sight – the glaciers and the aiguilles – I have only two things to say. One is that I don't think we are all 'called' to that ascent. 'If it were so, He would have told us.'

The second is this. The following position is gaining ground and is extremely plausible. Mystics (it is said) starting from the most diverse religious premises all find the same things. . . . I am doubtful about the premises. Did Plotinus and Lady Julian and St John of the Cross really find 'the same things'? . . .

I do not at all regard mystical experience as an illusion. I think it shows that there is a way to go, before death, out of what may be called 'this world' – out of the stage set. Out of this; but into what? That's like asking an Englishman, 'Where does the sea lead to?' He will reply, 'To everywhere on earth, including Davy Jones's locker, except England.' The lawfulness, safety, and utility of the mystical voyage depends not at all on its being mystical – that is, on its being a departure – but on the motives, skill, and constancy of the voyager, and on the grace of God. The true religion gives value to its mysticism; mysticism does not validate the religion in which it happens to occur.

I shouldn't be at all disturbed if it could be shown that a diabolical mysticism, or drugs, produced experiences indistinguishable (by introspection) from those of the great Christian mystics. Departures are all alike; it is the landfall that crowns the voyage. The saint, by being a saint, proves that his mysticism (if he was a mystic; not all saints are) led him aright; the fact that he has practised mysticism could never prove his sanctity.

Natural Gifts are Not Enough   *December 15*

If you are a nice person – if virtue comes easily to you – beware! Much is expected from those to whom much is given. If you mistake for your own merits what are really God's gifts to you through nature, and if you are contented with simply being nice, you are still a rebel: and all those gifts will only make your fall more terrible, your corruption more complicated, your bad example more disastrous. The Devil was an archangel once; his natural gifts were as far above yours as yours are above those of a chimpanzee.

But if you are a poor creature – poisoned by a wretched upbringing in some house full of vulgar jealousies and senseless quarrels – saddled, by no choice of your own, with some loathsome sexual perversion – nagged day in and day out by an inferiority complex that makes you snap at your best friends – do not despair. He knows all about it. You are one of the poor whom He blessed. He knows what a wretched machine you are trying to drive. Keep on. Do what you can. One day (perhaps in another world, but perhaps far sooner than that) He will fling it on the scrap-heap and give you a new one. And then you may astonish us all – not least yourself: for you have learned your driving in a hard school. (Some of the last will be first and some of the first will be last.)

'Niceness' – wholesome, integrated personality – is an excellent thing. We must try by every medical, educational, economic and political means in our power, to produce a world where as many people as possible grow up 'nice'; just as we must try to produce a world where all have plenty to eat. But we must not suppose that even if we succeeded in making everyone nice we should have saved their souls. A world of nice people, content in their own niceness, looking no further, turned away from God, would be just as desperately in need of salvation as a miserable world – and might even be more difficult to save.

For mere improvement is not redemption, though redemption always improves people even here and now and will, in the end, improve them to a degree we cannot yet imagine. God became man to turn creatures into sons: not simply to produce better men of the old kind but to produce a new kind of man. It is not like teaching a horse to jump better and better but like turning a horse into a winged creature. Of course, once it has got its wings, it will soar over fences which could never have been jumped and thus beat the natural horse at its own game. But there may be a period, while the wings are just beginning to grow, when it cannot do so: and at that stage the lumps on the shoulders – no one could tell by looking at them that they are going to be wings – may even give it an awkward appearance.

The Presence in Which You Have Always Stood

If what you want is an argument against Christianity (and I well remember how eagerly I looked for such arguments when I began to be afraid it was true) you can easily find some stupid and unsatisfactory Christian and say, 'So there's your boasted new man! Give me the old kind.' But if once you have begun to see that Christianity is on other grounds probable, you will know in your heart that this is only evading the issue. What can you ever really know of other people's souls – of their temptations, their opportunities, their struggles? One soul in the whole creation you do know: and it is the only one whose fate is placed in your hands. If there is a God, you are, in a sense, alone with Him. You cannot put Him off with speculations about your next door neighbours or memories of what you have read in books. What will all that chatter and hearsay count (will you even be able to remember it?) when the anaesthetic fog which we call 'nature' or 'the real world' fades away and the Presence in which you have always stood becomes palpable, immediate, and unavoidable?

The New Men in Christ

The thing has happened: the new step has been taken and is being taken. Already the new men are dotted here and there all over the earth. Some . . . are still hardly recognizable: but others can be recognized. Every now and then one meets them. Their voices and faces are different from ours; stronger, quieter, happier, more radiant. They begin where most of us leave off. They are, I say, recognizable; but you must know what to look for. They will not be very like the idea of 'religious people' which you have formed from your general reading. They do not draw attention to themselves. You tend to think that you are being kind to them when they are really being kind to you. They love you more than other men do, but they need you less. (We must get over wanting to be needed: in some goodish people, especially women, that is the hardest of all temptations to resist.) They will usually seem to have a lot of time: you will wonder where it comes from. When you have recognized one of them, you will recognize the next one much more easily. And I strongly suspect (but how should I know?) that they recognize one another immediately and infallibly, across every barrier of colour, sex, class, age, and even of creeds. In that way, to become holy is rather like joining a secret society. To put it at the very lowest, it must be great *fun*.

The Source of All Personalities   *December 19*

The more we get what we now call 'ourselves' out of the way and let Him take us over, the more truly ourselves we become. There is so much of Him that millions and millions of 'little Christs', all different, will still be too few to express Him fully. He made them all. He invented – as an author invents characters in a novel – all the different men that you and I were intended to be. In that sense our real selves are all waiting for us in Him. It is no good trying to 'be myself' without Him. The more I resist Him and try to live on my own, the more I become dominated by my own heredity and upbringing and sur- roundings and natural desires. In fact what I so proudly call 'Myself' becomes merely the meeting place for trains of events which I never started and which I cannot stop. What I call 'My wishes' become merely the desires thrown up by my physical organism or pumped into me by other men's thoughts or even suggested to me by devils. . . . Most of what I call 'Me' can be very easily explained. It is when I turn to Christ, when I give myself up to His Personality, that I first begin to have a real personality of my own. . . . There are no real personalities anywhere else. Until you have given up your self to Him you will not have a real self. Sameness is to be found most among the most 'natural' men, not among those who surrender to Christ. How monotonously alike all the great tyrants and conquerors have been: how gloriously different are the saints.

Keep Back Nothing   *December 20*

There must be a real giving up of the self. You must throw it away 'blindly' so to speak. Christ will indeed give you a real personality: but you must not go to Him for the sake of that. As long as your own personality is what you are bothering about you are not going to Him at all. The very first step is to try to forget about the self altogether. Your real, new self (which is Christ's and also yours, and yours just because it is His) will not come as long as you are looking for it. It will come when you are looking for Him. Does that sound strange? The same principle holds, you know, for more everyday matters. Even in social life, you will never make a good impression on other people until you stop thinking about what sort of impression you are making. Even in literature and art, no man who bothers about originality will ever be original: whereas if you simply try to tell the truth (without caring twopence how often it has been told before) you will, nine times out of ten, become original without ever having noticed it. The principle runs through all life from top to bottom. Give up your self, and you will find your real self. Lose your life, and you will save it. Submit to death, death of your ambitions and favourite wishes every day and death of your whole body in the end: submit with every fibre of your being, and you will find eternal life. Keep back nothing. Nothing that you have not given away will ever be really yours. Nothing in you that has not died will ever be raised from the dead. Look for yourself, and you will find in the long run only hatred, loneliness, despair, rage, ruin, and decay. But look for Christ and you will find Him, and with Him everything else thrown in.

The Coming of the Lord   *December 21*

Just as, on the factual side, a long preparation culminates in God's becoming incarnate as Man, so, on the documentary side, the truth first appears in *mythical* form and then by a long process of condensing or focusing finally becomes incarnate as History. This involves the belief that Myth is . . . a real though unfocused gleam of divine truth falling on human imagination. The Hebrews, like other peoples, had mythology: but as they were the chosen people so their mythology was the chosen mythology – the mythology chosen by God to be the vehicle of the earliest sacred truths, the first step in that process which ends in the New Testament where truth has become completely historical.

Incarnation Transcends Myth   *December 22*

Now as myth transcends thought, Incarnation transcends myth. The heart of Christianity is a myth which is also a fact. The old myth of the Dying God, *without ceasing to be myth*, comes down from the heaven of legend and imagination to the earth of history. It *happens* – at a particular date, in a particular place, followed by definable historical consequences. We pass from a Balder or an Osiris, dying nobody knows when or where, to a historical Person crucified (it is all in order) *under Pontius Pilate.* . . .

Those who do not know that this great myth became Fact when the Virgin conceived are, indeed, to be pitied. But Christians also need to be reminded . . . that what became Fact was a Myth, that it carries with it into the world of fact all the properties of a myth. God is more than a god, not less; Christ is more than Balder, not less. We must not be ashamed of the mythical radiance resting on our theology. We must not be nervous about 'parallels' and 'Pagan Christs': they *ought* to be there – it would be a stumbling block if they weren't.

Pagan 'Christs' and Christ Himself   *December 23*

Theology, while saying that a special illumination has been vouchsafed to Christians and (earlier) to Jews, also says that there is some divine illumination vouchsafed to all men. The Divine light, we are told, 'lighteneth every man'. We should, therefore, expect to find in the imagination of great Pagan teachers and myth-makers some glimpse of that theme which we believe to be the very plot of the whole cosmic story – the theme of incarnation, death, and rebirth. And the differences between the Pagan Christs (Balder, Osiris, etc.) and the Christ Himself is much what we should expect to find. The Pagan stories are all about someone dying and rising, either every year, or else nobody knows where and nobody knows when. The Christian story is about a historical personage, whose execution can be dated pretty accurately, under a named Roman magistrate, and with whom the society that He founded is in a continuous relation down to the present day. It is not the difference between falsehood and truth. It is the difference between a real event on the one hand and dim dreams or premonitions of that same event on the other. It is like watching something come

315

gradually into focus; first it hangs in the clouds of myth and ritual, vast and vague, then it condenses, grows hard and in a sense small, as a historical event in first-century Palestine.

Myth Became Fact   *December 24*

The essential meaning of all things came down from the 'heaven' of myth to the 'earth' of history. In so doing, it partly emptied itself of its glory, as Christ emptied Himself of His glory to be Man. . . . That is why the New Testament is . . . less poetical than the Old. Have you not often felt in church, if the first lesson is some great passage, that the second lesson is somehow small by comparison – almost, if one might say so, humdrum? So it is and so it must be. That is the humiliation of myth into fact, of God into Man; what is everywhere and always, imageless and ineffable, only to be glimpsed in dream and symbol and the acted poetry of ritual becomes small, solid – no bigger than a man who can lie asleep in a rowing boat on the Lake of Galilee.

Christmas Day   *December 25*

In Pantheism God is all. But the whole point of creation surely is that He was not content to be all. He intends to be 'all *in all*'.

One must be careful not to put this in a way which would blur the distinction between the creation of a man and the Incarnation of God. Could one, as a mere model, put it thus? In creation God makes – invents – a person and 'utters' – injects – him into the realm of Nature. In the Incarnation, God the Son takes the body and human

316

soul of Jesus, and, through that, the whole environment of Nature, all the creaturely predicament, into His own being. So that 'He came down from Heaven' can almost be transposed into 'Heaven drew earth up into it', and locality, limitation, sleep, sweat, footsore weariness, frustration, pain, doubt, and death, are, from before all worlds, known by God from within. The pure light walks the earth; the darkness, received into the heart of Deity, is there swallowed up. Where, except in uncreated light, can the darkness be drowned?

Jesus – God Incarnate   *December 26*

God could, had He pleased, have been incarnate in a man of iron nerves, the Stoic sort who lets no sigh escape him. Of His great humility He chose to be incarnate in a man of delicate sensibilities who wept at the grave of Lazarus and sweated blood in Gethsemane. Otherwise we should have missed the great lesson that it is by his *will* alone that a man is good or bad, and that *feelings* are not, in themselves, of any importance. We should also have missed the all-important help of knowing that He has faced all that the weakest of us face, has shared not only the strength of our nature but every weakness of it except sin. If He had been incarnate in a man of immense natural courage, that would have been for many of us almost the same as His not being incarnate at all.

The fact that God can make complex good out of simple evil does not excuse – though by mercy it may save – those who do the simple evil. And this distinction is central. Offences must come, but woe to those by whom they come; sins *do* cause grace to abound, but we must not make that an excuse for continuing to sin. The crucifixion itself is the best, as well as the worst, of all historical events, but the *role* of Judas remains simply evil. We may apply this first to the problem of other people's suffering. A merciful man aims at his neighbour's good and so does 'God's will', consciously co-operating with 'the simple good'. A cruel man oppresses his neighbour, and so does simple evil. But in doing such evil, he is used by God, without his own knowledge or consent, to produce the complex good – so that the first man serves God as a son, and the second as a tool. For you will certainly carry out God's purpose, however you act, but it makes a difference to you whether you serve like Judas or like John.

The Secret Signature of Each Soul   *December 28*

There have been times when I think we do not desire heaven; but more often I find myself wondering whether, in our heart of hearts, we have ever desired anything else. . . . Are not all lifelong friendships born at the moment when at last you meet another human being who has some inkling (but faint and uncertain even in the best) of that something which you were born desiring, and which, beneath the flux of other desires and in all the momentary silences between the louder passions, night and day, year by year, from childhood to old age, you are looking for, watching for, listening for? You have never *had* it. All the things that have ever deeply possessed your soul have been but hints of it – tantalizing glimpses, promises never quite fulfilled, echoes that died away just as they caught your ear. But if it should really become manifest – if there ever came an echo that did not die away but swelled into the sound itself – you would know it. Beyond all possibility of doubt you would say 'Here at last is the thing I was made for.' We cannot tell each other about it. It is the secret signature of each soul, the incommunicable and unappeasable want, the thing we desired before we met our wives or made our friends or chose our work, and which we shall still desire on our deathbeds, when the mind no longer knows wife or friend or work. While we are, this is. If we lose this, we lose all.

The House with Many Mansions   *December 29*

Be sure that the ins and outs of your individuality are no mystery to Him; and one day they will no longer be a mystery to you. The mould in which a key is made would be a strange thing, if you had never seen a key: and the key itself a strange thing if you had never seen a lock. Your soul has a curious shape because it is a hollow made to fit a particular swelling in the infinite contours of the divine substance, or a key to unlock one of the doors in the house with many mansions. For it is not humanity in the abstract that is to be saved, but you – you, the individual reader, John Stubbs or Janet Smith. Blessed and fortunate creature, your eyes shall behold Him and not another's. All that you are, sins apart, is destined, if you will let God have His good way, to utter satisfaction. The Brocken spectre 'looked to every man like his first love', because she was a cheat. But God will look to every soul like its first love because He is its first love. Your place in heaven will seem to be made for you and you alone, because you were made for it – made for it stitch by stitch as a glove is made for a hand.

The golden apple of selfhood, thrown among the false
gods, became an apple of discord because they scrambled
for it. They did not know the first rule of the holy game,
which is that every player must by all means touch the
ball and then immediately pass it on. To be found with it
in your hands is a fault: to cling to it, death. But when it
flies to and fro among the players too swift for eye to
follow, and the great master Himself leads the revelry,
giving Himself eternally to His creatures in the generation, and back to Himself in the sacrifice, of the Word,
then indeed the eternal dance 'makes heaven drowsy
with the harmony'. All pains and pleasures we have
known on earth are early initiations in the movements of
that dance: but the dance itself is strictly incomparable
with the sufferings of this present time. As we draw
nearer to its uncreated rhythm, pain and pleasure sink
almost out of sight. There is joy in the dance, but it does
not exist for the sake of joy. It does not even exist for the
sake of good, or of love. It is Love Himself, and Good
Himself, and therefore happy. It does not exist for us, but
we for it. . . . As our Earth is to all the stars, so doubtless
are we men and our concerns to all creation; as all the
stars are to space itself, so are all creatures, all thrones
and powers and mightiest of the created gods, to the
abyss of the self-existing Being, who is to us Father and
Redeemer and indwelling Comforter, but of whom no
man or angel can say or conceive what He is in and for
Himself, or what is the work that He 'maketh from the
beginning to the end'. For they are all derived and unsubstantial things. Their vision fails them and they cover
their eyes from the intolerable light of utter actuality,
which was and is and shall be, which never could have
been otherwise, which has no opposite.

Then Aslan turned to them and said: '. . . you are – as you used to call it in the Shadowlands – dead. The term is over: the holidays have begun. The dream is ended: this is the morning . . .'

And for us this is the end of all the stories, and we can most truly say that they all lived happily ever after. But for them it was only the beginning of the real story. All their life in this world and all their adventures in Narnia had only been the cover and the title page: now at last they were beginning Chapter One of the Great Story which no one on earth has read: which goes on for ever: in which every chapter is better than the one before.

Movable Fasts and Feasts

Year	Ash Wednesday	Maundy Thursday	Good Friday	Holy Saturday
1997	12 Feb	27 Mar	28 Mar	29 Mar
1998	25 Feb	9 Apr	10 Apr	11 Apr
1999	17 Feb	1 Apr	2 Apr	3 Apr
2000	8 Mar	20 Apr	21 Apr	22 Apr
2001	28 Feb	12 Apr	13 Apr	14 Apr
2002	13 Feb	28 Mar	29 Mar	30 Mar
2003	5 Mar	17 Apr	18 Apr	19 Apr
2004	25 Feb	8 Apr	9 Apr	10 Apr
2005	9 Feb	24 Mar	25 Mar	26 Mar
2006	1 Mar	13 Apr	14 Apr	15 Apr
2007	21 Feb	5 Apr	6 Apr	7 Apr
2008	6 Feb	20 Mar	21 Mar	22 Mar
2009	25 Feb	9 Apr	10 Apr	11 Apr
2010	17 Feb	1 Apr	2 Apr	3 Apr
2011	9 Mar	21 Apr	22 Apr	23 Apr
2012	22 Feb	5 Apr	6 Apr	7 Apr
2013	13 Feb	28 Mar	29 Mar	30 Mar
2014	5 Mar	17 Apr	18 Apr	19 Apr
2015	18 Feb	2 Apr	3 Apr	4 Apr
2016	10 Feb	24 Mar	25 Mar	26 Mar
2017	1 Mar	13 Apr	14 Apr	15 Apr
2018	14 Feb	29 Mar	30 Mar	31 Mar
2019	6 Mar	18 Apr	19 Apr	20 Apr
2020	26 Feb	9 Apr	10 Apr	11 Apr
2021	17 Feb	1 Apr	2 Apr	3 Apr
2022	2 Mar	14 Apr	15 Apr	16 Apr
2023	22 Feb	6 Apr	7 Apr	8 Apr
2024	14 Feb	28 Mar	29 Mar	30 Mar
2025	5 Mar	17 Apr	18 Apr	19 Apr

Easter	Ascension	Pentecost	Holy Trinity	Body/blood of Christ
30 Mar	8 May	18 May	25 May	29 May
12 Apr	21 May	31 May	7 Jun	11 Jun
4 Apr	13 May	23 May	30 May	3 Jun
23 Apr	1 Jun	11 Jun	18 Jun	22 Jun
15 Apr	24 May	3 Jun	10 Jun	14 Jun
31 Mar	9 May	19 May	26 May	30 May
20 Apr	29 May	8 Jun	15 Jun	19 Jun
11 Apr	20 May	30 May	6 Jun	10 Jun
27 Mar	5 May	15 May	22 May	26 May
16 Apr	25 May	4 Jun	11 Jun	15 Jun
8 Apr	17 May	27 May	3 Jun	7 Jun
23 Mar	1 May	11 May	18 May	22 May
12 Apr	21 May	31 May	7 Jun	11 Jun
4 Apr	13 May	23 May	30 May	3 Jun
24 Apr	2 Jun	12 Jun	19 Jun	23 Jun
8 Apr	17 May	27 May	3 Jun	7 Jun
31 Mar	9 May	19 May	26 May	30 May
20 Apr	29 May	8 Jun	15 Jun	19 Jun
5 Apr	14 May	24 May	31 May	4 Jun
27 Mar	5 May	15 May	22 May	26 May
16 Apr	25 May	4 June	11 Jun	15 Jun
1 Apr	10 May	20 May	27 May	31 May
21 Apr	30 May	9 Jun	16 Jun	20 Jun
12 Apr	21 May	31 May	7 Jun	11 Jun
4 Apr	13 May	23 May	30 May	3 Jun
17 Apr	26 May	5 Jun	12 Jun	16 Jun
9 Apr	18 May	28 May	4 Jun	8 Jun
31 Mar	9 May	19 May	26 May	30 May
20 Apr	29 May	8 Jun	15 Jun	19 Jun

Ash Wednesday

What cannot be admitted – what must exist only as an undefeated but daily resisted enemy – is the idea of something that is 'our own', some area in which we are to be 'out of school', on which God has no claim. . . . I do not think any efforts of my own will can end once and for all this craving for limited liabilities, this fatal reservation. Only God can. I have good faith and hope He will. Of course, I don't mean that I can therefore, as they say, 'sit back'. What God does for us, He does in us. The process of doing it will appear to me (and not falsely) to be the daily or hourly repeated exercises of my own will in renouncing this attitude, especially each morning, for it grows all over me like a new shell each night. Failures will be forgiven; it is acquiescence that is fatal, the permitted, regularized presence of an area in ourselves which we still claim for our own. We may never, this side of death, drive the invader out of our territory, but we must be in the Resistance, not in the Vichy government. And this, so far as I can yet see, must be begun again every day. Our morning prayer should be that in the *Imitation*: *Da hodie perfecte incipere* – grant me to make an unflawed beginning today, for I have done nothing yet.

Maundy Thursday

I do not know and can't imagine what the disciples understood Our Lord to mean when, His body still unbroken and His blood unshed, He handed them the bread and wine, saying *they* were His body and blood. . . . I find 'substance' (in Aristotle's sense), when stripped of its own accidents and endowed with the accidents of some other substance, an object I cannot think. . . . On the other hand, I get on no better with those who tell me that the elements are mere bread and mere wine, used

326

symbolically to remind me of the death of Christ. They are, on the natural level, such a very odd symbol of *that*. . . . And I cannot see why *this* particular reminder – a hundred other things may, psychologically, remind me of Christ's death, equally, or perhaps more – should be so uniquely important as all Christendom (and my own heart) unhesitatingly declare. . . . Yet I find no difficulty in believing that the veil between the worlds, nowhere else (for me) so opaque to the intellect, is nowhere else so thin and permeable to divine operation. Here a hand from the hidden country touches not only my soul but my body. Here the prig, the don, the modern, in me have no privilege over the savage or the child. Here is big medicine and strong magic. . . . The command, after all, was Take, eat: not Take, understand.

Good Friday

God, who needs nothing, loves into existence wholly superfluous creatures in order that He may love and perfect them. He creates the universe, already foreseeing – or should we say 'seeing'? there are are no tenses in God – the buzzing cloud of flies about the cross, the flayed back pressed against the uneven stake, the nails driven through the mesial nerves, the repeated incipient suffocation as the body droops, the repeated torture of back and arms as it is time after time, for breath's sake, hitched up. If I may dare the biological image, God is a 'host' who deliberately creates His own parasites; causes us to be that we may exploit and 'take advantage of' Him. Herein is love. This is the diagram of Love Himself, the inventor of all loves.

Holy Saturday

On the one hand Death is the triumph of Satan, the punishment of the Fall, and the last enemy. Christ shed tears at the grave of Lazarus and sweated blood in Gethsemane: the Life of Lives that was in Him detested this penal obscenity not less than we do, but more. On the other hand, only he who loses his life will save it. We are baptized into the *death* of Christ, and it is the remedy for the Fall. Death is, in fact, what some modern people call 'ambivalent'. It is Satan's great weapon and also God's great weapon: it is holy and unholy; our supreme disgrace and our only hope; the thing Christ came to conquer and the means by which He conquered.

Easter Day

I am not referring simply to the first few hours, or the first few weeks of the Resurrection. I am talking of this whole, huge pattern of descent, down, down, and then up again. What we ordinarily call the Resurrection being just, so to speak, the point at which it turns. Think what that descent is. The coming down, not only into humanity, but into those nine months which precede human birth, in which they tell us we all recapitulate strange pre-human, sub-human forms of life, and going lower still into being a corpse, a thing which, if this ascending movement had not begun, would presently have passed out of the organic altogether, and have gone back into the inorganic, as all corpses do. One has a picture of someone going right down and dredging the sea bottom. One has a picture of a strong man trying to lift a very big, complicated burden. He stoops down and gets himself right under it so that he himself disappears; and then he straightens his back and moves off with the whole thing swaying on his shoulders. Or else one has the picture of a diver, stripping off garment after garment, making himself naked, then flashing for a moment in the air, and then down through the green, and warm, and sunlit water into the pitch black, cold, freezing water, down into the mud and slime, then up again, his lungs almost bursting, back again to the green and warm and sunlit water, and then at last out into the sunshine, holding in his hand the dripping thing he went down to get. This thing is human nature; but, associated with it, all nature, the new universe.

The Ascension of the Lord

What really worries us is the conviction that, whatever we say, the New Testament writers meant something quite different. We feel sure that they thought they had seen their Master setting off on a journey for a local 'Heaven' where God sat in a throne and where there was another throne waiting for Him. And I believe that in a sense that is just what they did think. And I believe that, for this reason, whatever they had actually seen . . . they would almost certainly have remembered it as a vertical movement. What we must not say is that they 'mistook' local 'Heavens' and celestial throne-rooms and the like for the 'spiritual' Heaven of union with God and supreme power and beatitude. . . . *Heaven* can mean (1) The unconditioned Divine Life beyond all worlds. (2) Blessed participation in that Life by a created spirit. (3) The whole Nature or system of conditions in which redeemed human spirits, still remaining human, can enjoy such participation fully and forever. This is the Heaven Christ goes to 'prepare' for us. (4) The physical Heaven, the sky, the space in which Earth moves. What enables us to distinguish these senses and hold them clearly apart is not any special spiritual purity but the fact that we are the heirs to centuries of logical analysis: not that we are sons to Abraham but that we are sons to Aristotle. We are not to suppose that the writers of the New Testament mistook Heaven in sense four or three for Heaven in sense two or one. You cannot mistake a half-sovereign for a sixpence until you know the English system of coinage – that is, until you know the difference between them. In their idea of Heaven all these meanings were latent, ready to be brought out by later analysis. They never thought merely of the blue sky or merely of a 'spiritual' Heaven. When they looked up at the blue sky they never doubted that there . . . was the home of God: but on the other hand, when they thought of one ascending to that Heaven they never doubted He was 'ascending' in what we should call a 'spiritual' sense. . . . A man who really believes that 'Heaven' is in the sky may well, in his heart, have a far truer and more spiritual conception of it than many a modern logician who could expose that fallacy with a few strokes of his pen. For he who does the will of the Father shall know the doctrine. Irrelevant material splendours in such a man's idea of the vision of God will do no harm, for they are not there for their own sakes.

Pentecost

This third Person is called, in technical language, the Holy Ghost or the 'spirit' of God. Do not be worried or surprised if you find it (or Him) rather vaguer or more shadowy in your mind than the other two. I think there is a reason why that must be so. In the Christian life you are not usually looking *at* Him: He is always acting through you. If you think of the Father as something 'out there', in front of you, and of the Son as something standing at your side, helping you to pray, trying to turn you into another son, then you have to think of the third Person as something inside you, or behind you. Perhaps some people might find it easier to begin with the third Person and work backwards. God is love, and that love works through men – especially through the whole community of Christians. But this spirit of love is, from all eternity, a love going on between the Father and Son.

And now, what does it all matter? It matters more than anything else in the world. The whole dance, or drama, or pattern of this three-Personal life is to be played out in each one of us: or (putting it the other way round) each one of us has got to enter that pattern, take his place in that dance. There is no other way to the happiness for which we were made. Good things as well as bad, you know, are caught by a kind of infection. If you want to get warm you must stand near the fire: if you want to be wet you must get into the water. If you want joy, power, peace, eternal life, you must get close to, or even into, the thing that has them. . . . They are a great fountain of energy and beauty spurting up at the very centre of reality. If you are close to it, the spray will wet you: if you are not, you will remain dry. Once a man is united to God, how could he not live forever? Once a man is separated from God, what can he do but wither and die?

The Most Holy Trinity

A world of one dimension would be a straight line. In a two-dimensional world, you still get straight lines, but many lines make one figure. In a three-dimensional world, you still get figures but many figures make one solid body. In other words, as you advance to more real and more complicated levels, you do not leave behind you the things you found on the simpler levels: you still have them, but combined in new ways – in ways you could not imagine if you knew only the simpler levels.

Now the Christian account of God involves just the same principle. The human level is a simple and rather empty level. On the human level one person is one being, and any two persons are two separate beings – just as, in two dimensions (say on a flat sheet of paper) one square is one figure, and any two squares are two separate figures. On the Divine level you still find personalities; but up there you find them combined in new ways which we, who do not live on that level, cannot imagine. In God's dimension, so to speak, you find a Being who is three Persons while remaining one Being, just as a cube is six squares while remaining one cube. Of course we cannot fully conceive a Being like that: just as, if we were so made that we perceived only two dimensions in space we could never properly imagine a cube. But we can get a sort of faint notion of it. And when we do, we are then, for the first time in our lives, getting some positive idea, however faint, of something super-personal – something more than a person. . . . The thing that matters is being actually drawn into that three-personal life, and that may begin any time – tonight, if you like.

What I mean is this. An ordinary simple Christian kneels down to say his prayers. He is trying to get into touch with God. But if he is a Christian he knows that what is prompting him to pray is also God: God, so to speak, inside him. But he also knows that all his real knowledge of God comes through Christ, the Man who was God – that Christ is standing beside him, helping him to pray, praying for him. You see what is happening. God is the thing to which he is praying – the goal he is trying to reach. God is also the thing inside him which is pushing him on – the motive power. God is also the road or bridge along which he is being pushed to that goal. So that the threefold life of the three-personal Being is actually going on in that ordinary little bedroom where an ordinary man is saying his prayers.

The Body and Blood of Christ

Yes, you are always everywhere. But I,
Hunting in such immeasurable forests,
Could never bring the noble Hart to bay.

The scent was too perplexing for my hounds;
Nowhere sometimes, then again everywhere.
Other scents, too, seemed to them almost the same.

Therefore I turn my back on the unapproachable
Stars and horizons and all musical sounds,
Poetry itself, and the winding stair of thought.

Leaving the forests where you are pursued in vain
– Often a mere white gleam – I turn instead
To the appointed place where you pursue.

Not in Nature, not even in Man, but in one
Particular Man, with a date, so tall, weighing
So much, talking Aramaic, having learned a trade;

Not in all food, not in all bread and wine
(Not, I mean, as my littleness requires)
But this wine, this bread . . . no beauty we could desire.

Sources

Sources

January 1   *Letters* (20 January 1942)
January 2   *Mere Christianity*, Bk IV, ch. 8
January 3   *Problem of Pain*, ch. 7
January 4   *Letters to Malcolm*, ch. 17
January 5   *Surprised by Joy*, ch. 15
January 6   'The Grand Miracle'
January 7   'The Weight of Glory'
January 8   'Dogma and the Universe'
January 9   'The Weight of Glory'
January 10   *Problem of Pain*, ch. 3
January 11   *Ibid.*
January 12   *Ibid.*
January 13   'Religion Without Dogma?'
January 14   'On the Reading of Old Books'.
January 15   *Letters* (8 May 1939)
January 16   'Answers to Questions on Christianity'
January 17   *Screwtape Letters*, No. 25
January 18   *Great Divorce*, ch. 9
January 19   'Christian Apologetics'
January 20   *Ibid.*
January 21   *Ibid.*
January 22   *Miracles*, ch. 11
January 23   'On the Transmission of Christianity'
January 24   *Letters to Malcolm*, ch. 18
January 25   *Mere Christianity*, Bk III, ch. 12
January 26   'Modern Translations of the Bible'
January 27   *Ibid.*
January 28   'The Literary Impact of the Authorized
                   Version'
January 29   *Ibid.*
January 30   *Mere Christianity*, Bk II, ch. 1
January 31   'What Are We to Make of Jesus Christ?'
February 1   *Ibid.*
February 2   *Miracles*, ch. 14
February 3   *Mere Christianity*, Bk II, ch. 5
February 4   'Dogma and the Universe'
February 5   *Ibid.*
February 6   *Ibid.*
February 7   *Ibid.*
February 8   *Ibid.*

February 9	*Ibid.*
February 10	*Ibid.*
February 11	*Ibid.*
February 12	*Ibid.*
February 13	*Ibid.*
February 14	'The Seeing Eye'
February 15	*Ibid.*
February 16	'Religion and Rocketry'
February 17	*Ibid.*
February 18	*Surprised by Joy*, ch. 13
February 19	*Miracles*, ch. 11
February 20	*Mere Christianity*, Bk II, ch. 4
February 21	*Ibid.*
February 22	*Ibid.*
February 23	'Miserable Offenders'
February 24	*Ibid.*
February 25	'Dangers of National Repentance'
February 26	'On Forgiveness'
February 27	*Ibid.*
February 28	*Ibid.*
March 1	*Ibid.*
March 2	*Mere Christianity*, Bk III, ch. 1
March 3	*Ibid.*
March 4	*Ibid.*
March 5	*Ibid.*, Bk III, ch. 3
March 6	*Ibid.*
March 7	*Ibid.*
March 8	*Ibid.*
March 9	*Ibid.*
March 10	*Ibid.*, Bk III, ch.4
March 11	*Ibid.*
March 12	*Screwtape Letters*, No. 6
March 13	*Mere Christianity*, Bk III, ch. 2
March 14	*Ibid.*
March 15	*Ibid.*
March 16	*Ibid.*, Bk III, ch. 11
March 17	*Ibid.*
March 18	*Ibid.*
March 19	*Miracles*, ch. 7
March 20	'The Weight of Glory'
March 21	*Mere Christianity*, Bk III, ch. 7
March 22	*Ibid.*, Bk III, ch. 9

March 23	*Ibid.*, Bk III, ch. 12
March 24	*Ibid.*
March 25	'The Psalms'
March 26	*Pilgrim's Regress*, Bk IX, ch. 4
March 27	*Mere Christianity*, Bk III, ch. 5
March 28	*Ibid.*
March 29	*Screwtape Letters*, No. 9
March 30	*Mere Christianity*, Bk III, ch. 5
March 31	*Ibid.*
April 1	*Ibid.*, Bk III, ch. 8
April 2	*Ibid.*
April 3	*Ibid.*
April 4	*Ibid.*
April 5	*Letters to Malcolm*, ch. 8
April 6	*Ibid.*
April 7	*Ibid.*
April 8	'Miracles'
April 9	'Answers to Questions on Christianity'
April 10	'Miracles'
April 11	*Ibid.*
April 12	*Miracles*, ch. 15
April 13	*Ibid.*
April 14	*Ibid.*
April 15	*Ibid.*
April 16	*Ibid.*, ch. 16
April 17	*Ibid.*
April 18	*Ibid.*
April 19	'Religion Without Dogma?'
April 20	*Miracles*, ch. 16
April 21	*Ibid.*
April 22	*Ibid.*
April 23	'On Three Ways of Writing for Children'
April 24	'The Grand Miracle'
April 25	'The World's Last Night'
April 26	*Miracles*, ch. 16
April 27	*Ibid.*
April 28	'Transposition'
April 29	*Ibid.*
April 30	*Miracles*, ch. 16
May 1	'Good Work and Good Works'
May 2	'On the Reading of Old Books'
May 3	*Reflections on the Psalms*, ch. 11

May 4	*Miracles*, ch. 16
May 5	*Letters to Malcolm*, ch. 22
May 6	*Ibid.*, ch. 20
May 7	'The World's Last Night'
May 8	*Ibid.*
May 9	*Ibid.*
May 10	*Ibid.*
May 11	*Ibid.*
May 12	*Ibid.*
May 13	*Ibid.*
May 14	*Miracles*, ch. 16
May 15	'The World's Last Night'
May 16	'Some Thoughts'
May 17	*Problem of Pain*, ch. 6
May 18	'The World's Last Night'
May 19	*Ibid.*
May 20	*Great Divorce*, Preface
May 21	*Ibid.*
May 22	*Great Divorce*, ch. 5
May 23	*Ibid.*
May 24	*Ibid.*
May 25	*Ibid.*
May 26	*Ibid.*, ch. 9
May 27	*Ibid.*
May 28	*Reflections on the Psalms*, ch. 2
May 29	*Great Divorce*, ch. 8
May 30	*Ibid.*
May 31	*Ibid.*, ch. 9
June 1	*Perelandra*, ch. 9
June 2	'The Weight of Glory'
June 3	*Four Loves*, ch. 6
June 4	*Problem of Pain*, ch. 8
June 5	*Ibid.*
June 6	*Ibid.*
June 7	'The Weight of Glory'
June 8	*Four Loves*, ch. 1
June 9	*Ibid.*
June 10	*Ibid.*
June 11	*Problem of Pain*, ch. 4
June 12	*Four Loves*, ch. 3
June 13	*Ibid.*
June 14	*Ibid.*

June 15	*Ibid.*
June 16	*Ibid.*, ch. 4
June 17	*Ibid.*
June 18	*Ibid.*
June 19	*Ibid.*
June 20	*Ibid*
June 21	*Ibid.*
June 22	*Ibid.*
June 23	*Ibid.*
June 24	*Ibid.*, ch. 5
June 25	*Ibid.*
June 26	*Ibid.*
June 27	*Ibid.*
June 28	*Ibid.*
June 29	'Fern-Seed and Elephants'
	Letters to Malcolm, ch. 2
June 30	*Four Loves*, ch. 5
July 1	*Ibid.*
July 2	*Ibid.*
July 3	'On Obstinacy in Belief'
July 4	*Four Loves*, ch. 5
July 5	*Ibid.*, ch. 6
July 6	*Ibid.*
July 7	*Ibid.*
July 8	*Ibid.*
July 9	*Ibid.*
July 10	*Ibid.*
July 11	*Ibid.*
July 12	'Two Ways with the Self'
July 13	*Ibid.*
July 14	*Ibid.*
July 15	Letter to Walter Hooper (30 November 1954)
July 16	'First and Second Things'
July 17	*Ibid.*
July 18	*Ibid.*
July 19	'Is Progress Possible?'
July 20	'Membership'
July 21	'Equality'
July 22	*Letters to an American Lady* (1 November 1954)
July 23	'Equality'
July 24	'Myth Became Fact'

July 25	*Letters to Malcolm*, ch. 11
July 26	'Screwtape Proposes a Toast'
July 27	*Ibid.*
July 28	*Screwtape Letters*, No. 5
July 29	*Miracles*, ch. 14
July 30	'"Horrid Red Things"'
July 31	*Letters to Malcolm*, ch. 16
August 1	'Meditation in a Toolshed'
August 2	*Ibid.*
August 3	*Ibid.*
August 4	*Ibid.*
August 5	*Ibid.*
August 6	*Miracles*, ch. 16
August 7	*Experiment in Criticism*, ch. 3
August 8	*Letters to Malcolm*, ch. 16
August 9	'Answers to Questions on Christianity'
August 10	*Letters* (1 April 1952)
August 11	*A Preface to 'Paradise Lost'*, ch. 3
August 12	*Letters to Malcolm*, ch. 1
August 13	*Ibid.*
August 14	'Membership'
August 15	*Ibid.*
August 16	*Ibid.*
August 17	*Ibid.*
August 18	*Ibid.*
August 19	*Ibid.*
August 20	*Ibid.*
August 21	*Ibid.*
August 22	*Ibid.*
August 23	*Ibid.*
August 24	Letter to Stuart Robertson (6 May 1962)
August 25	'Christianity and Literature'
August 26	*Ibid.*
August 27	*Ibid.*
August 28	*Problem of Pain*, ch. 6
August 29	'Christianity and Culture'
August 30	*Ibid.*
August 31	*Ibid.*
September 1	*Ibid.*
September 2	*Ibid.*
September 3	*Ibid.*
September 4	'Learning in War-Time'

September 5	*Ibid.*
September 6	*Mere Christianity*, Bk IV, ch. 1
September 7	*Ibid.*
September 8	*Letters to Malcolm*, ch. 14
September 9	*Problem of Pain*, ch. 2
September 10	*Ibid.*
September 11	*Ibid.*
September 12	*Ibid.*
September 13	*Ibid.*
September 14	*Ibid.*
September 15	*Ibid.*, ch. 3
September 16	*Mere Christianity*, Bk II, ch. 3
September 17	*Ibid.*
September 18	*Screwtape Letters*, Preface to 1961 edition
September 19	*Mere Christianity*, Bk II, ch. 2
September 20	*A Preface to 'Paradise Lost'*, ch. 13
September 21	*Letters to Malcolm*, ch. 13
September 22	*Problem of Pain*, ch. 5
September 23	*Ibid.*
September 24	*Ibid.*, ch. 6
September 25	*Ibid.*
September 26	*Ibid.*
September 27	*Ibid.*
September 28	*Ibid.*
September 29	*Miracles*, Appendix A
September 30	*Ibid.*, ch. 4
October 1	*Mere Christianity*, Bk I, ch. 1
October 2	*Ibid.*
October 3	*Ibid.*, Bk I, ch. 2
October 4	*Four Loves*, ch. 5
October 5	*Abolition of Man*, ch. 1
October 6	*Ibid.*, ch. 2
October 7	'The Poison of Subjectivism'
October 8	*Mere Christianity*, Bk I, ch. 5
October 9	*Ibid.*, Bk II, ch. 1
October 10	'Is Theology Poetry?'
October 11	*Mere Christianity*, Bk I, ch. 4
October 12	*Miracles*, ch. 17
October 13	*Mere Christianity*, Bk II, ch. 2
October 14	*Ibid.*
October 15	*Ibid.*
October 16	*Screwtape Letters*, No. 7

October 17	*Mere Christianity*, Bk II, ch. 3
October 18	*Letters to Malcolm*, ch. 9
October 19	*Mere Christianity*, Bk II, ch. 3
October 20	*Ibid.*
October 21	*Ibid.*
October 22	*Reflections on the Psalms*, ch. 11
October 23	*Mere Christianity*, Bk II, ch. 4
October 24	*Ibid.*
October 25	*Ibid.*, Bk II, ch. 5
October 26	*Ibid.*
October 27	*Ibid.*
October 28	*They Stand Together* (10 January 1932)
October 29	*Mere Christianity*, Bk II, ch. 5
October 30	'Fern-Seed and Elephants'
October 31	*Mere Christianity*, Bk II, ch. 5
November 1	*Letters to Malcolm*, ch. 3
November 2	*Ibid.*, ch. 20
November 3	*Mere Christianity*, Bk IV, ch. 1
November 4	*Ibid.*
November 5	*Ibid.*, Bk IV, ch. 2
November 6	*Ibid.*
November 7	*Letters to Malcolm*, ch. 4
November 8	*Mere Christianity*, Bk IV, ch. 3
November 9	*Ibid.*
November 10	*Ibid.*
November 11	*Ibid.*
November 12	*Miracles*, Appendix B
November 13	'The Efficacy of Prayer'
November 14	*Ibid.*
November 15	*Ibid.*
November 16	*Ibid.*
November 17	*Ibid.*
November 18	*Ibid.*
November 19	*Letters to Malcolm*, ch. 5
November 20	*Ibid.*
November 21	*Ibid.*, ch. 15
November 22	'On Church Music'
November 23	*Ibid.*
November 24	'Man or Rabbit?'
November 25	*Ibid.*
November 26	*Ibid.*
November 27	*Ibid.*

November 28	*Ibid.*
November 29	*Mere Christianity*, Bk III, ch. 12
November 30	*Ibid.*, Bk III, ch. 10
December 1	*Ibid.*, Bk IV, ch. 9
December 2	*Ibid.*, Bk IV, ch. 5
December 3	*Ibid.*
December 4	*Ibid.*
December 5	*Ibid.*
December 6	*Ibid.*
December 7	Letter to Edward Dell (4 February 1949)
December 8	*Mere Christianity*, Bk IV, ch. 6
December 9	*Ibid.*, Bk IV, ch. 7
December 10	*Ibid.*
December 11	*Ibid.*
December 12	*Ibid.*
December 13	*Ibid.*
December 14	*Letters to Malcolm*, ch. 12
December 15	*Mere Christianity*, Bk IV, ch. 10
December 16	*Ibid.*
December 17	*Ibid.*
December 18	*Ibid.*, Bk IV, ch. 11
December 19	*Ibid.*
December 20	*Ibid.*
December 21	*Miracles*, ch. 15
December 22	'Myth Became Fact'
December 23	'Is Theology Poetry?'
December 24	*Ibid.*
December 25	*Letters to Malcolm*, ch. 13
December 26	*Letters* (c. October 1947)
December 27	*Problem of Pain*, ch. 7
December 28	*Ibid.*, ch. 10
December 29	*Ibid.*
December 30	*Ibid.*
December 31	*The Last Battle*, ch. 16

Movable Fasts and Feasts

Ash Wednesday	'A Slip of the Tongue'
Maundy Thursday	*Letters to Malcolm*, ch. 19
Good Friday	*Four Loves*, ch. 6
Holy Saturday	*Miracles*, ch. 14
Easter Day	'The Grand Miracle'
The Ascension of the Lord	*Miracles*, ch. 16
Pentecost	*Mere Christianity*, Bk IV, ch. 4
The Most Holy Trinity	*Ibid.*, Bk IV, ch. 2
The Body and Blood of Christ	*Poems*, 'No Beauty We Could Desire'

Works of C.S. Lewis quoted in this book

For details of all the published writings of C.S. Lewis, see the bibliography in *C.S. Lewis at the Breakfast Table and Other Reminiscences*, ed. James T. Como (New York: Macmillan, 1979; London: Collins, 1980).

Some of the books listed below are collections of essays, but only those essays actually quoted in the book are mentioned here. American editions, except when listed separately (those numbered 10 and 16), are given in brackets. Place of publication is London or New York unless otherwise stated.

Collins Publishers of London now handle the titles originally published by The Centenary Press and Geoffrey Bles Ltd. Fount Paperbacks and Fontana Lions are part of Fontana, the paperback house of Collins.

1. *The Pilgrim's Regress: An Allegorical Apology for Christianity, Reason and Romanticism*. J.M. Dent, 1933; Sheed and Ward, 1935; Geoffrey Bles, 1943, with the author's new Preface on Romanticism, footnotes, and running headlines. [Sheed and Ward, 1944; Eerdmans, Grand Rapids, 1958]
   * Fount Paperbacks, 1977
2. *The Problem of Pain*. The Centenary Press, 1940. [Macmillan, 1943]
   * Fount Paperbacks, 1977
3. *The Screwtape Letters*. Geoffrey Bles, 1942.

[Macmillan, 1943]; reprinted with 'Screwtape Proposes a Toast' as *The Screwtape Letters and Screwtape Proposes a Toast*, with a new and additional Preface. Geoffrey Bles, 1961. [Macmillan, 1962]
* Fount Paperbacks, 1977

4. *A Preface to 'Paradise Lost'*. Oxford University Press, 1942.
5. *Perelandra*. John Lane the Bodley Head, 1943. Also published as *Voyage to Venus (Perelandra)*, Pan Books, 1953. [First title, Macmillan, 1944]
6. *The Abolition of Man: or Reflections on Education with Special Reference to the Teaching of English in the Upper Forms of Schools*. Oxford University Press, 1943; Geoffrey Bles: The Centenary Press, 1946. [Macmillan, 1947]
   * Fount Paperbacks, 1978
7. 'Equality', *The Spectator*, CLXXI (27 August 1943), p 192.
8. *The Great Divorce: A Dream*. Geoffrey Bles: The Centenary Press, 1945. [Macmillan, 1946]
   * Fount Paperbacks, 1972
9. *Miracles: A Preliminary Study*. Geoffrey Bles: The Centenary Press, 1947. [Macmillan, 1947] With revision of Chapter III, Collins, 1960. [Macmillan, 1978]
   * Fount Paperbacks, 1977
10. *The Weight of Glory and Other Addresses*. New York: Macmillan, 1949. Revised and Expanded Edition, ed. Walter Hooper, 1980. ('The Weight of Glory', 'Learning in War-Time', 'Transposition', 'Is Theology Poetry?', 'Membership', 'On Forgiveness', 'A Slip of the Tongue')
11. *Mere Christianity: A revised and amplified edition, with a new introduction, of the three books 'Broadcast Talks', 'Christian Behaviour', and 'Beyond Personality'*. Geoffrey Bles, 1952. [Macmillan, 1952]
    * Fount Paperbacks, 1977
12. *Surprised by Joy: The Shape of My Early Life*. Geoffrey Bles, 1952. [Harcourt, Brace & World, 1956]
    * Fount Paperbacks, 1977
13. *The Last Battle*. The Bodley Head, 1956. Fontana Lions paperback, 1980. [Macmillan, 1956]
14. *Reflections on the Psalms*. Geoffrey Bles, 1958. [Harcourt, Brace & World, 1958]
    * Fount Paperbacks, 1977
15. *The Four Loves*. Geoffrey Bles, 1960. [Harcourt, Brace & World, 1958]
    * Fount Paperbacks, 1977

16. *The World's Last Night and Other Essays.* New York: Harcourt, Brace & World, 1960. ('The Efficacy of Prayer', 'On Obstinacy in Belief', 'Screwtape Proposes a Toast', 'Good Work and Good Works', 'Religion and Rocketry', 'The World's Last Night')

17. *An Experiment in Criticism.* Cambridge University Press, Cambridge, 1961.

18. *Letters to Malcolm: Chiefly on Prayer.* Geoffrey Bles, 1964. [Harcourt, Brace & World, 1964]
    * Fount Paperbacks, 1977

19. *Poems.* Ed. Walter Hooper. Geoffrey Bles, 1964. [Harcourt, Brace & World, 1965]

20. *Screwtape Proposes a Toast and Other Pieces.* Ed. Jocelyn Gibb. Collins, 1965. ('Screwtape Proposes a Toast', 'On Obstinacy in Belief', 'Good Work and Good Works', 'Is Theology Poetry?', 'Transposition', 'The Weight of Glory', 'A Slip of the Tongue')
    * Fount Paperbacks, 1977

21. *Letters of C.S. Lewis.* Ed. W.H. Lewis. Geoffrey Bles, 1966. [Harcourt, Brace & World, 1966]

22. *Christian Reflections.* Ed. Walter Hooper. Geoffrey Bles, 1967. [Eerdmans, Grand Rapids, 1967] ('Christianity and Literature', 'Christianity and Culture', 'The Poison of Subjectivism', 'On Church Music', 'The Psalms', 'Fern-Seed and Elephants' [As 'Modern Theology and Biblical Criticism' in the USA], 'The Seeing Eye')
    * Fount Paperbacks, 1981

23. *Letters to an American Lady.* Ed. Clyde S. Kilby. Hodder & Stoughton, 1969. [Eerdmans, Grand Rapids, 1967]

24. *Selected Literary Essays.* Ed. Walter Hooper. Cambridge University Press, Cambridge, 1969. ('The Literary Impact of the Authorized Version')

25. *Undeception: Essays on Theology and Ethics.* Ed. Walter Hooper. Geoffrey Bles, 1971. [As *God in the Dock: Essays on Theology and Ethics*, Eerdmans, Grand Rapids, 1970] ('Miracles', 'Dogma and the Universe', 'Answers to Questions on Christianity', 'Myth Became Fact', '"Horrid Red Things"', 'The Grand Miracle', 'Christian Apologetics', 'Man or Rabbit?', 'On the Transmission of Christianity', '"Miserable Offenders"', 'Religion Without Dogma?', 'Some Thoughts', 'What Are We to Make of Jesus Christ?', 'Dangers of National Repentance', 'Two Ways with the Self', 'On the Reading of Old Books', 'Meditation in a

Toolshed', 'Modern Translations of the Bible', 'First and Second Things', 'Is Progress Possible?']

26. *Fern-Seed and Elephants and Other Essays on Christianity.* Ed. Walter Hooper. Fount Paperbacks, 1975. ('Membership', 'Learning in War-Time', 'On Forgiveness', 'The World's Last Night', 'Religion and Rocketry', 'The Efficacy of Prayer', 'Fern-Seed and Elephants']

27. *God in the Dock: Essays on Theology.* Ed. Walter Hooper. Fount Paperbacks, 1979. ('Miracles', 'Dogma and the Universe', 'Myth Became Fact', 'The Grand Miracle', 'Man or Rabbit?', 'What Are We to Make of Jesus Christ?']

28. *They Stand Together: The Letters of C.S. Lewis to Arthur Greeves (1914-1963).* Ed. Walter Hooper. Collins, 1979. [Macmillan, 1979]

29. *Of This and Other Worlds.* Ed. Walter Hooper. Collins, 1982 and Fount Paperbacks, 1984. [As *On Stories and Other Essays on Literature,* Harcourt, Brace, Jovanovich, 1982] ('On Three Ways of Writing for Children']